Participating Days Inn® Hotels

IDAHO
Coeur d'Alene

ILLINOIS
Alsip
Barrington 💼
Champaign
Chicago - Lincoln Park North 💼
Chicago – Niles/Skokie 💼
Chicago – O'Hare/West
Elk Grove
Danville
El Paso
Elgin-Dundee
Libertyville
Macomb 💼
Morris
Mt. Vernon
North Chicago
Oglesby 💼
Quincy Riverside
Sheffield
Springfield 💼
Vandalia 💼
Waukegan
Woodstock 💼

INDIANA
Bloomington
Cloverdale
Columbus
Crawfordsville
Decatur 💼
Evansville - Airport
Evansville – East
Ft. Wayne – East/Downtown
Huntington
Indianapolis – Castleton
Indianapolis – Downtown 💼
Indianapolis – Franklin
Indianapolis – Northwest 💼
Indianapolis – Plainfield
Jasper 💼
Kokomo 💼
Louisville – Carefree
Louisville – Jeffersonville
Louisville – Sellersburg 💼
Merrillville
Muncie

Plymouth
Portage
Princeton
Richmond
Seymour
South Bend
South Bend – Mishawaka
Sullivan
Tell City
Terre Haute
West Lafayette

IOWA
Cedar Falls
Cedar Rapids
Coralville
Council Bluffs
Davenport – North
Des Moines – Ankeny
Des Moines – Merle Hay Road
Des Moines West – Urbandale
Dubuque 💼
Grinnell
Manchester
Mason City 💼
Missouri Valley
Newton 💼
Osceola
Shenandoah
Sioux City 💼
Toledo
Walcott
Williamsburg

KANSAS
Colby
Emporia 💼
Garden City
Hays
Junction City
Lawrence 💼
Newton 💼
Ottawa 💼
Russell
Salina
Wichita 💼
Wichita – West/Near Airport

KENTUCKY
Ashland 💼
Bardstown
Beaver Dam
Beree
Bowling Green
Carrollton
Cave City
Cincinnati – Fort Wright
Elizabethtown
Georgetown – North Lexington
Grayson
Kuttawa
Lexington
Lexington – Frankfort
Lexington – South 💼
London
Louisville
Louisville – Central
Louisville – La Grange
Louisville – Shelbyville
Louisville – Shepherdsville
Madisonville 💼
Morehead
Mt. Sterling
Murray 💼
Oak Grove
Owensboro – New Hartford
Richmond
Springfield
Williamstown 💼

MISSOURI
Boonville
Branson
Butler
Cameron
Carthage
Clienton
Columbia – Conference Center
Kansas City – South
Kansas City
Kingdom City
Kirksville
Mountain Grove

Rolla
Springfield – South 💼
St. Charles
St. Joseph
St. Louis – Lindbergh Blvd.
St. Louis – North Airport
St. Robert Waynesville/Ft. Leonard Wood

MONTANA
Billings 💼
Bozeman 💼
Great Falls
Helena 💼
Kalispell
Missoula
West Yellowstone 💼

NEBRASKA
Columbus
Kearney
Lexington
Lincoln
Lincoln – Airport
North Platte
Ogallala
Omaha
Omaha – Bellevue
Sidney
Paxton
York

NORTH DAKOTA
Bismarck 💼
Fargo – Airport/Dome/19th Ave. 💼
Jamestown
West Fargo – Main Ave. 💼

OREGON
Albany 💼
Burns
Eugene 💼
Medford
Portland – Airport
Portland – City Center
Portland – Gresham
Portland – North
Portland – South
Portland – Tigard
Portland – Wilsonville 💼

SOUTH DAKOTA
Chamberlain – Oacoma
Custer
Mitchell 💼
Murdo – Range Country
Pierre
Rapid City – Rapp Street
Rapid City – Jackson Blvd.
Sioux Falls – Airport
Sioux Falls – Empire
Spearfish
Wall
Watertown
Yankton

WASHINGTON
Bellingham
Mt. Vernon – Casino Area
Ocean Shores
Richland 💼
Seattle – Bellevue
Seattle – Downtown
Seattle – Kent 💼
Seattle – Int'l Airport
Seattle – North/Aurora Village
Spokane – Airport
Vancouver

**1-800-DAYS-INN® OR
DAYSINN.COM/TRAVELPLANNER**
PARA ESPAÑOL 1-888-709-4024

💼 Days Business Place® hotel which features rooms that include a microwave, refrigerator, large work desk, in-room coffee, iron/ironing boards, and dataports.

A family vacation that will change your whole altitude.

Howard Johnson welcomes you to the mountain states for your family vacation. Fresh air, beautiful scenery and a good night's sleep? Sounds like a recipe for memories that will last a lifetime. Bring the kids, bring the dog and bring yourself. We'll be waiting. And, while visiting Howard Johnson, join our TripRewards℠ program and become a member of the largest hotel program in the world.**

SAVE UP TO 30% off*

Howard Johnson

howardjohnson.com/mountain
1-800-I-GO-HOJO®
Request *LPHT* or the Hottest Deal Rate.

INTRODUCING
triprewards

Denver, CO
Howard Johnson Inn

Billings, MT
Howard Johnson Express Inn

Laurel, MT
Howard Johnson Inn

Rapid City, SD
Howard Johnson Express Inn & Suites

Spearfish, SD
Howard Johnson Express Inn

Salt Lake City, UT
Howard Johnson Express Inn

Laramie, WY
Howard Johnson Inn

* Discount is off regular rack rate. Rooms at the LPHT rate are limited and subject to availability at participating properties. Blackout dates and other restrictions may apply. Cannot be combined with any other discounts and offers. Pet Friendly rooms vary by location and additional charges may apply. © 2004 Howard Johnson International, Inc. All rights reserved. Hotels are independently owned and operated. © 2004 Travel Rewards, Inc. **Based on the number of participating hotels.

ALONG THE TRAIL WITH
LEWIS AND CLARK
Travel Planner and Guide : 2004-2005 Edition

Brad Hurd *Publisher*
Barbara Fifer *Author*
Joseph Mussulman *Cartographer*
John Thomas *Editor*
Jill Kuczmarski *Designer*

ADVERTISING
Larry Sem *Advertising Director*
Sheila Newlun
Advertising Representative
To Advertise Next Year:
P.O. Box 5630, Helena, Montana 59604
406-444-5100 or 1-800-654-1105
fax 406-443-5480
e-mail: ads@lewisandclark.com

SALES/MARKETING
Linda Netschert *Marketing Manager*
Lisa Juvik & Jason Savage
Sales Representatives
To Order Additional Copies
or Other Titles:
1-800-6821-3874
email: books@farcountrypress.com

OPERATIONS
Peggy Tobin *Business Manager*
Kathy Springmeyer *Production Director*
Matt Vanderwater *Warehouse/Mailroom*
Steve Morrison *Warehouse*

*The Travel Planner and Guide
is updated and published each spring.*

Cover portraits of William Clark and
Meriwether Lewis were painted by Charles
Willson Peale (1741-1847), and are used
with the permission of Independence
National Historic Park, Philadelphia. The
background map is a detail of Clark's third
and final map of lands the expedition traveled. It was published in 1814 and today is
housed in the Library of Congress,
Washington, D.C.

MONTANA
MAGAZINE

Find us on the World Wide Web
at www.lewisandclark.com
& at www.farcountrypress.com

This magazine may not be reproduced in whole or
in part by any means (with the exception of short
quotes for the purpose of review) without the permission of the publisher.

© 2004 Farcountry Press

CALENDAR OF EVENTS..................7
MAP LEGEND..................................7
MAKING READY............................9
ILLINOIS..16
MISSOURI......................................18
KANSAS...27
NEBRASKA....................................30
IOWA..38
SOUTH DAKOTA...........................43
NORTH DAKOTA..........................55
MONTANA....................................66
IDAHO..104
WASHINGTON............................110
OREGON......................................118

Please Read Before Using This Guide!

Our maps are to be used *along with state highway maps*, and do not show lack of pavement on some remote roads, or relative size of towns and cities. Take the yellow warning symbol seriously—it appears on roads you'll want to get local information about, if you even try them. It means extremely steep grades or tight curves, unpaved surfaces that are impassable when wet, or lack of services along the way. Since the Corps of Discovery traveled mostly by water, following their "trail" on modern roads means getting as close as is now possible.

In the Dakotas, Montana, and Idaho, population is light and distances between towns can be surprisingly long. You'll need to feed and water your vehicle and your passengers when you can, rather than when you feel like it.

Numerals in open-book symbols refer to maps.

Numerals in flags indicate text listings about significant Lewis and Clark sites: land that remains much the same as when they saw it, museums, monuments, etc., specific to the expedition.

Text and maps follow the Lewis and Clark Expedition from Monticello to the Pacific Ocean. Dividing the chapters into state-by-state treatment means that when the Corps traveled a river that today forms state boundaries, you'll find part of the story under one state and part under another. When looking for that night's campsite, they chose the best spot they saw, not the least concerned that someday it would mean that one night was in Iowa and the next in Nebraska. This guidebook is to help you know what they experienced at the place you are visiting.

Highlights of the return trip also are included in text and maps. The return is handled separately only in the Montana section, because the Corps split into groups there when heading home.

CALENDAR OF EVENTS

2004–2005 Lewis and Clark Expedition Related Annual Events

2004: Corps of Discovery II

Corps II is a bicentennial effort of federal and state agencies, private and nonprofit organizations, and American Indian tribes, coordinated by the National Park Service. The central feature of Corps II is the "Tent of Many Voices." This 150-seat auditorium tent (with air-conditioning/heating) hosts location-specific demonstrations, folklore, music, living history, and more.

Dates are tentative—please check www.lewisandclarkgnet.com before traveling.

April 7-11, Rend Lake, IL
April 17-25, Springfield, MO
May 1-4, Saint Genevieve, MO
May 13-16, Hartford, IL
May 10-15, St. Charles, MO
June 1-6, Jefferson City, MO
June 11-14, Booneville, MO
June 18-22, Fort Osage, MO
June 26-July 4, Kaw Point, Kansas City, KS
July 9-12, St. Joseph, MO
July 16-19, Nebraska City, NE
July 24-27, Omaha, NE
July 31-August 4, Blair, NE
Aug 9-12, Macy, NE
Aug 17-22, Sioux City, IA
Aug 26-30, Chamberlain, SD
Sept 4-12, Eagle Butte, SD
Sept 18-Oct 3, Fort Pierre, SD
Oct 9-13, Knife River, ND
Oct 22-31, Bismarck, ND
Nov 5-14, Washburn, ND

Corps II returns to the trail in April 2005.

2004

through June, OMSI, Portland, OR: "Lewis and Clark: Great Journey West," National Geographic Omnimax film

Jan. 14-Sept. 6, St. Louis, MO: Missouri History Museum in Forest Park. Lewis & Clark: The National Bicentennial Exhibition. www.lewisandclarkexhibit.org

April 14-18, Whittington, IL: Rend Lake Earth Day. Rend Lake Visitors Center (Interstate 57, exit 77). 618-998-9397

May 1-2, Hartsburg, MO: "Relive the Journey." On the Missouri River, re-enactors, period crafts, displays, workshops, film, music, children's play, black-powder shoots, Native American story-telling.

May 2, Maeystown, IL: "Lewis and Clark along the Kaskaskia Trace," commemoration of Clark's camp on Dec. 5, 1803, and Lewis's stay in Waterloo Dec. 3-5, 1803. 618-458-6660

May 13-16, Hartford & Wood River, IL: Expedition's Departure Signature Event.

May 14-16, Edwardsville, IL: "Spirit: The Seventh Fire." Traditional Native American music and dance blended with ultramodern visual effects. Southern Illinois University.

June 25-27, St. Joseph, MO: Sacred Hills Mini-Encampment. 816-232-1240

June 27-28, Weston, MO: Lewis & Clark Trad'n Days. Reenactors, demonstrations, journal readings.

July 3-4, Atchison & Fort Leavenworth, KS, & Kansas City, MO: "A Journey Fourth." Reenactors, period boats, exhibits, speakers, fireworks with music. 402-471-3368

July 16-18, Onawa, IA: Lewis and Clark Festival, reenactors in encampments, muzzleloader shoot.

August 3, Fort Calhoun, NE: First Tribal Council commemoration. Fort Atkinson Historical Park. 402-472-9333

August 1-4, Bismarck, ND: Lewis and Clark Trail Heritage Foundation Annual Conference.

August 6-9, Onawa, IA: Celebrates the Lewis & Clark Expedition's exact bicentennial at this site.

August 21-22, Sioux City, IA: Sergeant Floyd 1804 Living History Encampment. 712-279-0198

August 27-28, Chamberlain/Oacoma, SD: "Oceti Sakowin: Remembering & Education," recalls the expedition's visits with the Teton and Yankton Sioux.

Aug. 27-Sept. 26, Greenwood, SD: Educational tours of where Lewis & Clark met the Yankton Sioux.

Sept. 4-6, from Missoula, MT: Guided bus-coach tour of expedition's route in Lolo Pass area, western Montana & Idaho. Reservations required; contact Laura Fuller, mognop1@aol.com

October 22-31, Bismarck, ND: "Circles of Cultures, Time of Renewal and Exchange in Historical Homelands of the Mandan, Hidatsa, and Arikara." The winter of 1804-1805. 701-663-4758, www.fortlincoln.com or www.circleofcultures.com

November 2004 through March 2005, Philadelphia, PA: "Lewis & Clark: The National Bicentennial Exhibition." Academy of Natural Sciences. 215-299-1000

December 7, Cahokia, IL: "Lewis and Clark's Arrival Anniversary." Cahokia Courthouse State Historic Site. 618-332-1782

December 11-12, Hartford, IL: "Arrival at Camp River Dubois." Living history of the first winter and frontier military life. Lewis and Clark State Historic Site. 618-251-5811

2005

through March, Philadelphia, PA. Lewis & Clark: The National Bicentennial Exhibition at Academy of Natural Sciences. 215-299-1000

February 5, Cahokia, IL: "Fete du Bon Vieux Temps," colonial Mardi Gras celebration. Cahokia Courthouse State Historic Site. 618-332-1782

Apr. 29-May 1, Confluence of Yellowstone & Missouri Rivers, ND: Lewis & Clark at the Confluence: "This long wished for spot..."

May 28 to July 29, Kansas City, MO: "Lewis and Clark: Great Journey West" National Geographic Omnimax film at Union Center.

MAP LEGEND

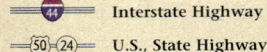

- Interstate Highway
- U.S., State Highway
- County Road
- Lewis & Clark Trail Highway
- Travel Restrictions (Local Inquiry)
- Streamflow Direction
- Bottom Lands (Roads may be impassable during certain seasons)
- Major Interpretive Site (See text for description)
- Water Route Direction: Westbound / Eastbound
- Land Route Direction: Westbound / Eastbound

Rediscover and Protect the Wild America Explored by Lewis & Clark

Two hundred years ago, the majesty of Mt. Hood stunned Captains Meriwether Lewis, William Clark and their Corps of Discovery. It's a sight that still causes jaws to drop today — and it's just one of the pristine American landscapes Lewis and Clark explored and that Sierra Club is working to protect. These places and the wildlife making them home are as wild today as they were in 1804, but many are threatened by development, drilling, clear-cutting, mining and other destructive activities. With your help we can keep them untamed and untouched. Commemorate the bicentennial of Lewis and Clark's journey by discovering and protecting what's left of the wild America Lewis and Clark saw — help us leave a legacy for future generations.

Learn more, pick up a travel or fishing guidebook, join us on an outing, volunteer and much more at
www.sierraclub.org/lewisandclark

SIERRA CLUB
FOUNDED 1892

Explore, enjoy and protect the planet

LEWIS & CLARK DISCOVERED THE WEST.
LET US TAKE CARE OF THE REST.

15% Off!*

Climb every mountain and cross every stream of the Corps Of Discovery to get to our front door. Every La Quinta. Every Time.

Discover the comforts Lewis & Clark were looking for and **save 15% off** our already great rates! You'll also enjoy our great amenities** like free continental breakfast with fresh waffles, in-room coffee maker, 25" TV with premium channels, indoor pool and spa, fitness center, evening snack, guest laundry, and kids stay free.

La Quinta Inn

Portland, OR
Convention Center
(503) 233-7933

Ritzville, WA
(509) 659-1007

Walla Walla, WA
(509) 525-2522

Coeur d'Alene, ID
US Hwy 95
(208) 765-5500

Sandpoint, ID
(208) 263-9581

La Quinta Inn & Suites

Portland, OR
Northwest
(503) 497-9044

Seattle, WA
Downtown
(206) 624-6820

Wenatchee, WA
(509) 664-6565

Kennewick, WA
Tri Cities
(509) 736-3326

Spokane, WA
Valley
(509) 893-0955

Coeur d'Alene, ID
East
(208) 667-6777

Kalispell, MT
(406) 257-5255

Great Falls, MT
Riverfront
(406) 761-2600

Bozeman/Belgrade, MT
(406) 388-2222

Visit LQ.com and use promotional code LCTP or call 1-800-531-5900 and ask for the Lewis & Clark Travel Planner Discount.

*15% discount on standard room only valid at participating La Quinta hotels in ID, MT, OR, and WA. Offer subject to availability, advance reservations required, tax extra. This offer cannot be combined with any other discount or offer, not valid during special events or blackout dates. Valid through 1/31/06.
**Amenities may vary.

Making Ready

Preparing to travel the newly obtained Louisiana Purchase filled Meriwether Lewis's time from April to August 1803, before he started down the Ohio River. At William Clark's home in Indiana, the two captains joined up at last, and Clark introduced the "young men from Kentucky" whom he'd enlisted in the Army. Then it was on down to the Mississippi River, which took them north to the St. Louis area. Lewis's sometimes sketchy journal of these early days is amplified by his letters to President Thomas Jefferson and to Clark, but we have to put up with frustrating holes in the record-keeping until August 30, 1803.

Monticello, Albemarle County, Virginia. CHARLES GURCHE

Statewide resources for Making Ready

Virginia Tourism Corporation
901 E. Byrd St., Richmond, VA 23219;
800-VISIT-VA_www.virginia.org

West Virginia Division of Tourism
90 MacCorkle Ave., SW, South Charleston, WV 25303
800-CALLWVA; www.callwva.com

Pennsylvania
800-VISITPA; www.experiencepa.com

Discover Ohio
800-BUCKEYE; www.ohiotourism.com

Kentucky Department of Travel
800-225-8747; www.kytourism.com

Indiana Tourism Division, Dept. of Commerce
One North Capitol, Suite 700, Indianapolis, IN 46204-2288
888-ENJOY-IN; www.in.gov/tourism

1803; return 1806

CHARLOTTESVILLE, VA

A planned town laid out in 1762, Charlottesville has grown as the pleasant seat of Albemarle County (population 82,000) in the Blue Ridge Mountain foothills. Revolutionary War and Civil War sites are scattered around the area. In a sense, the Lewis and Clark Trail begins here, where Jefferson first began thinking of an expedition to explore what now is the northwestern quarter of the contiguous United States.

So Very Virginia (Charlottesville/Albermarle County)
877-386-1102; www.soveryvirginia.com

Monticello
I-64, exit 121, follow signs; 434-977-1783
Thomas Jefferson's self-designed home from 1770 to his death on July 4, 1826 (except during two terms as the third president of the United States, 1801-1809) offers tours of the house, which exhibits specimens the Corps of Discovery brought back and some of Jefferson's inventions. Also to be explored are the gardens and the plantation community, including remains of Mulberry Row, site of the slave quarters.

Lewis & Clark & Sacagawea Memorial
Ridge & Main Streets
A statue honors the expedition's leaders and their Shoshone translator.

University of Virginia
Intersection of I-64 and US 29, follow signs
Tour information: 434-982-3200
Jefferson laid out the grounds and designed the first buildings, the Rotunda and the Pavilions on the Lawn. Along with James Monroe and James Madison, he attended the first cornerstone ceremony in 1817. After the Rotunda burned in 1895—except for the brick exterior walls—architect Stanford White redesigned it, but restoration according to Jefferson's original plans was accomplished between 1973 and 1976. Guided tours of the Rotunda and Lawn and of the Gardens are available.

Ash Lawn–Highland
James Monroe Parkway; 604-293-9539
Home to the fifth president (1817–1825) of the U.S., James Madison. His friend Jefferson arranged the purchase and planted orchards while Madison was in France in 1799 on a diplomatic mission. Unfortunately, Madison had to sell the estate in 1826 for financial reasons. Today, guided tours show visitors the rooms furnished in period from Madison's time.

1803; return 1806

WASHINGTON, DC

To President Thomas Jefferson, his official residence was President's House, Federal Town. George Washington, who never lived in the President's House, preferred calling the muddy little settlement Federal City. When Meriwether Lewis served as Jefferson's secretary, he lived in what we now call the White House, and his quarters were in today's East Room.

Visitor Information Center
1300 Pennsylvania Ave.; 202-328-4748
Closed Sundays from Labor Day to mid-March; open Sunday afternoons the rest of the year.

Making Ready

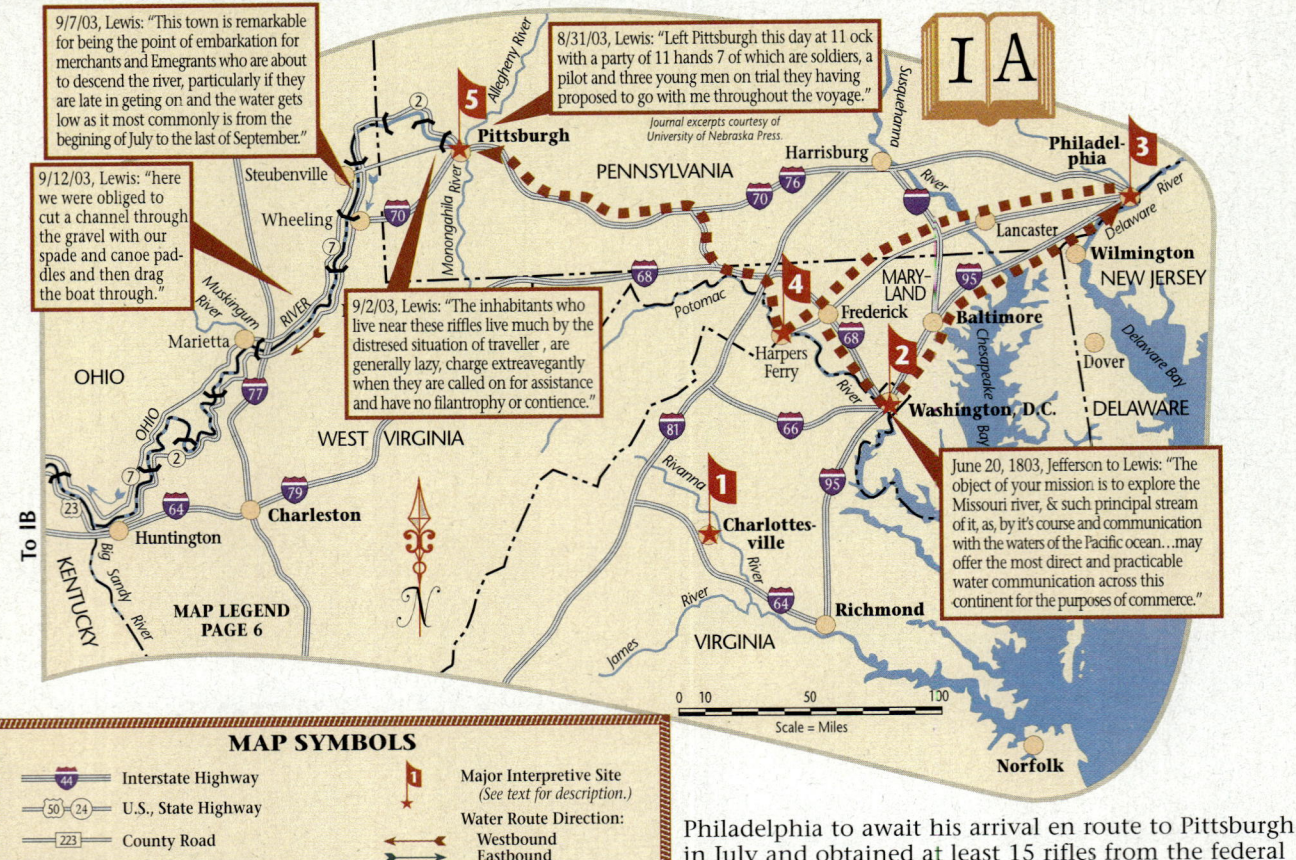

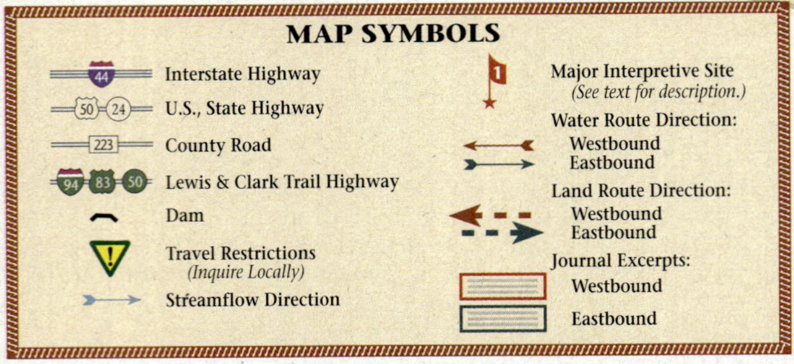

9/7/03, Lewis: "This town is remarkable for being the point of embarkation for merchants and Emegrants who are about to descend the river, particularly if they are late in geting on and the water gets low as it most commonly is from the begining of July to the last of September."

8/31/03, Lewis: "Left Pittsburgh this day at 11 ock with a party of 11 hands 7 of which are soldiers, a pilot and three young men on trial they having proposed to go with me throughout the voyage."
Journal excerpts courtesy of University of Nebraska Press.

9/12/03, Lewis: "here we were obliged to cut a channel through the gravel with our spade and canoe paddles and then drag the boat through."

9/2/03, Lewis: "The inhabitants who live near these riffles live much by the distressed situation of traveller, are generally lazy, charge extreavagantly when they are called on for assistance and have no filantrophy or contience."

June 20, 1803, Jefferson to Lewis: "The object of your mission is to explore the Missouri river, & such principal stream of it, as, by it's course and communication with the waters of the Pacific ocean...may offer the most direct and practicable water communication across this continent for the purposes of commerce."

MAP SYMBOLS

- Interstate Highway
- U.S., State Highway
- County Road
- Lewis & Clark Trail Highway
- Dam
- Travel Restrictions (Inquire Locally)
- Streamflow Direction
- Major Interpretive Site (See text for description.)
- Water Route Direction: Westbound / Eastbound
- Land Route Direction: Westbound / Eastbound
- Journal Excerpts: Westbound / Eastbound

Thomas Jefferson Memorial
S.E. side of Tidal Basin; 202-426-6821

Sample the third president's thoughts in quotations on panels that surround the 19-foot-tall bronze statue of Jefferson, standing under a classical dome reminiscent of his own architectural designs.

IA 2 — White House Visitor Center
1450 Pennsylvania Ave. NW (Dept. of Commerce) 800-717-1450

Jefferson was the second president in residence in the White House during his two terms (1801-1809). At this center, watch a half-hour video and see exhibits that describe the building's history and architecture. White House tours for the general public are not available.

March 16–April 8, July 5–8, 1803
Harpers Ferry, WV — IA

On his first visit, Lewis oversaw construction of the iron boat frame he had designed. (After the 800-pound frame was carried all the way to the Great Falls, Montana, he discovered that no trees in the area had pine pitch, which he'd counted on for caulking animal hides stitched over the metal frame; the boat sank upon launch.) Lewis had supplies shipped here from Philadelphia to await his arrival en route to Pittsburgh in July and obtained at least 15 rifles from the federal armory.

IA 3 — Harpers Ferry National Historic Park
US 340; 304-535-6223

The armory here was new—and then in the Commonwealth of Virginia—when Lewis came to supply the Corps; that building was destroyed by Confederates in 1861. An exhibit dedicated in 2003 tells of Lewis's two visits in 1803. Further exhibits recount abolitionist John Brown's 1859 raid, which he hoped would start a slave rebellion.

April 19–May 10, 1803
Lancaster, PA — IA

Meriwether Lewis began a summer of intensive study here, to prepare for the trip's requirement of drawing accurate maps, with prominent mathematician/astronomer Andrew Ellicott. Lewis learned the elements of celestial navigation and also how to figure longitude by calculations from charts the captains carried along. He later taught Clark, an experienced surveyor, who drew most expedition maps.

Lancaster is a gateway to touring Pennsylvania Dutch country and also has several museums showing area history from the colonial and revolutionary periods.

Pennsylvania Dutch Convention & Visitors Bureau
US30 at Greenfield Rd.; 800-723-8824

Sehner-Ellicott-von Hess House
123 N. Prince; 717-291-5861

The Historic Preservation Trust of Lancaster County

now has offices in Andrew Ellicott's former home. Self-guided tours are available Monday–Friday.

May 10–June, 1803
PHILADELPHIA, PA

Some people liken Meriwether Lewis's time here in 1803 to "boot camp." He received further training in navigation from mathematician Robert Patterson, studied botany and natural history with Benjamin Smith Barton, learned about anatomy and fossils from Caspar Wistar, and got a quick course in medicine from physician Benjamin Rush. All were friends of Jefferson, who asked them to prepare Lewis for the expedition's scientific aspects.

Lewis also shopped for supplies at the Schuylkill Arsenal and local stores, obtaining "blowing-trumpets" (long horns) for hailing people at a distance, metal cargo boxes, "portable soup" (rich broth condensed to a gelatin-like substance), ink powder, knives, axes, and more. He stocked up on such trade goods as glass lenses for fire-starting, beads, fishhooks, and flags. Lewis shipped a ton and a half of supplies to the Harpers Ferry Arsenal in Virginia to await him.

As a center of the War for Independence and a temporary capital for the new United States of America, Philadelphia is rich in historical sites relating to both, along with all the other amenities of city life.

Independence Visitor Center
Sixth & Market on Independence Mall; 800-537-7676
Film and exhibits on Independence National Park, City of Philadelphia, and southeastern Pennsylvania. Get tickets for Independence Hall tours here.

Independence National Historic Park
Sixth & Market; 800-537-7676
Orientation film and self-guided walking-tour brochures are available at Independence Visitor Center, listed above. Sites included in this park are reconstructed Declaration House at 7th & Market, where Jefferson drafted the Declaration of Independence; Liberty Bell Pavilion; Independence Hall, where both the Declaration of Independence and U.S. Constitution were signed; Congress Hall, which served 1790-1800; New Hall Military Museum, on the Army, Navy, and Marine Corps from 1775 to 1805.

Academy of Natural Sciences
19th & Benjamin Franklin Parkway; 215-299-1000
View more than 200 plant specimens collected by Lewis in the Lewis & Clark Herbarium, and also check out the dinosaur hall and live animal shows.

July 15–August 31, 1803
PITTSBURGH, PA

The city where the Ohio River begins was a riverboat-building headquarters in 1803, and Lewis came here to have a 55-foot-long keelboat built. It would be taken all the way to the Mandan-Hidatsa villages and spend the winter of 1804-1805 at Fort Mandan in future North Dakota. But Lewis spent six frustrating weeks here while the boatbuilder got drunk, fired employees, had to find new ones, and generally frittered away any chance the Corps of Discovery had for making it to the Mandan-Hidatsa villages in the fall of 1803.

Today's visitors can enjoy museums, the arts, all types of entertainment, professional sports, and the many ethnic neighborhoods and festivals.

Greater Pittsburgh Convention & Visitors Bureau
4 Gateway Center; 800-359-0758; www.pittsburgh-cvb.org

Point State Park
101 Commonwealth Place; 412-471-0235
At the Ohio River's headwaters stands the original blockhouse of Fort Pitt, part of the British colonial frontier post that was 45 years old when Lewis spent long summer weeks here awaiting the keelboat's completion.

September 6, 1803
STEUBENVILLE, OH

Lewis passed Steubenville on a windy day that pelted the keelboat with rain from time to time. He noted that the settlement "is [a] small well built thriving place. Has several respectable families residing in it, five years since it was a wilderness."

Old Fort Steuben
100 South St.; 740-264-6304
Restored American fort dating from 1787. Exhibits, bicycling trails, picnic area.

September 7, 1803
WELLSBURG, WV

Then called Charles Town, Wellsburg was three miles downstream from Lewis's camp of the day before. As he passed by, he thought it "a handsome little Village, containing about forty houses."

West Virginia broke off from the state of Virginia in 1863 because a majority of its residents favored being in the Union, which Virginia had left as the Civil War began.

Patrick Gass Grave
Brooke Cemetery, Pleasant Street
Above the Ohio River is the final resting place of the sergeant who outlived every other member of the Corps of Discovery, nearly reaching 100 years.

September 7–8, 1803
WHEELING, WV

As Lewis's keelboat docked here for two days, he attracted the attention of Dr. William Patterson, a young man who said he would go along when the boat pulled out the next day. He was the son of Robert Patterson, who trained Lewis in Philadelphia, but unfortunately was also an alcoholic who—for unknown reasons—never showed up and missed the trip of a lifetime. The Corps also missed having a "real" doctor along.

Lewis found Wheeling "a pretty considerable Village [that] contains about fifty houses." Today the population is around 30,000.

Making Ready

Wheeling Convention & Visitors Bureau
1401 Main St.; 800-828-3097; www.wheelingcvb.com

Wheeling Heritage Trail
This paved hiking/biking trail follows the Ohio River for 14 miles, with stairs to access downtown businesses.

September 13, 1803
MARIETTA, OH 1A

Ohio's oldest town was 15 when Lewis stopped overnight and wrote to Jefferson explaining how shallow the Ohio River was, and how he and his crew often had to cut a channel in the gravel bottom to get the keelboat through.

Historic Harmar Village
100 block, Maple St.; 800-288-2577

Fort Harmar, which stood here when Lewis stopped, is gone, but visitors now see museums and historic homes and shops in the area that served the fort. Riverboats still stop at the port of Marietta.

mid-September, 1803
MAYSVILLE, KY 1B

At the town then called Old Limestone, future privates John Colter and George Shannon may have joined Lewis on a test basis. Colter would become the most famous enlisted man in the party, as a mountain man who was the first white to see the geysers and mudpots of future Yellowstone National Park—too bad people thought he was just "yarning" them with his descriptions. Shannon, the youngest soldier, was just 18 that beginning year of the trip; he might have joined Lewis as early as the Pittsburgh stay.

September 28–October 4 or 5, 1803
CINCINNATI, OH 1B

Arriving here, Lewis found two letters from William Clark awaiting him—with news that Clark had found some men suitable for serving in the Corps of Discovery (see Clarksville, IN, below). Lewis and his group spent about a week in Cincinnati, but he had stopped keeping his journal.

Cincinnati Visitor Information Center
Fifth Third Center, Fountain Square
800-CINCYUSA; www.cincyusa.com

Serves 13 counties in Ohio, Kentucky, and Indiana.

October 6, 1803
COVINGTON, KY 1B

The wooly mammoth fossils here had been discovered in May of that year. Lewis visited with the Cincinnati physician William Goforth, who was making the dig, visited Bone Lick himself, and then reported the finds in great detail to Jefferson. He sent some specimens to the president, but they were lost in shipment.

Cincinnati Visitor Information Center
Fifth Third Center, Fountain Square, Cincinnati;
800-CINCYUSA

Serves thirteen counties in Ohio, Kentucky, and Indiana.

Big Bone Lick State Park 6
3380 Beaver Rd., 22 mi. SW on KY338;
859-384-3522

Today's visitors can tour the museum and stroll a trail through the re-created bog with life-sized wooly mammoth sculptures. Campsites are included in the park.

October 14, 1803
LOUISVILLE, KY 1B

Here began a horrific set of rapids, the Falls of the Ohio, a two-mile-long series of limestone ledges that the river snaked through, dropping from two to six feet at a time over the rock. Like all other travelers, Lewis stopped at Louisville and hired a local pilot to guide the keelboat through. Because the Ohio River was exceptionally low that year, the trip had to have been especially hard on the keelboat. Until leaving Clarksville, the co-captains often visited and did business in Louisville.

Today, Louisville calls itself "the southernmost northern city and the northernmost southern city" and recommends pronunciations of "Looavuhl" or "Looeyville."

Greater Louisville Convention & Visitors Bureau
400 S. First St.; 800-626-5646; www.gotolouisville.com

Filson Historical Society
1310 S. Third; 502-635-5083

Houses an extensive collection of photographs and documents on Kentucky history—including some documents and artifacts of the Lewis and Clark Expedition—with a small selection on exhibit at any one time.

Churchill Downs Kentucky Derby Museum
704 Central Ave.; 502-637-1111

Louisville's most famous annual event is the Kentucky Derby in May. Visitors to the museum can experience Derby Day here, any time of the year, in a multimedia presentation. Mon-Sat 9 to 5, Sun noon to 5.

October 15–26, 1803
CLARKSVILLE, IN 1B

At the town that took his name, George Rogers Clark lived on Clark's Point in a brand-new cabin in 1803, and younger brother William stayed with him awaiting his co-captain. The area at the end of the Falls of the Ohio had been called Point of Rocks before George Rogers chose this spot as his land grant for Revolutionary War service. Following Lewis's written request to recruit some good woodsmen (and not sissy "young gentlemen" who couldn't pull their weight) for the trip, Clark had signed up a hardy crew often called the "nine young men from Kentucky": Sgt. Charles Floyd, his cousin Sgt. Nathaniel Hale Pryor, Privates William Bratton, brothers Joseph and Reubin Field, George Gibson, John Shields. (To get nine out of that, you have to add the two men who had joined Lewis, possibly upriver at Maysville.) Clark also introduced York, the tall and then somewhat stout African-American slave who would make the trip with Clark and the Corps.

IB 7 Clark's Point
Falls of the Ohio State Park. I-65, exit 0; 812-280-9970

The same limestone that made the Falls of the Ohio so difficult for transportation in 1803 also supplied a magnificent record of ancient life forms on Earth. The creatures that lived 375 million years ago are described in multimedia exhibits in the interpretive center, and a wooly mammoth skeleton is exhibited. Outdoors, the park offers fishing, hiking, and picnicking facilities.

Return trip, 1806
ST. MATTHEWS, KY   IB

Locust Grove Historic Home
I-264, exit 22, 0.5 mi. W on US42
502-897-9845

There's no record that William and Meriwether visited here in 1803, although it seems likely they would have. It is recorded, however, that both captains visited this home of Lucy Clark Croghan and her husband William on their return trip to Washington, DC, in 1806. Today parts of Clark's sister's plantation and gardens are restored, and guided tours are offered.

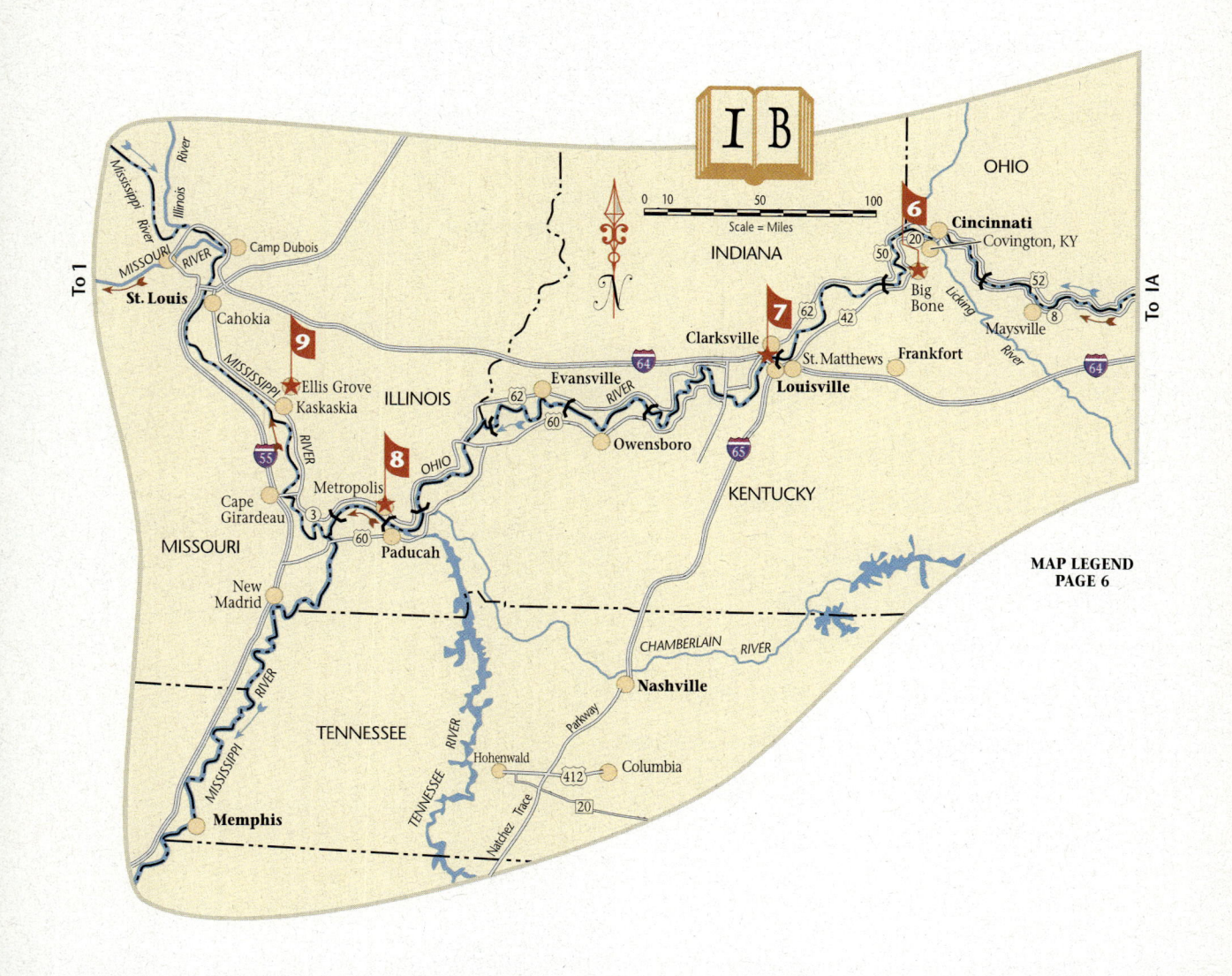

MAP LEGEND PAGE 6

MAKING READY   13

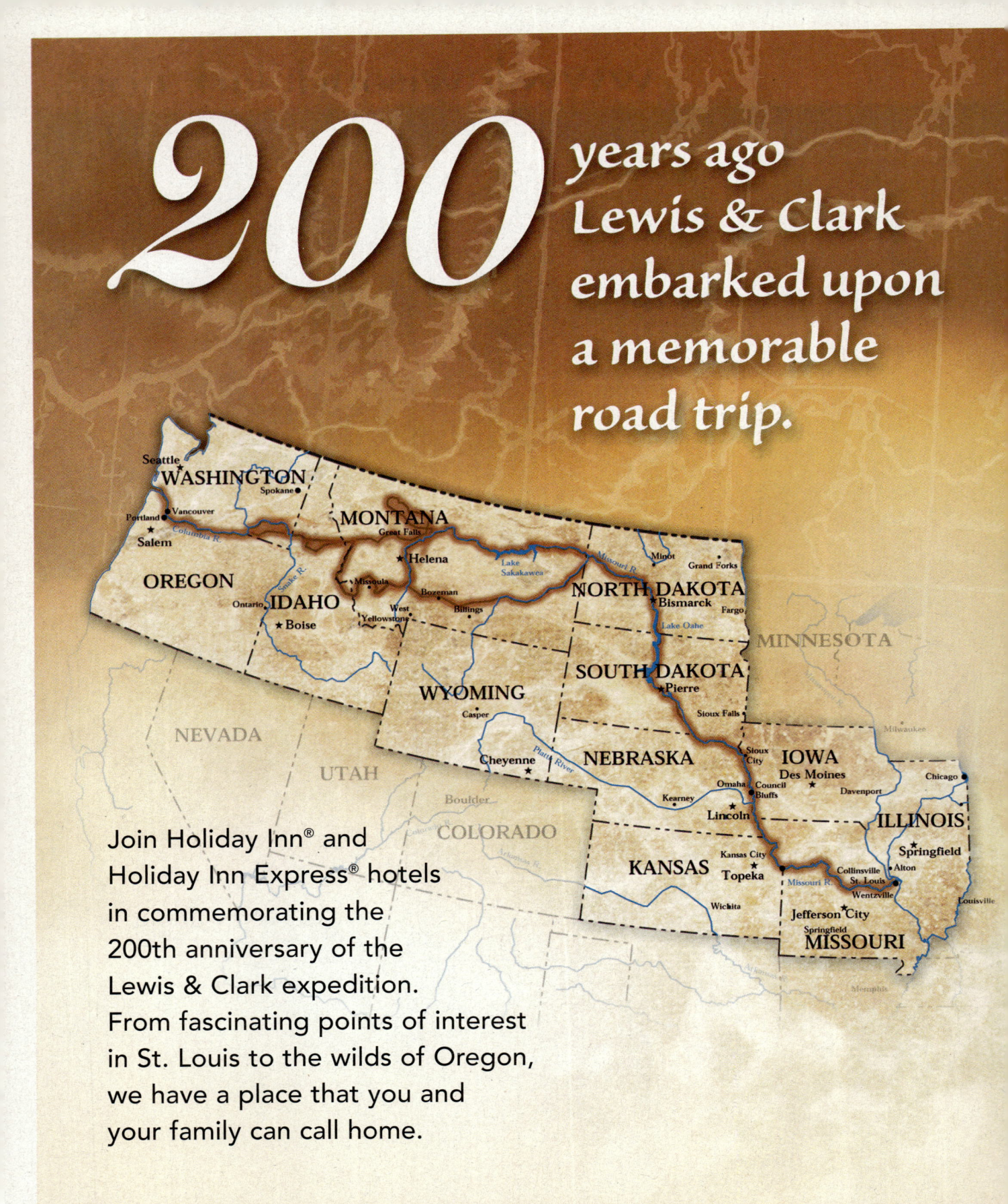

200 years ago Lewis & Clark embarked upon a memorable road trip.

Join Holiday Inn® and Holiday Inn Express® hotels in commemorating the 200th anniversary of the Lewis & Clark expedition. From fascinating points of interest in St. Louis to the wilds of Oregon, we have a place that you and your family can call home.

Visit us at holiday-inn.com/lewisandclark or hiexpress.com/lewisandclark

● Denotes Holiday Inn® Hotel & Suites location. ● Denotes Holiday Inn Select® hotel location. ● Denotes Holiday Inn Express® Hotel & Suites location.
©2004 InterContinental Hotels Group. All rights reserved. Most hotels are independently owned and/or operated.

Now it's your turn to explore the world they discovered.

IDAHO
Boise–Airport
(208) 344-8365
Lewiston
(208) 750-1600
Pocatello
(208) 237-1400
ILLINOIS
CHICAGO–DOWNTOWN AREA
Downtown •
(312) 957-9100
CHICAGO–O'HARE AIRPORT AREA
Elk Grove
(847) 437-6010
CHICAGO AREA
Midway Airport ■
(708) 594-5500
Skokie (North Shore Area)
(847) 679-8900
MOLINE
Airport Area
(309) 762-8300
Convention Center at the Airport
(309) 762-8811
IOWA
Davenport
(563) 391-1230
Newton (I-80)
(641) 792-7722
SIOUX CITY
Downtown
(712) 277-9400
Sioux City
(712) 274-1400
KANSAS
Topeka–West
(785) 272-8040

MISSOURI
KANSAS CITY AREA
Independence •
(816) 795-8889
Northeast–I-435 North
(at Worlds of Fun)
(816) 455-1060
ST. LOUIS AIRPORT AREA
Airport–Riverport
(314) 298-3400
Westport
(314) 434-0100
ST. LOUIS DOWNTOWN AREA
Forest Park (Hampton Avenue)
(314) 645-0700
St. Louis
(314) 773-6500
ST. LOUIS AREA
Alton, IL (Riverboat Gambling Area)
(618) 462-1220
Collinsville, IL
(618) 345-2800
South (I-55)
(314) 894-0700
Wentzville–O'Fallon
(636) 327-7001
MONTANA
Belgrade–Bozeman
(406) 388-0800
Billings–The Grand Montana
(406) 248-7701
Bozeman
(406) 587-4561
GREAT FALLS
Great Falls
(406) 727-7200
Great Falls •
(406) 455-1000
Miles City
(406) 234-1000
Missoula–Parkside
(406) 721-8550
NEBRASKA
Grand Island–Midtown
(308) 384-1330
Lexington •
(308) 324-9900
North Platte •
(308) 532-9500
Ogallala
(308) 284-2266

NEBRASKA (cont.)
Omaha–Central (I-80)
(402) 393-3950
Valentine •
(402) 376-3000
NORTH DAKOTA
Fargo
(701) 282-2700
Grand Forks •
(701) 772-7700
Minot–Riverside
(701) 852-2504
OHIO
Cleveland–Elyria/Lorain
(Ohio Turnpike Exit 145)
(440) 324-5411
OREGON
Astoria
(503) 325-6222
Bend •
(541) 317-8500
Corvallis–On the River
(541) 752-0800
Florence
(541) 997-7797
Ontario
(541) 889-8621
Pendleton
(541) 966-6520
PORTLAND AREA
Downtown
(503) 233-2401
East
(503) 492-2900
I-5 South (Wilsonville)
(503) 570-8500
Northwest Downtown •
(503) 484-1100
Salem (Oregon Capitol)
(503) 391-7000
SOUTH DAKOTA
Mitchell
(605) 996-6501
Pierre/Fort Pierre •
(605) 223-9045
Yankton •
(605) 665-3177
WASHINGTON
Pullman •
(509) 334-4337
Puyallup (Tacoma Area) •
(253) 848-4900

WASHINGTON (cont.)
SEATTLE AIRPORT AREA
Sea-Tac Airport •
(206) 824-3200
SEATTLE DOWNTOWN AREA
Seattle
(206) 728-8123
SEATTLE AREA
Issaquah
(425) 392-6421
SPOKANE AREA
Airport
(509) 838-1170
Downtown
(509) 328-8505
Valley
(509) 927-7100
Vancouver–North
(Salmon Creek Area) •
(360) 576-1040
WYOMING
Cheyenne–I-80
(307) 638-4466
Sheridan–Convention Center
(307) 672-8931
Thermopolis
(307) 864-3131

Hotel listings in blue are Holiday Inn Express® locations.
Hotel listings in green are Holiday Inn® locations.

Holiday Inn EXPRESS®

RELAX, it's Holiday Inn

or call 1-800-HOLIDAY for reservations.

Illinois

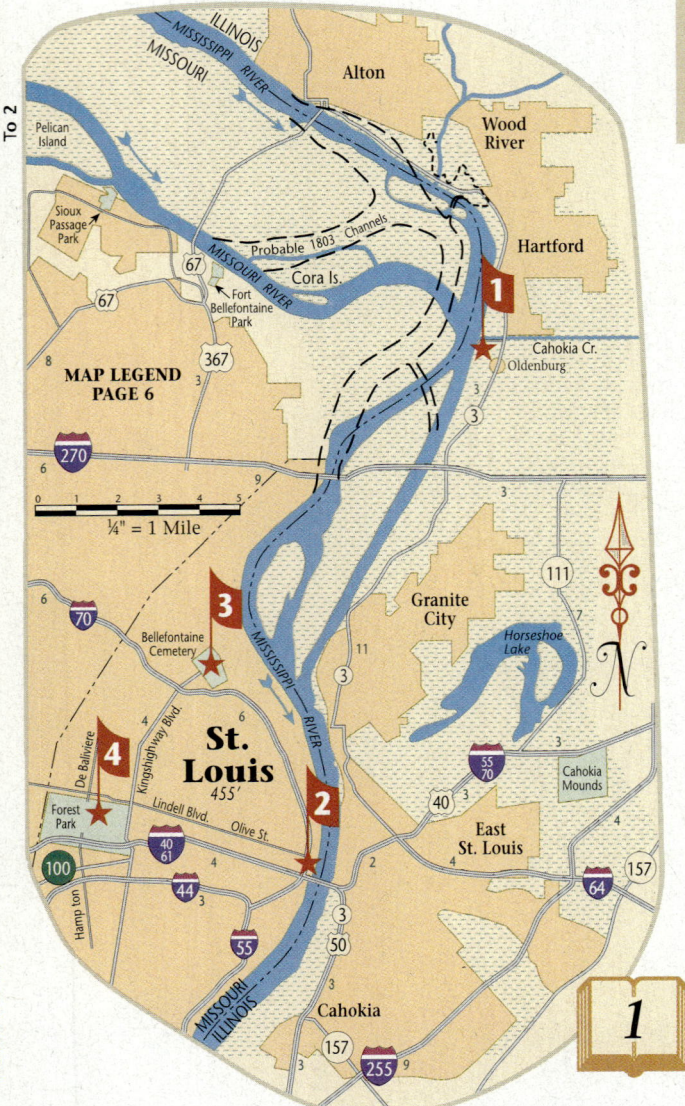

When we say the Lewis and Clark Expedition lasted from 1804 to 1806, that's just the time they were "on the road." Captain Meriwether Lewis, Lieutenant William Clark, and most of the enlisted men gathered in the fall of 1803, and with some hired civilians, spent the winter of 1803-1804 together. (Lewis could not get the army to allow Clark, a former captain and once Lewis's commanding officer, to grant him that rank for the expedition. He apologized to Clark, then lied to the men, and, in every way but on paper, Clark always was a co-captain.) This winter was an important time of preparation, while the captains assessed each man's strengths and weaknesses. They had to decide who would be in the "permanent party" going all the way to the Pacific. The expedition camp was on the east, Illinois, side of the Mississippi River, across from the mouth of the Missouri River. Illinois had become part of Indiana Territory that year of 1803, and had six years to wait until creation of Illinois Territory.

Fort de Chartres reenactment, Randolph County. SCOTT R. AVETTA

Statewide resources on Illinois

Illinois Dept. of Commerce & Community Affairs Bureau of Tourism
100 W. Randolph St., Suite 3-400, Chicago, IL 60601
800-2CONNECT; www.enjoyillinois.com

November 11-13, 1803

METROPOLIS, IL

Here the Corps hired the most George Drouillard, son of a Shawnee mother and French-Canadian father. Besides speaking French, English, and Shawnee, he knew Plains Indian sign language. His French allowed the captains to talk to Toussaint Charbonneau, who conversed in Hidatsa with Sacagawea, who spoke her native Shoshone to obtain horses for crossing the Rockies. Besides Drouillard's language abilities, he was brave, intelligent, and got along well with all the men. Both captains regularly selected him to go out on his own or in their small advance parties.

In the comic book, Metropolis was the small town where Superman spent his boyhood, and today's Metropolis has great fun with that fiction.

Southernmost Illinois Tourism Bureau
P.O. Box 278, Ullin IL 62992
800-248-4373; www.southernmostillinois.com

Fort Massac State Park
On US 45 east of Metropolis; 618-524-9321
Reconstructed Fort Massac now sits in a large park, which offers camping and a museum on 18th-

century frontier life in the area. Living-history events during the summer portray French voyageurs who traded here, and French, British, and American troops stationed here, 1757-1814. A major encampment occurs the third weekend of October, with demonstrations, costumed interpreters, period foods, and activities.

November 27–December 3, 1803
ELLIS GROVE, IL IB

The Corps of Discovery visited a rebuilt Fort Kaskaskia here, a U.S. Army post. The first one had been built in 1734 by French residents, who destroyed it in 1766 during the French and Indian War when capture by the British was imminent.

IB **Fort Kaskaskia State Historic Site**
618-859-3741

Today, remnants of the second fort can be seen. The park includes an overlook of the confluence of the Kaskaskia and Mississippi rivers, along with tent/RV campsites.

CAHOKIA, IL 1

Lewis spent a good deal of the winter of 1803-1804 here, where any mail to or from men of the Corps arrived and departed. He undoubtedly received some information about what lay ahead up the Missouri River from Nicholas Jarrot and other fur men in the area. Clark didn't get here too often—until finally he complained that he needed a change of pace.

Cahokia State Historic Sites
107 Elm St., Cahokia, IL 62206; 888-666-8624

Includes visitor center at above address and Cahokia Courthouse, Jarrot Mansion, Holy Family Parish Log Church (open to public June-August), and French-Creole–style Martin-Boismenue House in Prairie duPont.

Cahokia Courthouse
Among the handful of surviving human-made structures that Lewis and Clark visited, this building is an example of French colonial architecture on the American frontier. Cahokia, the Mississippi's oldest existing Euro-American village, was founded by missionaries in 1699. A century later it was the government center for the western portion of Indiana Territory, which the captains knew as "the Illinois." Built in 1740, the courthouse was a vibrant place to meet and do business for the area's varied residents: Indians, freed and enslaved blacks, French, Spanish, English, and Americans. Closed Sun-Mon.

Jarrot Mansion
Constructed over the turn of the 19th century, this is the oldest brick structure in Illinois. Fur trader Nicholas Jarrot translated for Meriwether Lewis when he met the French commandant at St. Louis late in 1803, and they became friends. Lewis probably stayed at Jarrot's previous home sometimes, but this one was begun in 1807. Open for tours on advance notice.

Cahokia Mounds State Historic Site
Collinsville, IL off I 55-70 & I-255, & IL 111; 618-346-5160

Interpretive center tells the story of the settlement that was occupied from 800 to 1400 by Mississippian Indians. Archaeological digs at this United Nations World Heritage Site are ongoing each summer. Closed Mon-Tue.

Dec. 13, 1803–May 14, 1804
HARTFORD 1

Clark arrived at the mouth of River Dubois in a keelboat with at least eight soldiers, two civilians, and "nine young men from Kentucky" that Clark had gathered. The wary Spanish captain at St. Louis told them to stay on the other side of both the Missouri and the Mississippi from his tiny fort. That, he knew for sure, was U.S. territory.

They built their own small log fort, the first of three winter quarters most of them would share, and called it Camp River Dubois.

How many men should the captains take along, what skills would be needed, and who had them? Mysterious lists in Clark's handwriting show names with pluses, checkmarks, and zeros beside some of them.

Jefferson had warned Lewis to take not "young gentlemen" but hardy frontiersmen. This winter's recreation included footraces and shooting contests. The young men enjoyed themselves while, off to the side, Clark watched and rated them.

The captains also quizzed anyone in St. Louis who could tell them what to expect up the Missouri River. Lewis often went to St. Louis to buy supplies and trade goods (adding two tons to the eight or so tons carried this far). The company's two blacksmiths crafted tools. Others parched corn to take along. And, in the spring, they boiled maple sap for sugar—to the later delight of Sacagawea, among others.

When the men left here, it was the official start of the expedition, for purposes of recording mileage from the mouth of the Missouri.

Greater Alton Convention & Visitors Bureau
200 Piasa; 800-258-6645

1 Lewis & Clark State Historic Site, National Trail Site #1
Across from confluence of Missouri with Mississippi, IL Route at Poag Road; 618-251-5811

This 14,000-square-foot multimedia center and museum tells the story of the entire trip, with an emphasis on the winter of preparations at and around Camp River Dubois. Includes a filmed presentation, a full-size, 55-foot, cutaway keelboat, and exhibits on how the men worked and played. Outdoor camp reconstruction features living history during summers.

Lewis and Clark State Confluence Memorial
IL Route 3, three-fifths of a mile N of I-270

Supporting a rotunda, the monument's 11 pillars represent the future states the expedition traveled, and plaques tell of their journey.

Missouri

Missouri River, Callaway County. CHARLES GURCHE

Imagine being the commander of a small, isolated frontier outpost (home to maybe 1,400 souls) of New Spain. One winter day, the leader of a U.S. military expedition arrives and informs you that his country is buying this land from France, for whom Spain manages it. Word just hasn't gotten to you yet—trust me, I had a letter from my president on the way here.

That happened to Carlos Dehault Delassus, lieutenant governor of Upper Louisiana, on December 8, 1803, when Meriwether Lewis introduced himself. On March 9, 1804, the official transfer occurred. Delassus formally ceded the Louisiana Purchase to U.S. artillery captain Amos Stoddard, as France's representative. The following day, Stoddard completed transfer to the U.S., nearly doubling the young nation's size.

Statewide resources on Missouri

Missouri Division of Tourism
301 W. High St., Box 1055 Jefferson City, MO 65701
800-877-1234; www.missouritourism.org

Missouri Department of Natural Resources (State Parks)
Box 176 Jefferson City, MO 65102
800-334-6946; www.dnr.state.mo.us

National Park Service Midwest Region
1709 Jackson St. Omaha, NE 65102-2571
402-221-3471; www.nps.gov

November 23, 1803

CAPE GIRARDEAU, MO

Sending the boats and an ill Captain Clark two miles north to Old Cape Girardeau for the night, Lewis stopped in Cape Girardeau to visit its creator and commandant, Louis Lorimier. Lewis carried a letter of introduction from George Drouillard, Lorimier's nephew. Lorimier's appearance fascinated Lewis, who detailed how the French Canadian had long, thick and still black (at age 60) hair, worn in a braid to his knees, and held in place by a "leather girdle" at his waist. After being burned out of his Ohio trading post by George Rogers Clark, Lorimier had started over here eight years before and prospered. His Shawnee wife "presided" at dinner, and the family included a "remarkably handsome" daughter.

The Red House Interpretive Center modeled after Louis Lorimier's French colonial home and trading post that Lewis visited opened in the fall of 2003. Panels portray Lewis and Clark, members of the Expedition who returned to Cape Girardeau, the Lorimier family, local settlers, African Americans, Native Americans, the Mississippi River, and transportation.

Cape Girardeau Convention & Visitors Bureau
100 Broadway; 800-777-0068

Cape Girardeau Cape River Heritage Museum
538 Independence St., Cape Girardeau; 573-334-0405
Mississippi River transportation exhibits; area heritage and history. Open Wednesday, Friday, Saturday.

Trail of Tears State Park
10 miles north on MO 177; 573-334-1711
Hiking trails mark the route followed by Cherokee people when they were forced to Oklahoma in 1838-1839. Wildlife viewing; camping, including RV sites.

November 28 to December 3, 1803

STE. GENEVIEVE

The Corps of Discovery camped across the Mississippi River from "old Ste. Genevieve" and practiced with the navigational instruments. The old townsite had been abandoned after a great flood in 1785.

Ste. Genevieve's National Historic Landmark District today holds restored homes and businesses that combine frontier, American-Federal and French Colonial architectural influences. Tours are offered daily, and special events occur year-round.

Great River Road Interpretive Center
66 S. Main St., Ste. Genevieve, MO, 800-373-7007
Rotating exhibits about life along the Mississippi, and the place to get town walking-tour brochures.

December 8, 1803; return: September 23, 1806

ST. LOUIS

The Corps reached journey's end at St. Louis at noon, and people on the banks cheered them. In his journal the next day, Clark admitted that he slept "but little last night." He and Lewis began writing letters to announce their return, including Lewis's official one to Jefferson. With that entry, the expedition journals end.

St. Louis became the commercial center of the American fur trade in the early 1800's, and the starting point for the California, Oregon, and Santa Fe trails west. When William Clark later served as Indian agent for the vast Louisiana Territory, many Indian people called St. Louis "Red Head's Town."

Free* Lewis & Clark Souvenir at Holiday Inn®

200 years ago Lewis & Clark embarked upon a memorable road trip.

Participating Holiday Inn® Hotels

ST. LOUIS AIRPORT AREA

1. Airport
(314) 731-2100
2. Airport (Oakland Park)
(314) 427-4700
3. Airport–Riverport
(314) 298-3400
4. St. Peters/St.Charles ▪
(636) 928-1500
5. Westport
(314) 434-0100

ST. LOUIS DOWNTOWN AREA

6. Downtown (Convention Center) ▪
(314) 421-4000
7. Forest Park (Hampton Avenue)
(314) 645-0700

ST. LOUIS AREA

8. Alton, IL (National Trail Site #1)
(618) 462-1220
9. Collinsville, IL
(618) 345-2800
10. South County Center
(314) 892-3600
11. South (I-55)
(314) 894-0700
12. Southwest (Viking)
(314) 821-6600
13. Wentzville–O'Fallon
(636) 327-7001

▪ Denotes Holiday Inn Select® hotel location.

Follow the Footsteps of Lewis & Clark

A. National Trail Site #1: The Lewis & Clark State Historic Site (Hartford, IL)
B. The Lewis & Clark Centers
C. Jefferson National Expansion Memorial: The Gateway Arch
D. Museum of Westward Expansion
E. Lewis & Clark: Great Journey West (at the St. Louis Science Center)
F. The Missouri History Museum
G. Powder Valley Conservation Nature Center
H. St. Louis Walk of Fame
I. William Clark's Grave
J. Fort Belle Fontaine
K. General Daniel Bissell House
L. Cahokia Courthouse
M. Holy Family Church
N. Jarrot Mansion
O. Cahokia Mounds Historic Site
P. The Lewis & Clark Boat House and Nature Center
Q. Katy Trail (trailhead begins in St. Charles)
R. Daniel Boone Home and Boonesfield Village (Defiance, MO)

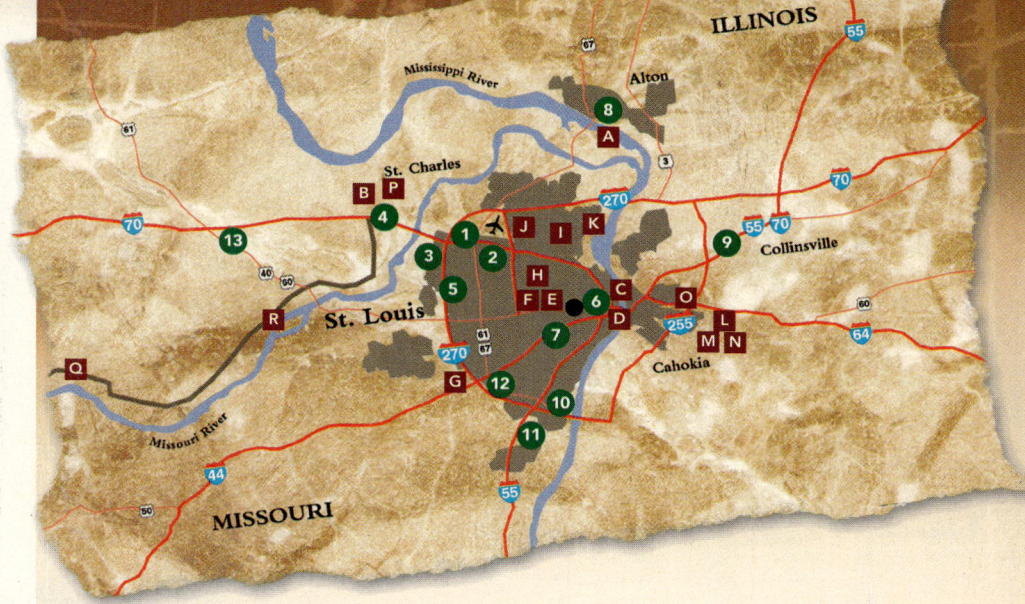

Now it's your turn to explore the world they discovered.

Join the St. Louis Area Holiday Inn® hotels in commemorating the 200th anniversary of the Lewis & Clark expedition. From Trail Site #1 near Alton to points of interest in St. Louis to the richly historic city of St. Charles, we have a place that you and your family can call home.

RELAX, it's Holiday Inn

Visit **holidayinnstlouis.com** or call **1-800-HOLIDAY** to reserve your room.

Lewis & Clark Holiday Inn 200th Anniversary

Present this coupon at check-in to receive a complimentary* Lewis & Clark souvenir.

*Must present this coupon at check-in. Limit one offer per room. Offer valid while supplies last at participating St. Louis Holiday Inn® hotels only. ©2003 InterContinental Hotels Group. All rights reserved. Most hotels are independently owned and/or operated.

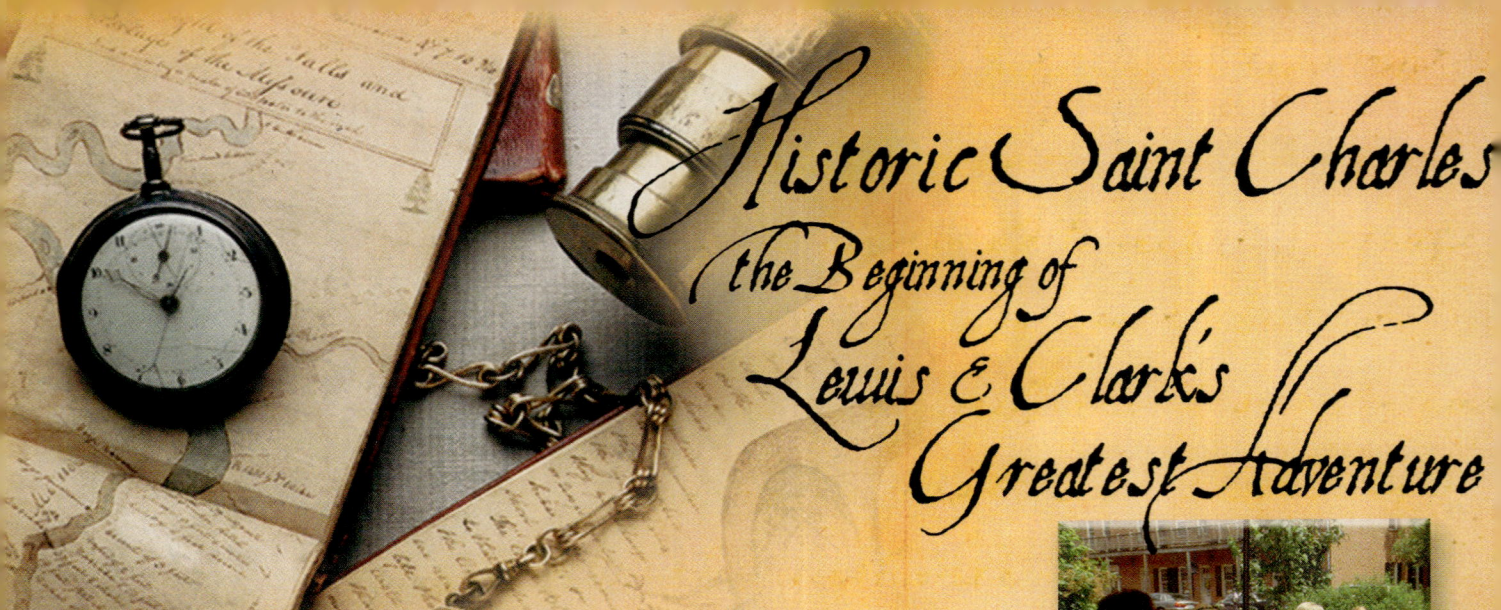

Historic Saint Charles
the Beginning of Lewis & Clark's Greatest Adventure

Follow in the footsteps of Captains Meriwether Lewis and William Clark and America's pioneers. Explore more than 125 unique shops. Choose from more than 30 restaurants, menus ranging from casual pubs to elegant cuisine. All set in the 18th century ambiance of this nationally Historic District.

Discover Missouri's First State Capitol or the Lewis & Clark Boat House and Nature Center. Experience Missouri's beautiful Wine Country and Daniel Boone's home. Spend a night in a quaint bed and breakfast or a comfortable hotel.

Commemorate the epic journey that Lewis & Clark began in Saint Charles, the journey that changed the course of American history. Visit Saint Charles - "Where History Comes Alive Everyday!"

★★★ PREPARATIONS COMPLETE ★★★
Lewis & Clark
the EXPEDITION FACES WEST
1804 2004
MAY 14-23, 2004 SAINT CHARLES, MO

GREATER SAINT CHARLES
CONVENTION & VISITORS BUREAU

1-866-301-9770
www.lewisandclarkstcharles.com
www.historicstcharles.com

25 minutes from downtown St. Louis

www.lewisandclark.com

St. Louis Convention & Visitors Commission
1 Metropolitan Sq., Suite 1100,
St. Louis, MO 63102
800-916-0092; www.st-louis-cvc.com

Jefferson National Expansion Memorial
11 N. 4th St., St. Louis, MO 63102; 314-655-1700; www.nps.gov/jeff

Beneath the Gateway Arch, the Museum of Westward Expansion covers the Lewis and Clark Expedition, a peace medal collection, other westward explorers and pioneers, native peoples, and natural history of the American West. The 90-acre complex is on the original St. Louis town site.

Tickets required (and summertime lines are slow), but advance tickets are available.

Missouri History Museum
in Forest Park; 314-746-4599

On the grounds of the 1904 Louisiana Purchase Exposition, the four-story Jefferson Memorial Building holds exhibits of Native Americans, the Lewis and Clark Expedition, and westward expansion.

Bellefontaine Cemetery
4947 W. Florissant Ave., St. Louis, MO

At William Clark's grave here is a monument dedicated in 1904, during the expedition's centennial.

May 16, 1804

St. Stanislaus Conservation Area
in St. Louis County: MO 370 to Earth City Expressway, then 3.5 miles north (road becomes Aubuchon Rd.); 314-441-4554

Clark wrote that, early this morning, the men passed "a remarkable coal hill" called La Charbonniere by local French residents. Hike that bluff and other trails throughout the park.

return: September 22, 1806

Fort Belle Fontaine County Park
13300 Bellefontaine Rd.

Near the site of the U.S. Army's first post in Upper Louisiana Territory, built by 1805. The Corps stopped to see the new fort in 1806 and spend their last night before reaching in St. Louis. Interpretive trail on the Missouri bluffs allows a view of their May 14, 1804, camp—the first on the expedition.

May 16–21, 1804

ST. CHARLES

Lewis was still making arrangements in St. Louis when Clark and the men set off from Camp Dubois. The Corps waited for Lewis in this village of 450 residents, whom Clark called "poor and extremely kind." When the French villagers held a party honoring their guests, three Corps members had too much fun and stayed out all night. Clark held their court martial the next day. One of the men was given 50 lashes; military discipline had to be sure and swift if the expedition was to survive. Lewis arrived on horseback three days later.

return: September 21, 1806

When men of the expedition saw St. Charles ahead, they rowed hard even though they were riding the Missouri's current toward town. It was a Sunday afternoon, and people on the banks were saluted with gunfire as the Corps announced its arrival. Residents again vied with each other in offering hospitality.

Lewis and Clark Boathouse & Nature Center
1050 Riverside Dr.; 636-947-3199

Combines the exhibits of the former Lewis and Clark Center with replicas of the keelboat and the two pirogues, boat construction in progress, campsite with living history year-round, and the story of how St. Charles residents affected the expedition and many other Missouri River travelers.

Frontier Park
Missouri Hwy. 91; 636-949-3372

The Corps camped near here as they repacked the boats and enjoyed local hospitality in 1804. Signs along trails tell the story.

May 21–June 8, 1804

Katy Trail State Park

This 250-mile hike/bike gravel trail follows the Missouri's north side from St. Charles to Boonville, in the former railbed of the Missouri-Kansas-Texas Railroad (the "Katy"). Most of its 36 entrances offer parking and restrooms; some also have other services. The Corps, pushing upstream against spring run-off, moved very slowly along here—as few as 4 miles a day. Motorized wheelchairs permitted.

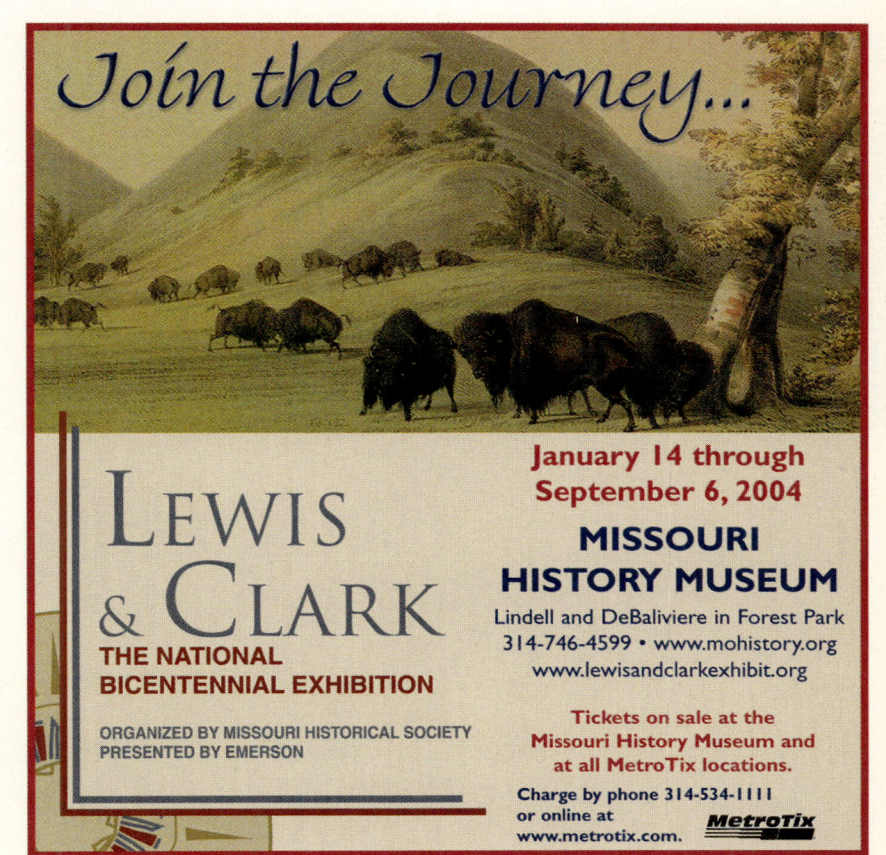

Join the Journey...

LEWIS & CLARK
THE NATIONAL BICENTENNIAL EXHIBITION

ORGANIZED BY MISSOURI HISTORICAL SOCIETY
PRESENTED BY EMERSON

January 14 through September 6, 2004

MISSOURI HISTORY MUSEUM
Lindell and DeBaliviere in Forest Park
314-746-4599 • www.mohistory.org
www.lewisandclarkexhibit.org

Tickets on sale at the Missouri History Museum and at all MetroTix locations.

Charge by phone 314-534-1111
or online at
www.metrotix.com.

MetroTix

Missouri

May 25, 1804

Washington

Nearly opposite today's Washington, in 1804, was La Charette, a village of seven French families who traded with local indians. "The people at this Village is pore," Clark wrote, "houses Small, they Sent us milk & eggs to eat." This welcoming place was the last white settlement up the Missouri River in 1804.

J.E. Rennick Riverfront Park
Front & Jefferson; 636-390-1080
Picnic sites, benches for viewing the Missouri, interpretive sign, recreation areas, and boat and fishing access make this a great place to enjoy the river.

June 3-4, 1804

Jefferson City

After a cloudy, uneventful day of slogging upriver and making only five miles, the Corps camped at the mouth of the Moreau River, east of today's state capital. Clark wrote that, in addition to having a cold and a sore throat, he was "tormented with mosquitoes and small ticks." The next morning they passed and named Cedar Island. Madison Street Overlook, where that street reaches the Missouri River, offers interpretive signs on the expedition and a picnic area.

Jefferson City Convention & Visitors Bureau
213 Adams St., Jefferson City, MO 65102
800-769-4183; www.visitjeffersoncity.com

Jefferson Landing State Historic Site
Jefferson & Water Sts.; 573-751-3475
Original buildings that once served the steamboat trade now house exhibits about those days of the 1800s.

Arrow Rock

June 9, 1804

Arrow Rock State Historic Site
4th & Van Buren; 816-837-3330
The Corps camped overnight on a small island two miles upstream from what Indians called "The Prairie of the Arrows." Today's park brings to life Missouri villages of the 19th century, with historic homes and businesses. Picnic site overlooks the river.

west of Arrow Rock

Higginsville

Confederate Memorial State Historic Site
1 mile N on MO 13; 660-584-2853
A day-use park honoring Missouri's 40,000 members of the Confederate army. Chapel, cemetery, fishing lakes, picnic sites.

June 22, 1804

Sibley

The Corps ate well here, with Sgt. Ordway killing a goose and interpreter Drouillard downing a bear.

Fort Osage
1 mile N; 816-650-5737
Clark founded this fort in 1808. Today's visitors tour a restoration of this first permanent U.S. Army fort in the Louisiana Purchase.

June 23, 1804

Independence

East of today's city, Clark hunted miles ahead of the main party, expecting them to catch up. But the day was so windy that Lewis and the boats didn't leave from the previous night's camp. By the time Clark realized they'd been detained, he couldn't reach camp by nightfall. So he simply peeled tree bark to make a bed and built a campfire to keep away the mosquitoes. About dark, Drouillard found Clark's campsite, and the two "feasted" on venison and water.

National Frontier Trails Center
W. Pacific & Osage; 816-325-7575
Exhibits and films tell of the Lewis and Clark Expedition and pioneers and traders who left here on the Oregon, Santa Fe, and California trails.

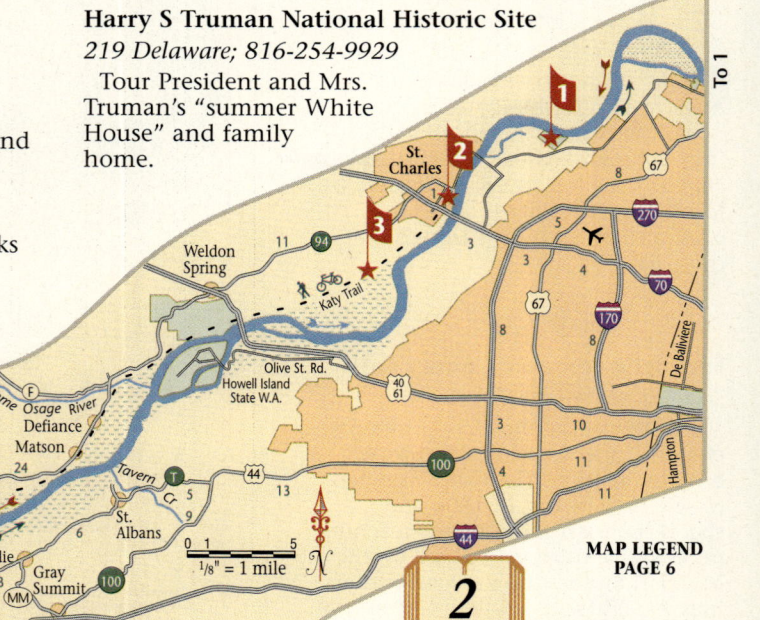

Harry S Truman National Historic Site
219 Delaware; 816-254-9929
Tour President and Mrs. Truman's "summer White House" and family home.

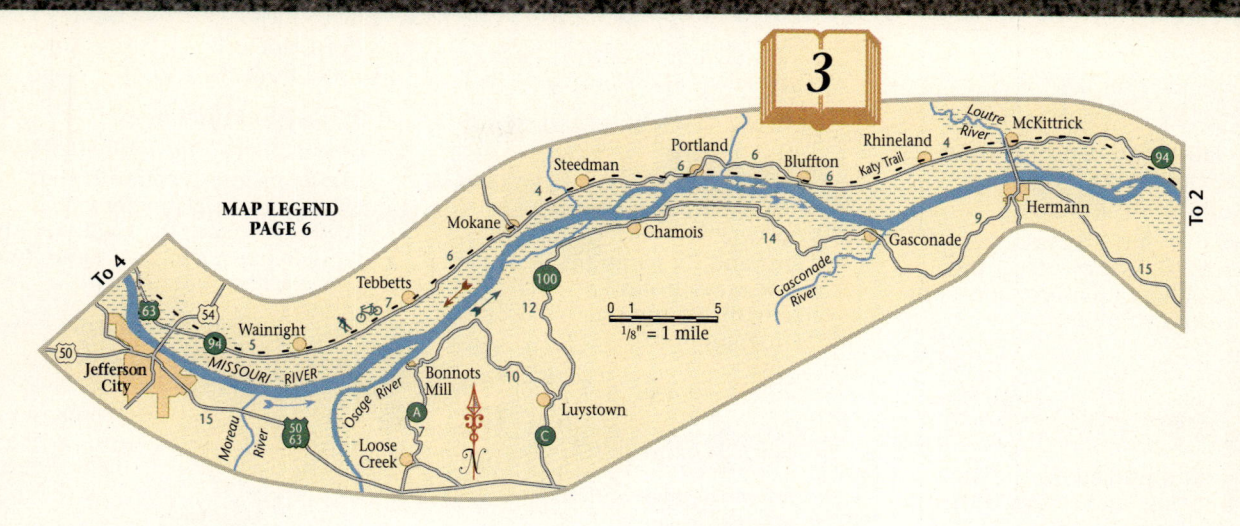

www.lewisandclark.com

June 26-29, 1804

Kansas City

The expedition took a sorely needed rest at a camp on the Kansas side, drying out wet clothing, gear, and trade goods. See also Kansas City, Kansas, under these dates.

return: September 15, 1806

Going with the Missouri River's current, the Corps passed the mouth of the Kansas River. There was a quick stop on the Missouri side, where the captains climbed the hill they thought good for a fort. Today this site is in downtown Kansas City.

No army fort was built on that hill, but a trading post that opened in 1821 began permanent white settlement here. In the 1860s, railroads and the first bridge over the Missouri River made Kansas City a center for agricultural shipping and processing. Today it's also a manufacturing and insurance center.

Convention & Visitors Bureau of Greater Kansas City
1100 Main, Suite 2550, Kansas City, MO 64105
800-767-7700; www.gointokansascity.com

Clark's Point
in Case Park, 8th & Jefferson; 816-871-5630

This city park, named for a local official and not William Clark, overlooks the confluence of the Kansas and Missouri rivers. Statue grouping honors the Corps.

Science City at Union Station
30 W. Pershing Rd.; 816-460-2222

In the restored 1914 Union Depot and an adjoining modern building, Science City offers 50 interactive "neighborhoods" where visitors explore scientific principles by becoming astronauts, broadcasters, doctors, railroad switchers, artists, and more. Films, live performances, and laser shows; restaurants, shops, and tours of the historic depot.

18th & Vine Historic District
1616 E. 18th St.

The revitalized home of Kansas City jazz includes American Jazz Museum (with Blue Room jazz club, an exhibit by day and a working club four nights a week), Gem Theater, and Negro Leagues Baseball Museum, with memorabilia and interactive exhibits.

HISTORIC
Arrow Rock
MISSOURI

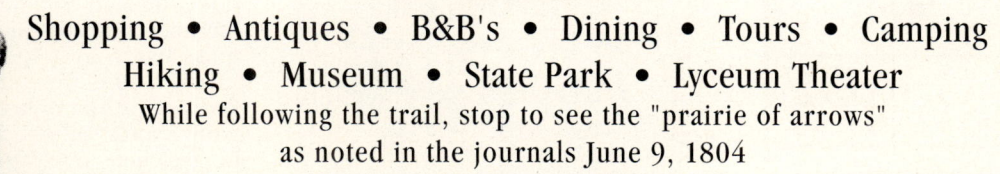

Shopping • Antiques • B&B's • Dining • Tours • Camping
Hiking • Museum • State Park • Lyceum Theater

While following the trail, stop to see the "prairie of arrows" as noted in the journals June 9, 1804

On the bluff of the Missouri River. Join us in our commemoration of the Lewis & Clark Expedition June 8-9, 2004
Visit our web site: www.arrowrock.org
Or write for more info: Box 147L, Arrow Rock, MO 65320

"Woodboatman," by George Caleb Bingham, courtesy of the People of Missouri

Missouri

south of Kansas City
Blue Springs

Burr Oak Woods Conservation Nature Center
1 mile N of I-70 Exit 20
More than a thousand acres of nature trails. Visitor center includes a 3,000-gallon aquarium and natural history exhibits.

July 2, 1804
Platte City

Drouillard walked on the Missouri side, hunting, and reported that the land was "generally very fine."

Ben Ferrel Platte County Museum
3rd and Ferrel; 816-431-5121
From April through October, tour this Victorian mansion built in 1882. It is restored and has some original furnishings along with other period items.

July 4, 1804
Rushville

Clark commented on how many nearly grown geese the Corps saw.

FORT OSAGE
National Historic Landmark

* Established by William Clark in 1808
* Reconstructed Frontier Fort & Factory
* Expedition camped June 23, 1804
* Living History Interpretation

JACKSON COUNTY PARKS & RECREATION
3 miles N. of Buckner, MO • 23 miles E. of Kansas City
816-795-8200, Ext. 1-260
www.jacksongov.org

Today, birding is one of the ways to enjoy Lewis and Clark State Park.

Lewis and Clark State Park
On MO 45, 3 miles south of US 59, then a mile west on MO 138; 816-579-5564
Tent and RV camping, and shaded picnic areas around a lake with swimming, fishing, and boating.

July 7, 1804
St. Joseph

One of the men suffered sunstroke, so Lewis "bled" him (drained about a pint of blood) and dosed him with saltpeter to lower his fever. The Missouri was running very swiftly, so the men had to walk ashore and tow their boats with ropes.

return: September 12, 1806
The Corps reused this campsite, landing when they met a trading party on its way up the Missouri. In it was Joseph Gravelines, who interpreted for them at Fort Mandan during the winter of 1804-1805. The

---

Preserving the Legacy & the Legend

at the Original Pony Express Stables

The Pony Express National Museum
914 Penn Street
St. Joseph, Missouri 64503
1-800-530-5930
www.ponyexpress.org

"Financial support for this ad provided by the St. Joseph Convention & Visitors Bureau."
1-800-785-0360

Corps got as much news as they could from the traders.

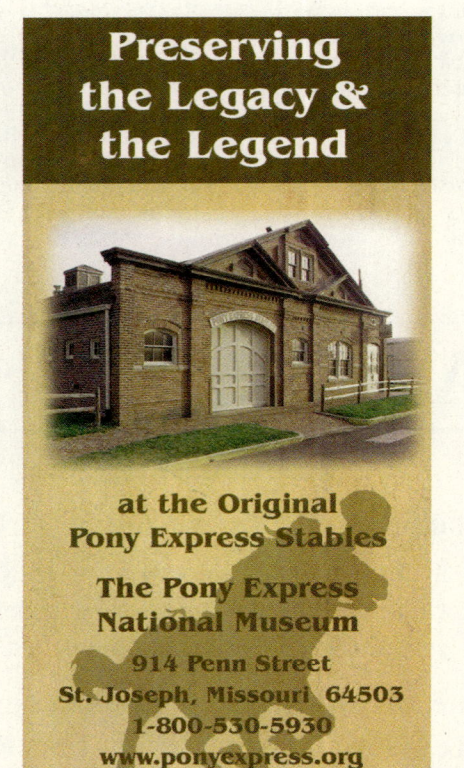

St. Joseph Museum
Charles St. at 11th; 800-530-8866
Local history is colorful, and exhibits cover Native Americans, Lewis and Clark, the Civil War, the Pony Express, and Jesse James (who was killed in St. Joseph).

Glore Psychiatric Museum
3406 Frederick Ave.; 877-387-2310
Dr. Benjamin Rush, Lewis's medical teacher for the trip, also is considered the father of American psychiatry. Museum exhibits full-sized replicas of early treatment devices and illustrates how perception and treatment of mental illness have evolved for 450 years. Includes medical aspects of the expedition, with instruments and medicines taken along. Certified Site on the Lewis and Clark National Historic Trail.

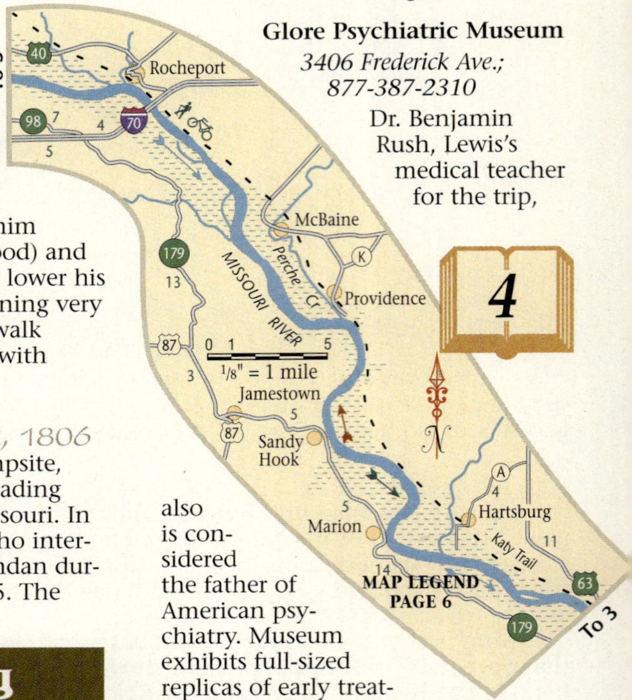

Pony Express Museum
914 Penn St.; 800-530-5930
The Pony Express lasted for only 18 months, beginning in 1860, but its romance still attracts visitors to this museum's stables from which the first rider left. Passed from rider to rider, the mail would reach sacramento, California—more than 1,900 miles away—in only 10 days!
Patee House Museum at 12th & Penn was a luxury hotel that housed Pony Express offices. Also includes house where Jesse James was killed.

July 9, 1804
Nodaway

The Corps of Discovery were tense when they camped on an island near here this windy night, having been

www.LewisandClark.com

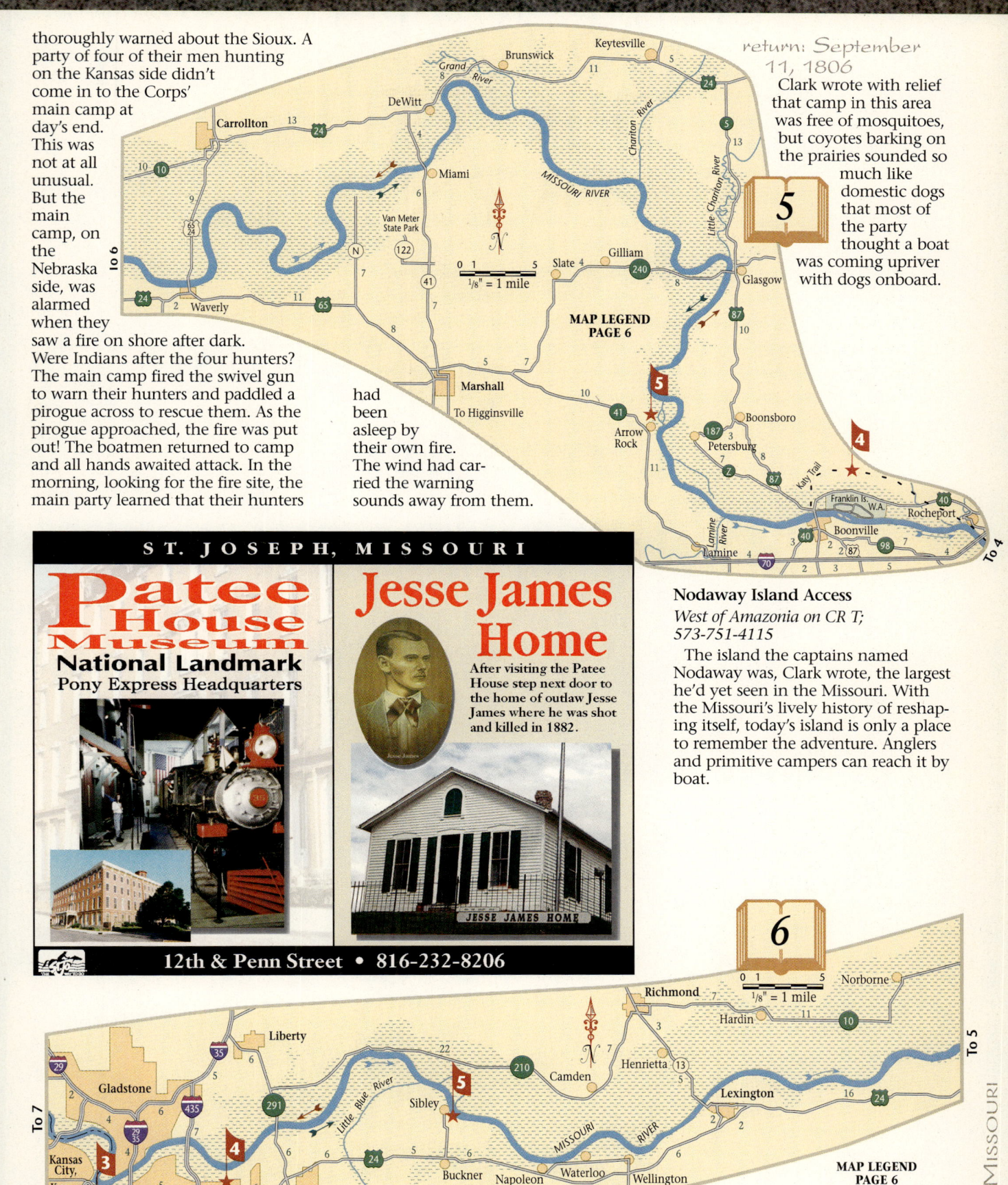

thoroughly warned about the Sioux. A party of four of their men hunting on the Kansas side didn't come in to the Corps' main camp at day's end. This was not at all unusual. But the main camp, on the Nebraska side, was alarmed when they saw a fire on shore after dark. Were Indians after the four hunters? The main camp fired the swivel gun to warn their hunters and paddled a pirogue across to rescue them. As the pirogue approached, the fire was put out! The boatmen returned to camp and all hands awaited attack. In the morning, looking for the fire site, the main party learned that their hunters had been asleep by their own fire. The wind had carried the warning sounds away from them.

return: September 11, 1806
Clark wrote with relief that camp in this area was free of mosquitoes, but coyotes barking on the prairies sounded so much like domestic dogs that most of the party thought a boat was coming upriver with dogs onboard.

ST. JOSEPH, MISSOURI

Patee House Museum
National Landmark
Pony Express Headquarters

Jesse James Home
After visiting the Patee House step next door to the home of outlaw Jesse James where he was shot and killed in 1882.

12th & Penn Street • 816-232-8206

Nodaway Island Access
West of Amazonia on CR T; 573-751-4115

The island the captains named Nodaway was, Clark wrote, the largest he'd yet seen in the Missouri. With the Missouri's lively history of reshaping itself, today's island is only a place to remember the adventure. Anglers and primitive campers can reach it by boat.

IT WAS AMERICA'S EPIC TALE OF ADVENTURE.

CONSIDER US CHAPTER ONE.

Gary R. Lucy · Washington, MO · www.garylucy.com

Lewis and Clark began the country's greatest military expedition in Missouri almost 200 years ago. Celebrate the upcoming bicentennial commemoration by retracing their historic steps, from their starting point in St. Charles to their triumphant return in St. Louis.

For information on these and other Missouri sites, call **1-800-519-6800 ext. 275** or explore **www.VisitMO.com.** Your journey awaits.

MISSOURI®
Where the rivers run

KANSAS

On the way upriver, the Corps of Discovery camped on the Kansas or the Missouri side of the river, wherever a good spot appeared at the right time of day. At the future site of Atchison, they celebrated the United States' 28th birthday by distributing an extra ration of whiskey and firing the keelboat's swivel gun.

Missouri River, Doniphan County. STEVE MULLIGAN

Kaw Point Riverfront Park
1 Rivercity Dr.; 800-264-1563

At the site where the Corps rested, today's visitors enjoy interpretive walking trails with historical and ecological information. Riverfront boardwalk, boat ramp.

Wyandotte County Historical Museum
631 N. 126th St.; 913-721-1078

Designated a National Lewis and Clark Historic Trail site. The story of the Corps' Kaw Point stay is told with exhibits including reproductions of Clark's and York's clothing, children's hands-on area where they can try on similar copies, a 200-year-old dugout canoe.

July 1, 1804
LEAVENWORTH [7]

Knowing they were nearing Sioux territory, the Corps were on alert as they camped on the Missouri side across from here. The temperature had been in the 90s that day, but the men managed to move 15 miles upstream—despite stopping for three hours at midday. Still, when one of the sentries "challenged either a man or beast" during the night, all hands instantly prepared for action. Whatever the creature was, it ran off.

return: September 14, 1806

Camping on Leavenworth Island, the captains passed out "a dram" of whiskey recently bought from upward-bound traders, and "our party…sung songs until 11 o'clock at night in the greatest harmony."

Fort Leavenworth
Reynolds Ave.; 913-684-3191

Self-guided tours are offered of one of the U.S.'s oldest continuously used military sites; photo identification is required for entry. On the grounds, the Buffalo Soldiers Monument honors black cavalrymen; Cheyenne Indians supplied that nickname because of the soldiers' valor in battle.

Frontier Army Museum on the grounds has exhibits on the Lewis and Clark Expedition (an army project), and artifacts from the frontier military, pioneers, and Indians.

Welcome Center
KS 7 North, Leavenworth, KS; 800-844-4114

Pick up a map for the self-guided Historic Wayside Tour for walking the downtown riverfront and driving to additional sites; all have interactive kiosks to help tell the city's story.

Statewide resources on Kansas

Kansas Travel & Tourism
700 S.W. Harrison, Suite 1300, Topeka, KS 66603
800-2-KANSAS; www.travelKS.com

Kansas Wildlife & Parks
Public Information Office
512 S.E. 25th Ave., Pratt, KS 67124-8174
316-672-5911; www.kdwp.state.ks.us

National Park Service Midwest Region
1709 Jackson St., Omaha, NE 65102-2571
402-221-3471; www.nps.gov

June 26-29, 1804
KANSAS CITY [7]

The Kansas River, an expected landmark, was a good place to rest. The Corps camped just north of the Kansas's mouth. Clark thought the site a "beautiful" one for a fort, even though Kansas River water "is very disagreeably tasted to me." The men unpacked boats and dried out the soaked provisions and trade goods.

Two of the men who had gone AWOL back in St. Charles were standing guard duty the night of the 28th. They helped themselves to the whiskey supply and were court martialed the next day. One received 100 lashes for getting drunk, and the other 50 lashes for allowing him to get into the whiskey.

Kansas City Kansas Convention and Visitors Bureau
727 Minnesota Ave., Kansas City, KS 66101
913-321-5800; 800-264-1563
www.kckcvb.org

BEYOND LEWIS & CLARK
The Army Explores the West

December 10, 2004 - August 14, 2005

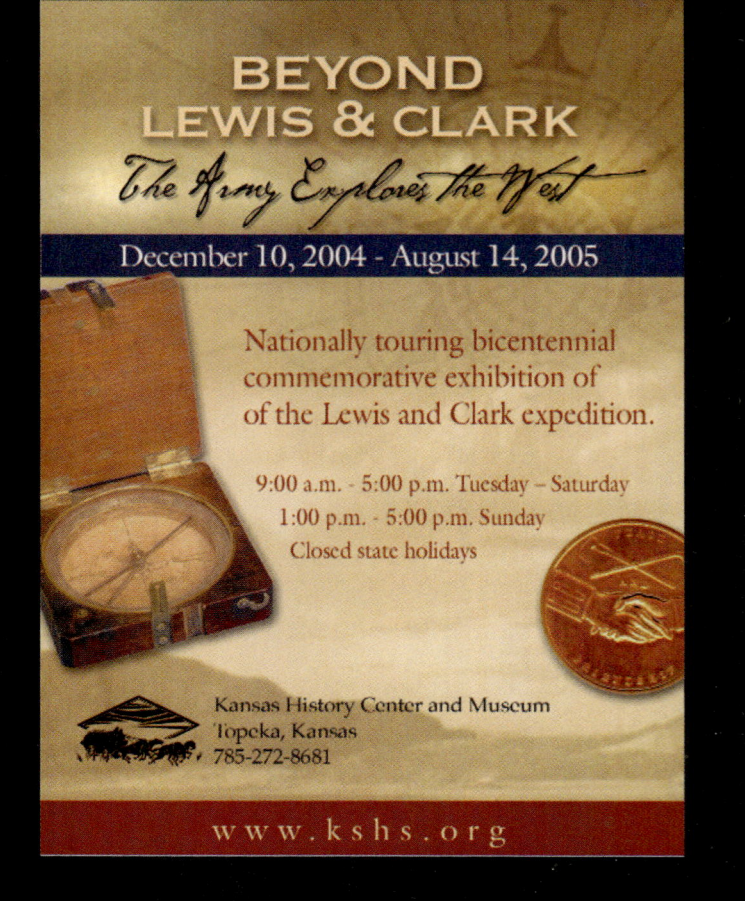

Nationally touring bicentennial commemorative exhibition of the Lewis and Clark expedition.

9:00 a.m. - 5:00 p.m. Tuesday – Saturday
1:00 p.m. - 5:00 p.m. Sunday
Closed state holidays

Kansas History Center and Museum
Topeka, Kansas
785-272-8681

www.kshs.org

We salute the Corps of Discovery in historic
Atchison, Kansas

See where expedition members celebrated Independence Day with a "discharge from our bow piece" and an extra gill of whiskey, and admire the "butifull" plain where they camped July 4, 1804.

Plus . . . impressive Victorian mansions, fascinating museums, Amelia Earhart heritage, narrated trolley tours, unique shopping and dining, and lovely bed & breakfasts!

www.atchisonkansas.net   **1-800-234-1854**
email: tours@atchisonkansas.net

Host city for *"A Journey Fourth"* A National Signature Event of the Lewis and Clark Bicentennial

Rediscover

the Lewis and Clark Trail.

We invite you to follow in the legendary explorers' wake and rediscover the natural and cultural wonders that await you in Kansas.

Join us for festive commemorative activities, June 25 – July 11, 2004 and for *A Journey Fourth*, July 3 – 4, 2004, A National Signature Event of the Lewis and Clark Bicentennial

For more information E-mail:
kslewisandclark@charter.net

1-800-2KANSAS   MM44
www.lewisandclarkinkansas.com

Photo by Bill Stephens

www.lewisandclark.com

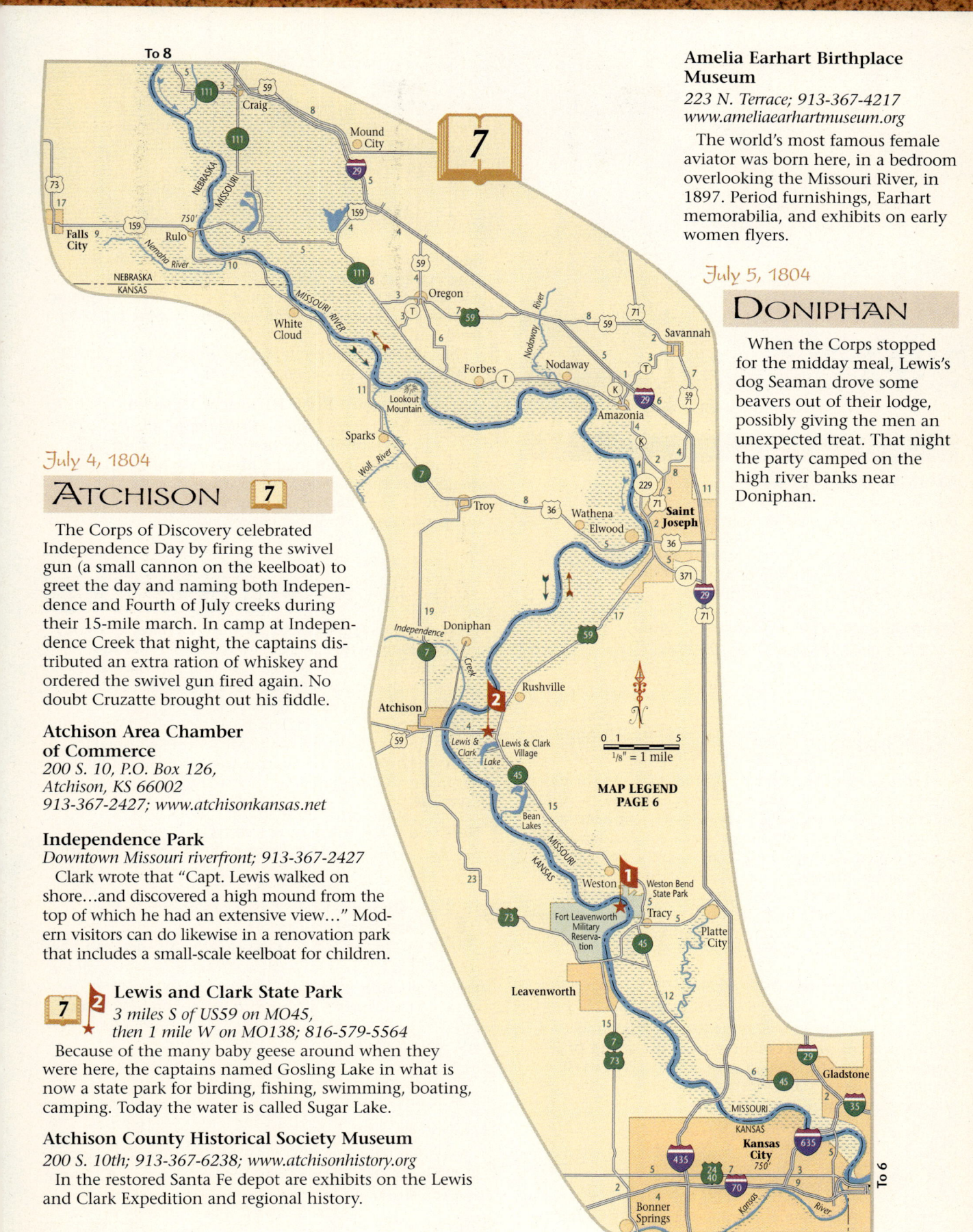

Amelia Earhart Birthplace Museum
223 N. Terrace; 913-367-4217
www.ameliaearhartmuseum.org

The world's most famous female aviator was born here, in a bedroom overlooking the Missouri River, in 1897. Period furnishings, Earhart memorabilia, and exhibits on early women flyers.

July 5, 1804

DONIPHAN

When the Corps stopped for the midday meal, Lewis's dog Seaman drove some beavers out of their lodge, possibly giving the men an unexpected treat. That night the party camped on the high river banks near Doniphan.

July 4, 1804

ATCHISON

The Corps of Discovery celebrated Independence Day by firing the swivel gun (a small cannon on the keelboat) to greet the day and naming both Independence and Fourth of July creeks during their 15-mile march. In camp at Independence Creek that night, the captains distributed an extra ration of whiskey and ordered the swivel gun fired again. No doubt Cruzatte brought out his fiddle.

Atchison Area Chamber of Commerce
200 S. 10, P.O. Box 126, Atchison, KS 66002
913-367-2427; www.atchisonkansas.net

Independence Park
Downtown Missouri riverfront; 913-367-2427
Clark wrote that "Capt. Lewis walked on shore…and discovered a high mound from the top of which he had an extensive view…" Modern visitors can do likewise in a renovation park that includes a small-scale keelboat for children.

Lewis and Clark State Park
3 miles S of US59 on MO45, then 1 mile W on MO138; 816-579-5564
Because of the many baby geese around when they were here, the captains named Gosling Lake in what is now a state park for birding, fishing, swimming, boating, camping. Today the water is called Sugar Lake.

Atchison County Historical Society Museum
200 S. 10th; 913-367-6238; www.atchisonhistory.org
In the restored Santa Fe depot are exhibits on the Lewis and Clark Expedition and regional history.

Nebraska

Niobrara River, Knox County. STEVE MULLIGAN

Captain William Clark, who must have loved open spaces, used the word "beautiful" over and over in his descriptions of the plains. The Corps of Discovery was on the lookout for Sioux Indians; traders in St. Louis had warned the captains to fear them. But when they met Yankton people near today's Gavin Point, the visit was peaceful. The Yankton, however, warned them about the Teton Sioux farther upriver.

Statewide resources on Nebraska

Nebraska Travel & Tourism
Box 94666 Lincoln, NE 68509-4666
800-228-4307; www.visitnebraska.org

Nebraska Game & Parks Commission
P.O. Box 30370 Lincoln, NE 68503-0370
800-826-PARK; www.ngpc.state.ne.us

National Park Service Midwest Region
1709 Jackson St. Omaha, NE 65102-2571
402-221-3471; www.nps.gov

July 14, 1804

SHUBERT

Hard rain kept the men in camp until 7 a.m., then after they'd traveled a mile, the weather got even worse. Clark observed, "We were in a situation." A violent windstorm turned the keelboat and one of the pirogues sideways and gave the men all they could do to keep the boats from being dashed to pieces on a sandbar. This kept up for 40 minutes. Then suddenly the storm stopped, the river smoothed out, and a nice stern breeze allowed the Corps to proceed under sail. Camp that night was in the area of Indian Cave State Park.

Indian Cave State Park
On NE 64 5 miles E of NE 67; 402-883-2575
Extends 3 miles along the Missouri, and includes reconstructed buildings from the village of St. Deroin (founded in 1854), a cave, petroglyphs, wildlife, 20 miles of hiking trails, weekend frontier craft demonstrations, and campsites (some RV).

July 16, 1804

BROWNVILLE

Passing through here, the captains began to see the open Great Plains, and Clark commented on how the "high prairies" were "good land covered with grass[,] entirely void of timber" except along the river. Happily for the men's monotonous meat diet, bushes were full of ripe fruits and berries.

The village of Brownville is a National Historic District recalling the steamboat era.

Missouri River Historical Museum
South of US 136 Brownville Bridge; 402-825-3341
Exhibits on exploration and use of the river. This museum is in a retired 20th-century Missouri River dredgeboat, the *Captain Meriwether Lewis,* at dock in Brownville State Recreation Area, where you may also camp and boat. Steamboat cruises available.

July 18, 1804

NEBRASKA CITY

A pleasant day's travel took the boats 22 miles upriver, pushed along by their sails. Clark walked on shore and wrote one of his many passages of praise for wide-open places: "...an open and bound less Prarie," where grass grew two feet high as far as the horizon, like an endless ocean.

Over four decades later, Fort Kearny was built on these bluffs, the first fort west of the Missouri established to protect travelers on the Oregon Trail. More emigrants began the trail here than at almost any other Missouri River site.

Nebraska City Tourism & Events
806 1st Avenue, Nebraska City, NE 68410
800-514-9113; www.nebraskacity.com

Missouri River Basin Lewis & Clark Interpretive Center
911 Central Ave., Nebraska City, NE: 402-873-3388
Scheduled to open in 2004, a 12,000-square-foot center that emphasizes flora, fauna, and other scientific "discoveries" of the expedition. Full-size keelboat reproduction, IMAX theater. Great Hall of Large Animals, Young Explorers' Activity Room.

July 21, 1804

PLATTSMOUTH

Just north is the mouth of the Platte River. For a Missouri River man in those days, passing the Platte was as big an event as an oceangoing sailor's first crossing of the equator.

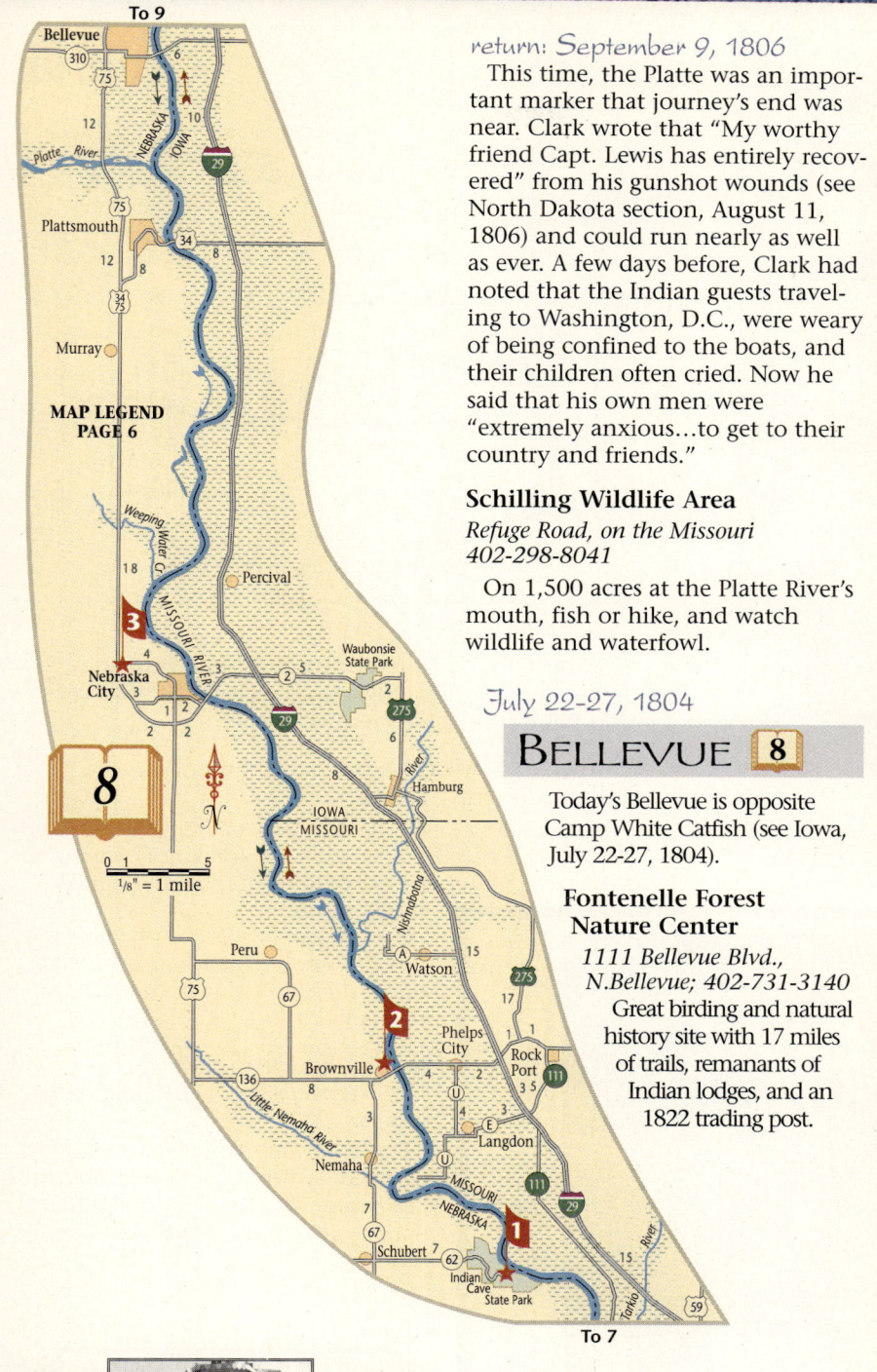

www.lewisandclark.com

return: September 9, 1806

This time, the Platte was an important marker that journey's end was near. Clark wrote that "My worthy friend Capt. Lewis has entirely recovered" from his gunshot wounds (see North Dakota section, August 11, 1806) and could run nearly as well as ever. A few days before, Clark had noted that the Indian guests traveling to Washington, D.C., were weary of being confined to the boats, and their children often cried. Now he said that his own men were "extremely anxious…to get to their country and friends."

Schilling Wildlife Area
Refuge Road, on the Missouri
402-298-8041

On 1,500 acres at the Platte River's mouth, fish or hike, and watch wildlife and waterfowl.

July 22-27, 1804

BELLEVUE 8

Today's Bellevue is opposite Camp White Catfish (see Iowa, July 22-27, 1804).

Fontenelle Forest Nature Center
1111 Bellevue Blvd., N.Bellevue; 402-731-3140
Great birding and natural history site with 17 miles of trails, remanants of Indian lodges, and an 1822 trading post.

July 26, 1804

OMAHA 9

The Corps spent a miserable night in the area of today's Douglas Street Bridge, the mosquitoes were as big as houseflies "raging all night."

return: September 9, 1806

Zooming downriver by rowing with the current, the Corps passed here on a day that saw 73 miles traveled.

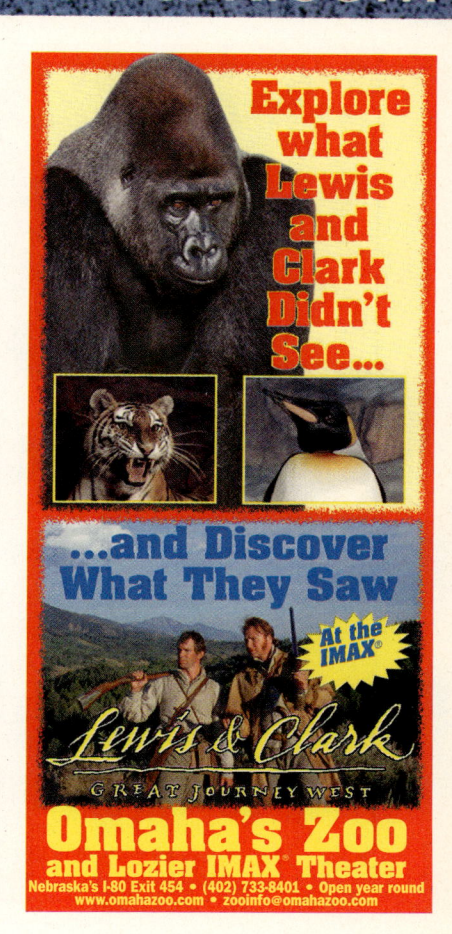

CRUISE THE RIVER OF LEWIS & CLARK
- See the Lewis & Clark campsite of July 15, 1804
- Dinner & sightseeing cruises
- Private charters
- All day river country adventures
- 150 passengers

April - October

Call (402) 825-6441
Box 96, Historic
Brownville, NE 68321

Spirit of Brownville

Explore what Lewis and Clark Didn't See…

…and Discover What They Saw
At the IMAX
Lewis & Clark GREAT JOURNEY WEST

Omaha's Zoo and Lozier IMAX Theater
Nebraska's I-80 Exit 454 • (402) 733-8401 • Open year round
www.omahazoo.com • zooinfo@omahazoo.com

A Lewis & Clark-style Adventure!

Wildlife Safari

Take a drive-through adventure and discover North American animals just like Lewis & Clark saw on their great journey west!

Nebraska's I-80 Exit 426
Open April-October 9:30 a.m. – 5 p.m.
(402) 944-WILD or (402) 733-8401
www.omahazoo.com
Operated by Omaha's Henry Doorly Zoo

NEBRASKA 31

NEBRASKA

Sarpy County

Lewis & Clark Children's Interpretive Art Wall Unveiling May, 2004

Haworth Park
Bellevue, Nebraska

Call for FREE visitors information.
1-800-gosarpy • 1-402-593-4143
www.gosarpy.com

Just South of Metro Omaha

Sarpy County Nebraska

Sarpy County Tourism
NEBRASKA CROSSING WELCOME CENTER
I-80, Exit 432 • 14333 S. Hwy 31 • Gretna, NE 68028

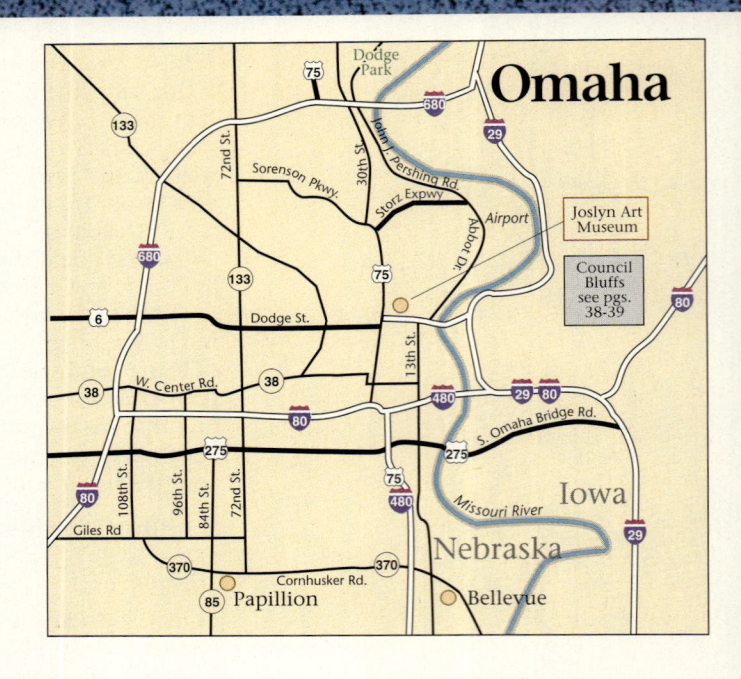

Come Experience Nebraska City

Award-Winning Celebrations
Arbor Day April 30–May 2, 2004 • AppleJack Festival September 18–19, 2004

Visit our many attractions including the Arbor Lodge State Historical Park.

Visit www.nebraskacity.com or call 800-514-9113 Dept. 4LCA for your FREE Nebraska City Visitor Guide to see all Nebraska City has to offer.

Paid for by Otoe County Visitors Committee

Omaha

Greater Omaha Convention & Visitor Bureau
6800 Mercy Rd., Suite 202, Omaha, NE 68106-2627;
866-YES-OMAHA; www.visitomaha.com

Joslyn Art Museum
2200 Dodge; 402-342-3300

Lewis and Clark buffs flock to view paintings by George Catlin, who traveled far up the Missouri only 17 years after the expedition returned. He painted some Indians the captains had met. Works by Karl Bodmer, who toured the upper Missouri in 1833, are on exhibit, along with impressionist and 20th-century American art.

N.P. Dodge Park
11005 Pershing Drive, via I-680 North;
402-444-4673

This riverfront park in the city offers tent and RV camping, boat ramps, fishing, picnic shelters, bicycling, walking, horse trails, softball fields, and horseshoe pits.

Visit the
John G. Neihardt Center
State Historical Site
Bancroft, Nebraska

- Author of *Black Elk Speaks* and *Cycle of the West*
- Nebraska's Poet Laureate
- Neihardt's Study
- Sacred Hoop Garden
- Museum Exhibits

Open year-round. Call ahead for Winter & Holiday hours: **1-888-777-4667** or e-mail: Neihardt@gpcom.net

www.lewisandclark.com

July 30–August 3, 1804 **9**

FORT CALHOUN

On July 28, the Corps met a Missouri Indian who was part of a bison-hunting party of Missouris and Otos. The captains invited him to bring the party for a council, and bluffs at this site were agreed upon as the place to meet. (The Missouri has since shifted to the east.) The Corps arrived here on the 30th, named it the Council Bluff, and waited four days until the hunting party arrived. These men were experienced traders and received Lewis's gifts and speech about their new "father" agreeably. From them, the captains learned that Santa Fe was only 25 days away, and people from this area traveled there to trade.

return: September 8, 1806

As they'd done elsewhere on the return, the Corps paused here long enough for the captains to climb the hill and see whether it was a good place for a a military fort.

9 ★ **2** **Fort Atkinson State Historic Park**
7th and Madison;
402-468-5611 or 800-826-PARK

This frontier post, the first army base west of the Missouri River, opened in 1820 to protect fur traders and Indians, was staffed by as many as 1,000 soldiers, and abandoned in 1827. Reconstruction began in 1961 and continues today, even while the park is open year-round. Visitor center; living history demonstration weekends once a month, July through October.

August 4, 1804

BLAIR **10**

As the Corps passed near here, Pvt. Pierre Cruzatte pointed out the remains of a post where he'd spent two years trading with the Omahas, Pawnees, and Otos. It may have been built by James McKay, retired and living in St. Louis, who was one of the captains' important informants the previous winter.

August 8, 1804

TEKAMAH **10**

Lewis killed one of hundreds of pelicans on what they named Pelican Island, which the shifting river has since joined to the bank. For three miles below the island, feathers had covered the Missouri's surface to a width of 70 feet. Lewis wrote a few hundred words in his journal describing the bird, commenting that they'd seen few waterfowl before.

Lewis N Clark
An Authentic 1804 Experience

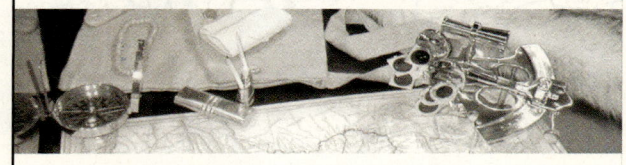

See exhibits featuring scientific findings and replica tools of the Corps of Discovery at White Catfish Camp

Explore the lands along Lewis & Clark's journey with a new audio kiosk & interpretive exhibits* along FNA's boardwalks & 17 miles of trails
*opening March 20th

www.fontenelleforest.org

Fontenelle Nature Association
Fontenelle Forest Nature Center
1111 N Bellevue Blvd
Bellevue, NE

LEWIS AND CLARK NATIONAL HISTORIC TRAIL

NEBRASKA
possibilities...endless.™
1-877-NEBRASKA
www.VisitNebraska.org

Sarpy County Visitors Committee

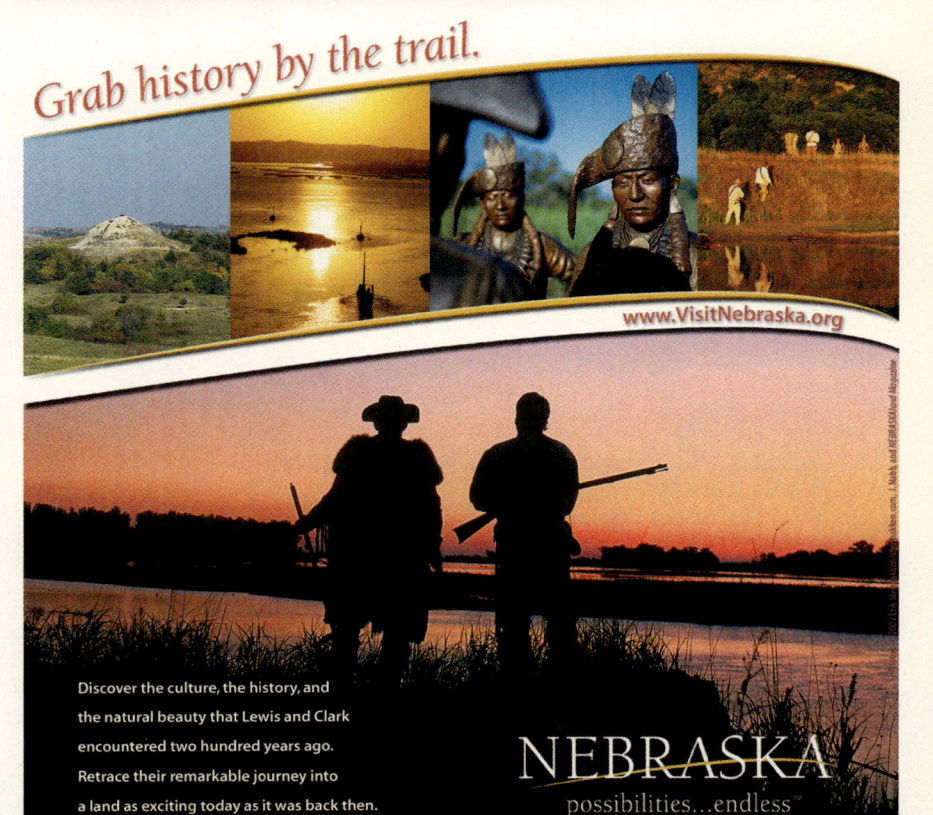

Grab history by the trail.

www.VisitNebraska.org

Discover the culture, the history, and the natural beauty that Lewis and Clark encountered two hundred years ago. Retrace their remarkable journey into a land as exciting today as it was back then.

NEBRASKA
possibilities...endless.™

For a FREE travel packet, call **1-877-NEBRASKA** Dept. 4ALA or visit **www.VisitNebraska.org**

Nebraska

Pelican Point State Recreation Area
From Tekamah, 4 miles E, then 4 miles N
Hike, fish, boat, or tent-camp on the Missouri, just above & across from the mouth of the Little Sioux River.

August 11, 1804

Decatur

The Corps stopped respectfully at the site of a common frontier tragedy, but one that was not yet really understood. North of today's Decatur were buried Omaha Chief Blackbird and 400 of his people, all victims of smallpox. The Omahas had caught the disease from the whites, who had some natural immunity that Native Americans did not. On the burial mound—where Chief Blackbird was said to be interred astride a horse, and facing the river—the captains placed a white flag bordered in red, white, and blue.

Blackbird Hill Overview
At milepost 152 on US 75, three miles N; 402-837-5301
Modern visitors can pay their respects from this highway stop, which includes informative signs, on the Omaha Indian Reservation.

Bancroft

West of Homer on NE 51, the village of Bancroft was home from 1900 to 1920 to John G. Neihardt, the state's poet laureate. Neihardt also wrote the 1932 book *Black Elk Speaks,* in which Oglala Sioux holy man Black Elk (1863-1950) recalled his pre-reservation childhood and Sioux culture.

John G. Neihardt Center
Washington & Elm Sts.; 800-727-8323
This Nebraska State Historical Society site includes exhibits, the poet's study, and a prayer garden based on Black Elk's Great Vision, experienced at age 9. It taught of the fading and then resurgence of traditional Sioux beliefs.

August 12, 1804

Homer

The Omahas' "Big Village" (Tonwantonga) was empty as the Corps passed by, the people out hunting bison. As Clark marveled at the number of burial mounds in sight, he mistakenly figured that another Indian nation's war party had brought smallpox here.

Tonwantonga
8 miles SW of South Sioux City on US 77
Today, the site of historic Big Village has interpretation on Omaha Indian history and life, and hiking trails.

August 13-20, 1804

Dakota City

South of here, on the west side of the river, the Corps of Discovery made what they named "Fish Camp" and sent five men to Tonwantonga (see above) to await the Omahas' return and invite them to a council. One day, they dragged the river with brush and caught 318 fish of several species, and another day, 800!

The Omahas didn't return from hunting, and the Corps pushed on without meeting them.

Moses B. Reed (see also Iowa section, August 6, 1804) was brought in, court martialed on August 18, and found guilty of desertion and stealing army property—his gun. He was sentenced to run the gantlet four times, while each man struck him with a handful of switches. Reed was drummed out of the army but allowed to stay with the Corps through the coming winter rather than being turned out alone on the prairie. The French boatman who had deserted with him wasn't found.

In the evening, after Reed's punishment, the captains held a dance until 11:00, to celebrate Lewis's 30th birthday!

return: September 4, 1806

The captains passed out one cup of flour per person for evening supper. Although an upward-bound trader had just given them a barrel of flour in exchange for corn, some of the flour was from the supply carried upriver in 1804 and cached at the Marias River over the winter of 1805-1806.

Cottonwood Cove Park
13th and Hickory; 402-987-3448
This city park right on the Missouri offers picnicking, camping (with RV sites), fishing, and boating.

August 20, 1804

South Sioux City

Scenic Park Campground
I29, exit 147B; 1021 E. 6th Street; 402-494-7531; www.cityofsouthsiouxcity.org
Park includes boat ramp, hiking trails, fishing access, playground, swimming pool. Tree-shaded campground offers parking pads, grills, picnic tables, and a dump station.

August 21, 1804

Ponca

Look downstream at the Missouri from here and you see the channeled river, with dredged shipping ways. Upstream, the river is unchanneled and, where not dammed, still appears as the Lewis and Clark Expedition saw it.

Ponca State Park
NE to Hwys. 9 and 12; 402-755-2284
Scenic river overlooks are along some of this large park's hiking trails. Horseback riding, swimming, fishing, picnic sites, campsites (some for RVs), and cabin rentals are offered.

August 28–September 1, 1804

CROFTON AND GAVINS POINT 12

The Corps camped below what they named Calumet Bluff, using the French term for peace pipe. About 70 Yankton Sioux warriors and some women joined them on the 29th and stayed for a two-day council. Interpreting was Pierre Dorion, Sr., a French trader who'd lived among the Yankton for 20 years. During the first day, the captains talked about the new American government, gave presents, and demonstrated the astonishing rifle that fired from air pressure rather than gunpowder. The Sioux were invited to make peace with area tribes, and go to visit President Jefferson next spring. After saying they'd give their answer tomorrow, the chiefs "looked on with much dignity" during a long evening of Sioux-warrior dancing.

The following afternoon, the chiefs agreed to negotiate peace and go to Washington. But they warned that the Teton Sioux, upstream, would probably not be as easy to convince.

Corps of Discovery Welcome Center
US 81, Crofton; 402-667-6557

A riverside overlook with interpretation, exhibits, special events, and information on the Corps' path.

12 4 Gavins Point Dam, Lewis and Clark Lake Regional Visitor Center
9 miles N of Crofton; 402-667-7873

The story of the Calumet Bluff council is among exhibits on Upper Missouri native peoples, history, Gavins Point Dam construction, and Lewis and Clark Lake recreation.

Lewis and Clark Lake—South Shore
West of NE 121; 402-388-4169

Gavins Point Dam forms this lake on the Missouri River. The Nebraska side has three recreation areas; modern and primitive campsites, boat access, swimming, fishing, picnic sites available. (See North Shore listing in South Dakota section, August 29-30, 1804.)

September 3-4, 1804

NIOBRARA 12

The Corps camped east of town on the 3rd and traveled upstream only eight miles the next day, spending that night west of the Niobrara River mouth. Clark walked three miles up the Niobrara to a Ponca Indian earth-lodge village but found that its people were on a buffalo hunt.

12 5 Niobrara State Park
NE 12 W of Niobrara; 402-857-3373

Indian history from Lewis and Clark's visit to the time of Mormon pioneers. Hiking and horse trails, cabins, camping (some RV sites), fishing, picnic sites, pool.

September 7, 1804

LYNCH 12

The Corps saw its first prairie dog town, which the captains explored by poking a stick into and pouring five barrels of water down burrows to see how deep it was and to flush out some of the animals.

The Tower/Old Baldy
6 miles N on Missouri River; 402-569-2706

Self-guided tour describes the same prairie dog site.

The beaver's fur was valued for men's hats until the 1860s.

South Sioux City, Nebraska on the Lewis & Clark Trail

Come Experience The Adventure Today!

Fish Camp II
A Lewis & Clark Bicentennial Event
August 14, 2004
www.FishCampII.com

Best Value Inn - 4402 Dakota Ave.
Call 402-494-4114 or 800-553-2666

Marina Inn - 4th & B Street
Call 402-494-4000 or 800-798-7980

South Ridge Motel - 1001 W. 29th St
Call 402-494-4213

Cardinal Inn & Suites - 2829 Dakota
Call 402-494-8874

Regency Inn - 400 Dakota Ave
Call 402-494-3046 or 800-478-7878

Scenic Park Campground - 4th & D
Call 402-494-7531

Park Plaza - Dakota Ave & 13th
Call 402-494-2021

ATTRACTIONS
Lewis & Clark Interpretive Center
Sgt. Floyd Monument
Southern Hills Mall "An American Adventure" Mural Collection
Sgt. Floyd Riverboat Museum & Welcome Center
Cottonwood Cove Park
Chief Blackbird Overlook
Site of Tonwantonga

South Sioux City Visitors Bureau   3900 Dakota Ave. Suite 11, South Sioux City, NE 68776
800-793-6327 www.southsiouxcity.org   Exit 148 from I-29 • Exit 2 from Hwy 20

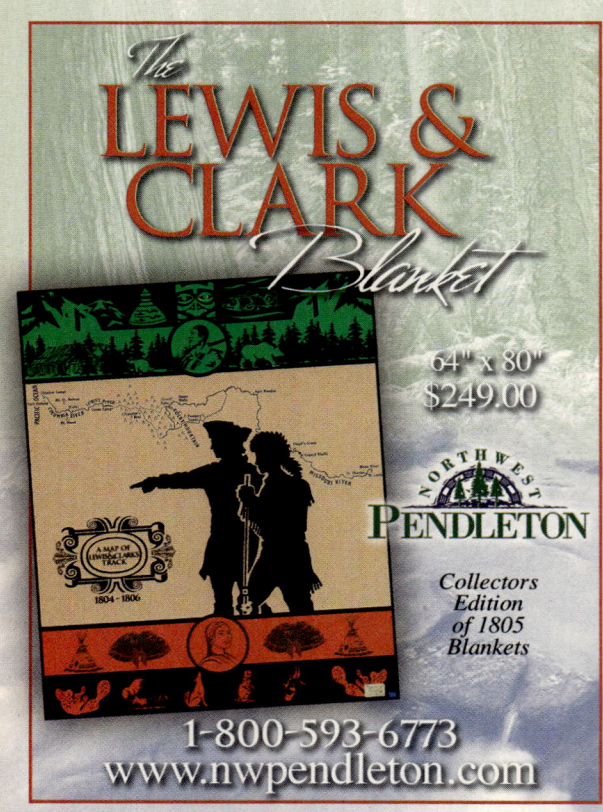

LEWIS AND CLARK TRADE GOODS

A SPECIAL ADVERTISING SECTION

The Lewis & Clark Blanket

64" x 80"
$249.00

NORTHWEST PENDLETON

Collectors Edition of 1805 Blankets

1-800-593-6773
www.nwpendleton.com

Woven by Pendleton Woolen Mills

NEWLY RELEASED!

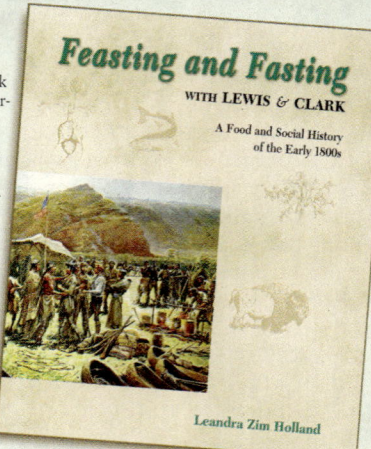

What did the Lewis and Clark Expedition live on? Leandra Holland's narrative about what the expedition members ate on their journey makes this book a rich treat as well as a solid reference for historians, researchers, and re-enactors. Extensive illustrations, authentic recipes, their food preparation, preservation and storage methods are included. A detailed index, separate recipe and menu index, and item-by-item appendices of food groups further assist food lovers and Lewis and Clark buffs.

Feasting and Fasting with LEWIS & CLARK
A Food and Social History of the Early 1800s
Leandra Zim Holland

288 pages, 8½" x 10". Full color.
Softbound.   **$20.00**
1-59152-010-X $24.95
Hardbound.   **$30.00**
1-59152-007-X $35.00

Published by Old Yellowstone Publishing, Inc.
Produced and Distributed by Farcountry Press

"Congratulations on a truly scrumptious book -- a remarkable soup to nuts answer to the persistent question: How did they do it? Leandra's no-stone-unturned research technique takes us back to the early 1800s and gives us a crystal clear understanding of the amount of time, effort, and ingenuity it took to feed the Expedition up the river, across the plains, over the mountains, and back. Devour this book and keep it handy as an excellent reference guide."
STEPHENIE AMBROSE TUBBS, AUTHOR

"Leandra ... she knows what she's talking about."
TIME MAGAZINE, JULY 8, 2002 ISSUE

In memory of Leandra, who's tragic accidental death occurred just as the book went to press, all net proceeds of this book will go to the **Leandra Zim Holland Memorial Research Fund** established in the Lewis and Clark Trail Heritage Foundation.

To Order - see: www.lewisandclark-food.com; FAX 480-396-0089; or call: 888-733-8452

Order your Lewis & Clark gifts ONLINE
or purchase them at the Helena Dillard's "MONTANA SHOP"

www.helenadillards.com

Dillard's Montana Shop

Capital Hill Mall
(406) 443-3000

Lewis and Clark Trade Goods

A SPECIAL ADVERTISING SECTION

"THE LEWIS AND CLARK BICENTENNIAL COLLECTION"

Lewis and Clark Bicentennial™ Medals
Lewis and Clark Bicentennial™ Buckles
Lewis and Clark Bicentennial® Clothing
Lewis and Clark Bronze Sculpture
Lewis and Clark Lithographs
Lewis and Clark Poster
Sacajawea Medals • Sacajawea Buckles
Sacajawea Clothing • Sacagawea Bronze Sculpture
Sacajawea Jewelry • Sacagawea Poster

Sacagawea is a registered Federal Trademark

39mm, 1oz. .999 silver

www.lewisandclarkproducts.com

P.O. Box 675 • Lakeside, MT 59922 • PH: 406-844-3630 • sacajawea@centurytel.net

Original Journals of the Lewis and Clark Expedition
(8 Volumes, 15 Parts including the Atlas)

This is a reprint of the Dodd Mead edition as published in 1904. It has been described as the most accurate and elaborate work on the expedition. 8 volumes including a digitized atlas. Edited, with Introduction, Notes, and Index by Reuben Gold Thwaites.

Order online at HTTP://WWW.DIGITALSCANNING.COM or call toll free 1-888-349-4443 (9-5 M-F, ET) or send Check or MO to address below. Shipping Approximately $12.00

ISBN#s:
TP Set: 1582186510   TP Set: $219.95
HC Set: 158218660X   HC Set: $349.95

DSP — Digital Scanning & Publishing

Digital Scanning, Inc. · 344 Gannett Road · Scituate, MA · 02066
toll free: 888.349.4443 · tel: 781.545.2100 · fax: 781.545.4908

Iowa Simply Beautiful II

Photography by Larsh K. Bristol, Kent Foster, and Curt Maas.

Come home to Iowa once again with this second collection of photographs from Bristol and Maas, this time joined by Kent Foster. These are scenes of hard work and hard play in a land with four strong seasons; images of past history and cultures; and the natural beauty of all the Iowa landscapes between the Mississippi and the Missouri. If Iowa is home, you will find a family album here. If not, you will know from these photographs that visitors are always welcome in Iowa.

138 color photographs. 120 pages, 10½" x 12". Hardbound. 29.95 + S&H*

South Dakota Simply Beautiful

Photography by J. C. Leacock.

Contrast the incomparable ruggedness of wintery peaks in Badlands National Park and the prairie's soft rolling hills covered in yellow sweet clover and you'll agree it's simply beautiful!

Approx. 120 color photographs. 120 pages, 10½" x 12". Hardbound. $29.95 + S&H*

FARCOUNTRY PRESS
800-821-3874 • www.farcountrypress.com
See our Ad Featuring Lewis & Clark products on pages 76 & 77
*S&H = $6 for 1st item - $2 for each additional items.

While passing along future Iowa in 1804, the newly-begun expedition wasn't going too well. One of the privates had deserted, then one of the men became ill and died of a mysterious ailment. Shortly after that, Meriwether Lewis was testing a rock specimen and inhaled fumes that made him very sick. But, always, the Corps of Discovery kept "proceeding on," to use their words.

Sergeant Floyd Monument, Sioux City. CHUCK HANEY

Statewide resources on Iowa

Iowa Division of Tourism
200 E. Grand Ave., Des Moines, IA 50309
800-345-IOWA; www.traveliowa.com

Department of Natural Resources (State Parks)
Wallace State Office Bldg., Des Moines, IA 50319-0034
www.state.ia.us/dnr/organiza/ppd

July 16-17, 1804

HAMBURG 8

The area's loess hills with plants adapted to a dry climate look much as they did when Clark wrote, "This prairie I call bald-pated prairie," about land extending north from the future state of Missouri. The Corps paused to hunt and take celestial measurements, important for the maps they were to draw.

Waubonsie State Park
at IA 2 & IA 239; 712-382-2786

Hiking trails, including Ridge Trail with view of Missouri River, horse trails, picnic sites, camping (with RV sites).

July 22-27, 1804

COUNCIL BLUFFS 9

The Corps camped south of today's city to rest, dry out their cargo, make new oars and boat poles, and arrange to meet the Oto Indians. They built willow bowers and erected a flagpole. They named the site White Catfish Camp. George Drouillard and Pierre Cruzatte went looking for the Otos and found their village emptied for the summer bison hunt. A meeting with the Oto was held August 2-3, under a bluff on the Nebraska side, at a site the captains named The Council Bluff. Since then, the Missouri has shifted farther east. (See also Nebraska, July 30–August 3, 1804.)

return: September 8, 1806

Having floated 78 miles downstream this day, the Corps camped again at White Catfish Camp, even though they'd hoped to reach the milestone Platte River .

Founded by Mormons in 1846 and once called Kanesville, Council Bluffs was renamed in 1852 to honor the Corps' meeting with the Otos 42 years earlier. Today it offers outdoor recreation, gaming casinos, and access to the National Loess Hills Scenic Byway.

Council Bluffs Convention & Visitors Bureau
7 N. 6th St., Council Bluffs, IA 51503
800-228-6878; 712-325-1000
www.councilbluffsiowa.com

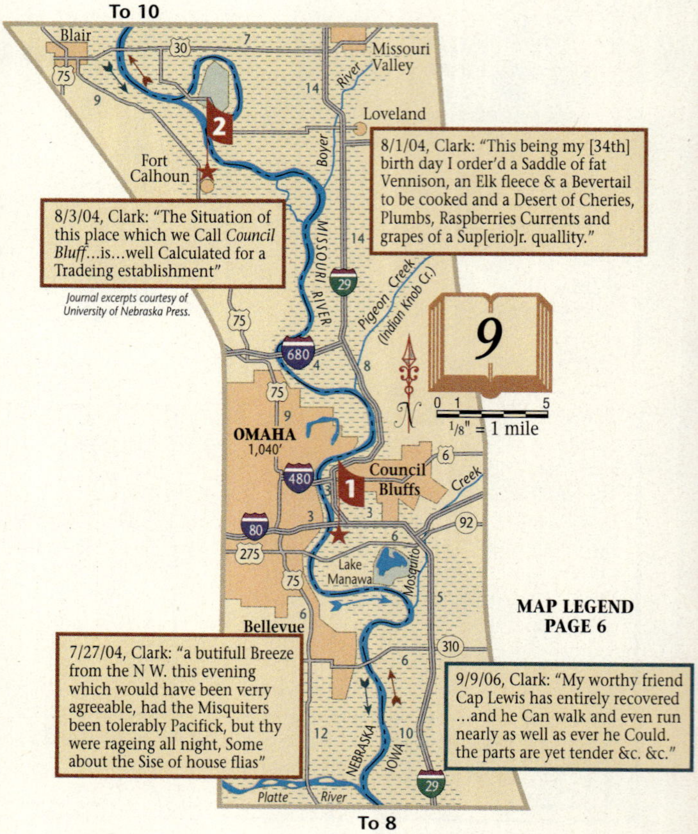
To 10
Blair
Missouri Valley
Loveland
Fort Calhoun
Boyer
River
MISSOURI RIVER
Pigeon Creek
(Indian Knob Cr.)
8/1/04, Clark: "This being my [34th] birth day I order'd a Saddle of fat Vennison, an Elk fleece & a Bevertail to be cooked and a Desert of Cheries, Plumbs, Raspberries Currents and grapes of a Sup[erio]r. quallity."
8/3/04, Clark: "The Situation of this place which we Call *Council Bluff*...is...well Calculated for a Tradeing establishment"
Journal excerpts courtesy of University of Nebraska Press.
9
0 1 5
1/8" = 1 mile
OMAHA
1,040'
Council Bluffs
Creek
Lake Manawa
Mosquito
Bellevue
MAP LEGEND PAGE 6
7/27/04, Clark: "a butifull Breeze from the N W. this evening which would have been verry agreeable, had the Misquiters been tolerably Pacifick, but thy were rageing all night, Some about the Sise of house flias"
9/9/06, Clark: "My worthy friend Cap Lewis has entirely recovered ...and he Can walk and even run nearly as well as ever he Could. the parts are yet tender &c. &c."
NEBRASKA
IOWA
Platte River
To 8

www.lewisandclark.com

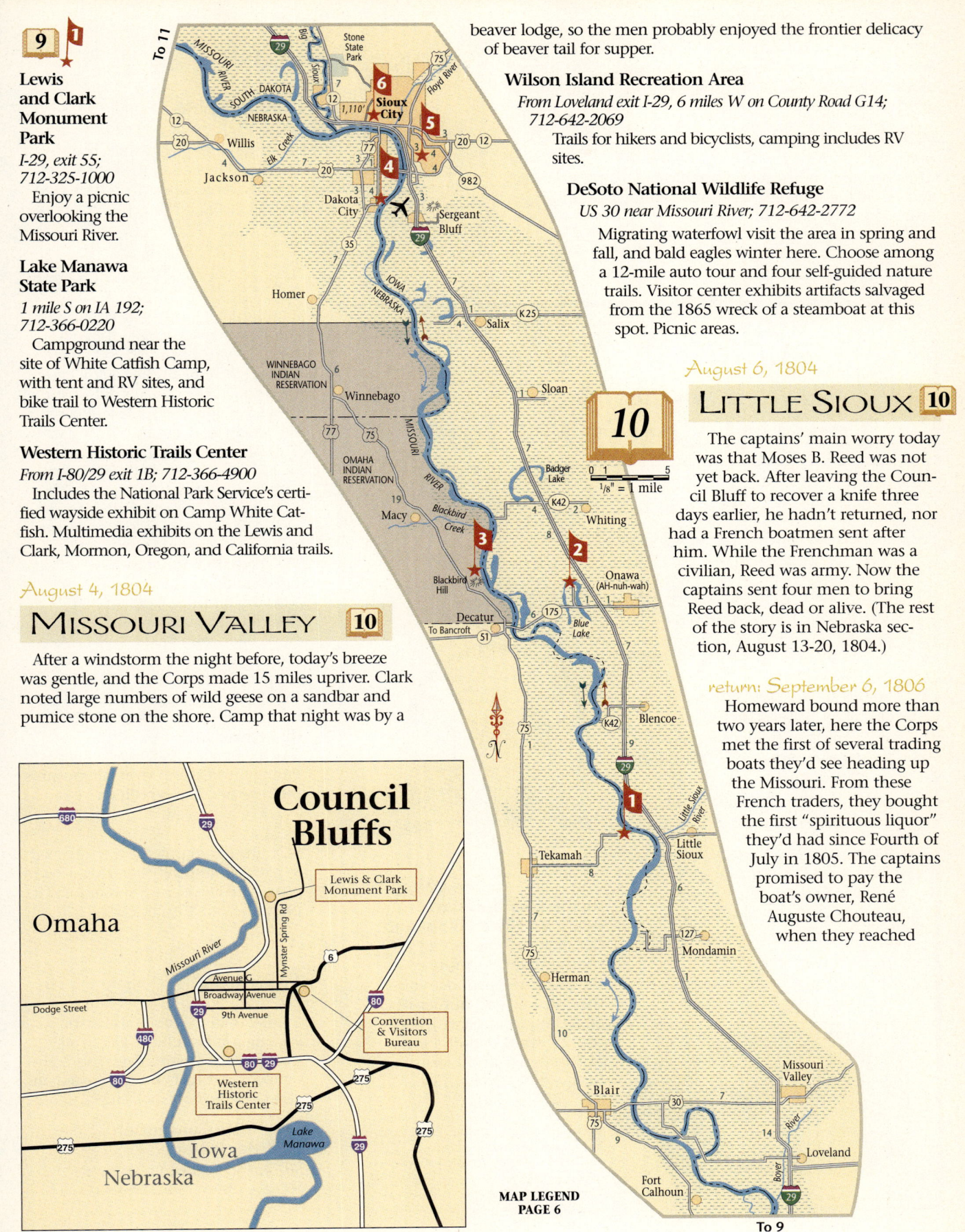

9. Lewis and Clark Monument Park
I-29, exit 55; 712-325-1000
Enjoy a picnic overlooking the Missouri River.

Lake Manawa State Park
1 mile S on IA 192; 712-366-0220
Campground near the site of White Catfish Camp, with tent and RV sites, and bike trail to Western Historic Trails Center.

Western Historic Trails Center
From I-80/29 exit 1B; 712-366-4900
Includes the National Park Service's certified wayside exhibit on Camp White Catfish. Multimedia exhibits on the Lewis and Clark, Mormon, Oregon, and California trails.

August 4, 1804
MISSOURI VALLEY
After a windstorm the night before, today's breeze was gentle, and the Corps made 15 miles upriver. Clark noted large numbers of wild geese on a sandbar and pumice stone on the shore. Camp that night was by a beaver lodge, so the men probably enjoyed the frontier delicacy of beaver tail for supper.

Wilson Island Recreation Area
From Loveland exit I-29, 6 miles W on County Road G14; 712-642-2069
Trails for hikers and bicyclists, camping includes RV sites.

DeSoto National Wildlife Refuge
US 30 near Missouri River; 712-642-2772
Migrating waterfowl visit the area in spring and fall, and bald eagles winter here. Choose among a 12-mile auto tour and four self-guided nature trails. Visitor center exhibits artifacts salvaged from the 1865 wreck of a steamboat at this spot. Picnic areas.

August 6, 1804
LITTLE SIOUX
The captains' main worry today was that Moses B. Reed was not yet back. After leaving the Council Bluff to recover a knife three days earlier, he hadn't returned, nor had a French boatmen sent after him. While the Frenchman was a civilian, Reed was army. Now the captains sent four men to bring Reed back, dead or alive. (The rest of the story is in Nebraska section, August 13-20, 1804.)

return: September 6, 1806
Homeward bound more than two years later, here the Corps met the first of several trading boats they'd see heading up the Missouri. From these French traders, they bought the first "spirituous liquor" they'd had since Fourth of July in 1805. The captains promised to pay the boat's owner, René Auguste Chouteau, when they reached

MAP LEGEND PAGE 6

IOWA
39

IOWA

St. Louis. The traders told the corps that Zebulon Pike had left on an army exploration two months earlier; they didn't know that among his troops was John Boley, who'd slogged up the Missouri with them in 1804 and was in the keelboat return crew of 1805.

Little Sioux Delta Park
From I-29 & IA K45, 1 mile W; 712-647-2785
Interpretation of the return trip meeting with Chouteau's traders. Hiking, fishing, picnic area, primitive campsites, boat access to Missouri.

August 8, 1804
ONAWA   10

10 2 Lewis and Clark State Park
3 miles W on Hwy. 175; 712-423-2829
This park features an interpretive trail about the Lewis and Clark Expedition, and replicas of the Corps' keelboat and pirogues; interpretive center opens in 2004. Campsites with electricity, lake fishing and boating, playground.

August 20, 1804   10
SERGEANT BLUFF

Beginning July 30, journal entries mention that Sgt. Charles Floyd was quite ill, with a bad cold and upset stomach. Eventually he couldn't keep food down. The captains did what they could, including bleeding and purging the young man, but he only worsened. This day, the Corps stopped at noon to make Floyd a warm bath, but before water was heated, he died, probably from appendicitis and peritonitis. It would be twenty years before doctors began to understand the illness, so Floyd's death was not because of frontier conditions.

He was buried at Sergeant Bluff (which the captains named Sergeant Floyd Bluff) with full Honors of War. A cedar post marking his grave was a Missouri River landmark at least into the 1830s. The Corps traveled on and camped above the mouth of a river they named for Floyd.

Despite many illnesses and injuries during the next two years, all the other men survived the expedition.

return: September 4, 1805
On the return trip, the men stopped to pay their respects, found Sgt. Floyd's grave partially opened, and reclosed it. (See also Sioux City, below.)

August 20, 1804
SIOUX CITY   10

Other than mentioning that the evening was beautiful, Clark wrote nothing more on this date. The Corps camped overnight and "proceeded on" very early the next morning.

Sioux City Convention & Visitor Bureau
801 4th St., Sioux City, IA 51101
800-593-2228; 712-279-4800

Onawa, Iowa
on the
Trail of Lewis & Clark

Along I-29, Onawa is the home to a state-of-the-art Lewis & Clark Interpretive Center, Located in Lewis & Clark State Park. This mulit-purpose facility will be open in August 2004 and will feature:

- KeelBoat Storage/Display/Work area
- Journals and Maps
- Trail Exhibit Area
- Children's Discovery Zone
- Native American Displays
- Gift Shop
- Outdoor Boat Viewing Platform on Blue Lake

Make Plans to Join Us as We Celebrate the Bicentennial of Lewis & Clark's Journey with a Special Celebration / Grand Opening of Onawa's Lewis & Clark Interpretive Center to be held August 6-9, 2004.

Come and see the **ONLY authentic, life-size replica of the Lewis and Clark keelboat** afloat today. Experience the Buckskinner's rendezvous, the music, food and crafts of a time long past. Held the 2nd weekend of June at the Lewis and Clark State Park, Onawa, IA

Contact Onawa Chamber of Commerce
@712-423-1801, chamber@onawa.com

www.lewisandclark.com

Lewis and Clark Interpretive Center
900 Larsen Park Rd.; 721-224-5242

Explore the many interactive exhibits that look closely at the Corps experiences in the area of Sgt. Floyd's death. Right on the Missouri River.

Sergeant Floyd Monument
I-29 exit 143, on US 75S; 712-279-4800

The ever-shifting (before dam construction) Missouri River had eaten into Sergeant Bluff by 1857, and Floyd's grave was moved to Sioux City. In 1901, the 100-foot monument was erected at his final resting site on Floyd's Bluff.

Sergeant Floyd Riverboat Museum
I-20, exit 149 to 1000 S. Larsen Park Rd.; 712-279-0198

Missouri River transportation history, beginning with the Lewis and Clark Expedition. Exhibits include a life-size figure of Sgt. Charles Floyd, reconstructed by a forensics expert based on a cast of Floyd's skull made in 1901, and scale models of various types of riverboats that traveled the Missouri.

Stone State Park
5 miles N on IA Hwy. 12; 712-255-4698

Overlooks the Missouri and Big Sioux confluence, and has camping (some RV sites), picnic sites, fishing, and hiking trails.

Sioux City Riverfront Trail
I-29 exit 147; 712-279-0198

Hiking trail along the Missouri to the mouth of the Floyd River, with trailheads of other hiking and bicycling trails. Visitor center is housed in the M.V. *Sgt. Floyd*.

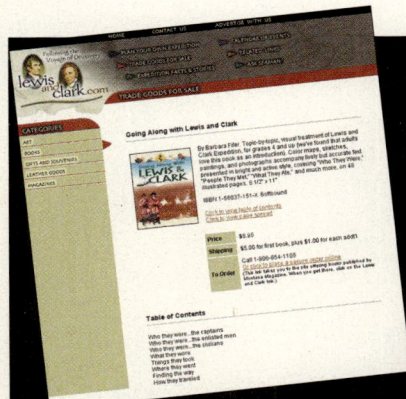

Lewis & Clark
AN AMERICAN ADVENTURE
Sioux City, Iowa

Experience the Journey!

- Barnes & Noble opening Spring 2004
- JCPenney opening Summer 2004
- 12-Screen Stadium Seating Theater
- Over 110 Specialty Shops
- 38 original mural paintings stretching 296 feet in length

Southern Hills Mall
Where your friends are

SERGEANT ROAD & LAKEPORT ROAD
I-29 TO HIGHWAY 20-EAST
EXIT 1 TO LAKEPORT ROAD
www.southernhillsmall.com

Visit Us Online!
www.lewisandclark.com

South Dakota
Lewis and Clark Signature Event
Oceti Sakowin Experience: Remembering and Educating
Aug. 26 – Sept. 27, 2004

Commemorate the bicentennial of the Lewis and Clark Expedition with the Lakota, Nakota and Dakota people. Travel the tribal lands and reservations of South Dakota and learn about American Indian experiences before, during and after the Lewis and Clark Expedition.

The event kicks off Aug. 26 – 27 in Chamberlain/Oacoma, S.D. at the Native American Art Show and Auction. Contact the Alliance of Tribal Tourism Advocates at (605) 870-5144 or visit www.attatribal.com for event information.

Call 1-800-S-DAKOTA for a free South Dakota Vacation Guide or visit **TravelSD.com** for vacation packages.

South Dakota
GREAT FACES. GREAT PLACES.

SOUTH DAKOTA

On August 21, 1804, traveling under a gentle breeze, the Corps of Discovery passed the mouth of the Big Sioux River, today's South Dakota–Iowa border. Today, four dams on the Missouri River have changed the river greatly from what the Corps saw. The dams back up lakes that offer camping and outdoor recreation ranging from primitive camping to marinas and resorts.

Missouri River, Bon Homme County. CHAD COPPESS/SOUTH DAKOTA TOURISM

August 22, 1804
ELK POINT 11

The captains Meriwether Lewis and William Clark had to replace the late Sgt. Floyd, and they had the men act as nominating committee. Each was to vote for his choice, and from the three highest vote-getters, the captains would select. The most votes went to Patrick Gass, followed by William Bratton and George Gibson. Gass was promoted to sergeant.

11 2 Gass Election Site
Heritage Park
A wayside exhibit telling of this vote, the first American election held west of the Missouri, includes a bust of Patrick Gass, who lived until 1870.

return: September 3, 1806
Just below the Vermillion River on their return, the Corps met two trading boats going up. Clark was disappointed that the St. Louis-based traders didn't know more news from back east but was glad to hear that President Jefferson was well. He also learned that Vice President Aaron Burr had killed Secretary of the Treasury Alexander Hamilton in a duel.

Clark recorded that the Indians called the Vermillion "White Stone River." They mined white and red pigments from its clay banks, and eventually red (vermillion) won the name game.

Statewide resources on South Dakota

South Dakota Department of Tourism
711 E. Wells Ave., Pierre, SD 57501
800-SDAKOTA; www.travelsd.com

South Dakota State Parks/Recreation Areas
www.state.sd.us/gfp/sdparks

Alliance of Tribal Tourism Advocates
P.O. Box 232, Lower Brule, SD 57548
605-473-0560; www.nativetourismalliance.org

Great Lakes of South Dakota Association
605-224-4617; www.sdgreatlakes.org

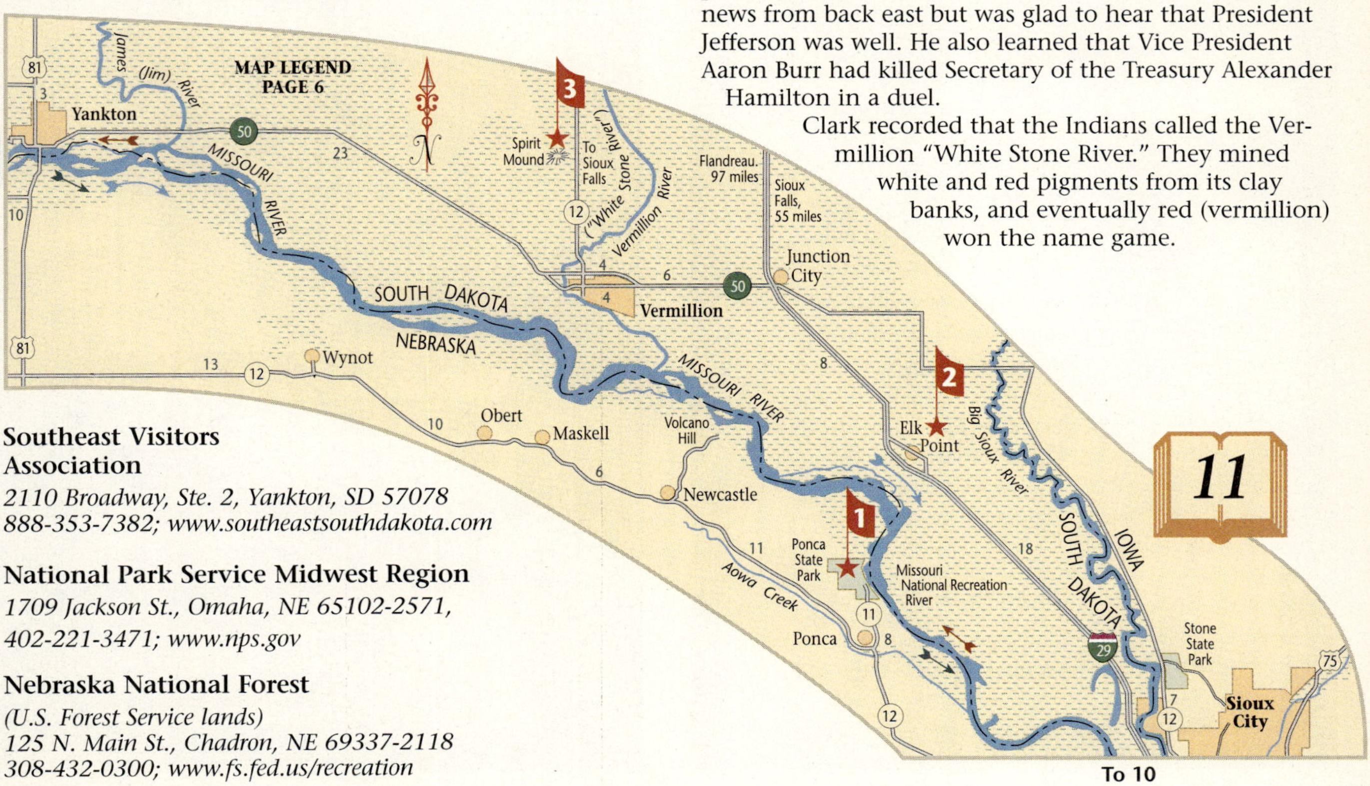

Southeast Visitors Association
2110 Broadway, Ste. 2, Yankton, SD 57078
888-353-7382; www.southeastsouthdakota.com

National Park Service Midwest Region
1709 Jackson St., Omaha, NE 65102-2571,
402-221-3471; www.nps.gov

Nebraska National Forest
(U.S. Forest Service lands)
125 N. Main St., Chadron, NE 69337-2118
308-432-0300; www.fs.fed.us/recreation

South Dakota

August 24, 1804

Vermillion [11]

The day before the Corps passed here, the wind had blown hard, sending sand flying "like a cloud of smoke," and turning the grass white, Clark wrote. But today the hunters did well. Four deer, an elk, a goose, and the first bison the expedition had killed were bagged.

Since 1882, the city has been home to the University of South Dakota.

Spirit Mound [11-3]
SD 19, six miles N; 605-987-2263

On the 24th, while the boats continued past the Vermillion River's mouth, the captains, York, and eight other men hiked north to view Spirit Mound. Otos, Sioux, Omahas, and other area tribes told of "merciless" spirits that lived there, appearing as 18-inch-tall, giant-headed creatures and killing people who had the nerve to approach.

After many years of private ownership, the site now is a state park, with interpretive signs and a hiking trail to the top. The land has been reseeded with native prairie vegetation to look as it did in 1804.

W. H. Over State Museum
SD 50 & Ratigen St.; 705-677-5228

One of four South Dakota State Historical Society museums, this site houses artifacts, dioramas, and exhibits on the state's heritage, including the Spirit Mound story.

north of Vermillion

Sioux Falls

Sixty miles north of Vermillion on I-29, Sioux Falls is a regional commerce center that was settled in the 1850s because of natural resources including waterpower available from the Big Sioux River, plus nearby stone quarries. Self-guided walking tours of the late–19th-century historic districts are outlined in brochures available at Siouxland Heritage Museums.

Sioux Falls Convention and Visitors Bureau
200 N. Phillips, Suite 102; P.O. Box 1425
Sioux Falls, SD 57012; 800-333-2072

Siouxland Heritage Museums

Old Courthouse Museum at 200 W. 6th has changing exhibits in a restored late–19th-century courthouse. 605-367-4211

Pettigrew Home and Museum is an 1889 Queen Anne home at 131 N. Duluth Ave., with guided tours, and exhibit on prairie living. 605-367-7096

Center for Western Studies
2201 S. Summit Ave. at Augustana College
605-274-4007

Permanent and changing exhibits on the history and many cultures of the Northern Plains, art gallery, library and archives, including exhibit on Joseph Desomet, who claimed to be the son of an expedition member, was born in the area, and is buried near Chamberlain.

ALL TRAILS LEAD TO Yankton! SOUTH DAKOTA

Visit Yankton on the Lewis & Clark Trail for recreation, history, shopping and fun. Explore Lewis & Clark Lake and Gavins Point Dam and enjoy swimming, fishing, camping, boating and more!

Lewis & Clark Festival Dates 2004-2005
August 27-29, 2004
August 27-28, 2005

To learn more, contact the Yankton Area Chamber of Commerce at 1-800-888-1460. Or see us on the web at www.yanktonsd.com

GREAT SERVICE
Photos provided by South Dakota Tourism

Royal River Casino, Bingo & Motel...

South Dakota's Premier Entertainment Complex!

- Slots • Blackjack
- Meeting Facilities
- Bingo • 120-Room Motel
- Award-Winning Restaurant

ROYAL RIVER CASINO BINGO & MOTEL

Flandreau, South Dakota
Exit 114 on I-29
7 miles East on Hwy 32

Must be 21 to enter casino or play bingo.

Great Plains Zoo
805 S. Kiwanis Ave.; 605-367-7059

Nearly 400 animals of 70 species from around the world live in simulated natural habitats scattered over 45 acres. Kids of all ages love the Animal Nursery. Delbridge Museum of Natural History exhibits more than 150 mounted animals.

Washington Pavilion of Arts and Sciences
11th & Main Ave.; 877-WASHPAV

Art museum, science center, and performing arts center under one roof. Art by Native American, regional, and contemporary Americans, and changing exhibits in six galleries. Over 80 hands-on exhibits at the science center. IMAX cinema and live performances.

north of Sioux Falls
FLANDREAU

This center for outdoor recreation nestles in South Dakota's glacial lakes and prairies region. The Flandreau-Santee Sioux Tribe Wacipi, on the third weekend of July, welcomes the public to traditional Indian dances from all over the nation.

Glacial Lakes & Prairies Tourism Association
in Redlin Art Center, Watertown
P.O. Box 244, Watertown, SD 57201
605-886-7305; 800-244-8860

Flandreau-Santee Sioux
P.O. Box 283
Flandreau, SD 57028

August 29-30, 1804
YANKTON [11]

Yankton Sioux camped west of here during their council below "Calumet Bluff," while the Corps camped at Gavins Point on the Nebraska side of the Missouri. Sgt. Pryor noted the Sioux's "conical" lodges—the first Plains tipi the Corps had seen. The Yanktons warned the captains that the Teton Sioux upriver wouldn't be so friendly.

return: Sept. 1, 1806

The Corps camped in future Yankton County at the site where the Sioux had stayed two years before, and Clark noted their flagpole from 1804 still standing across the river.

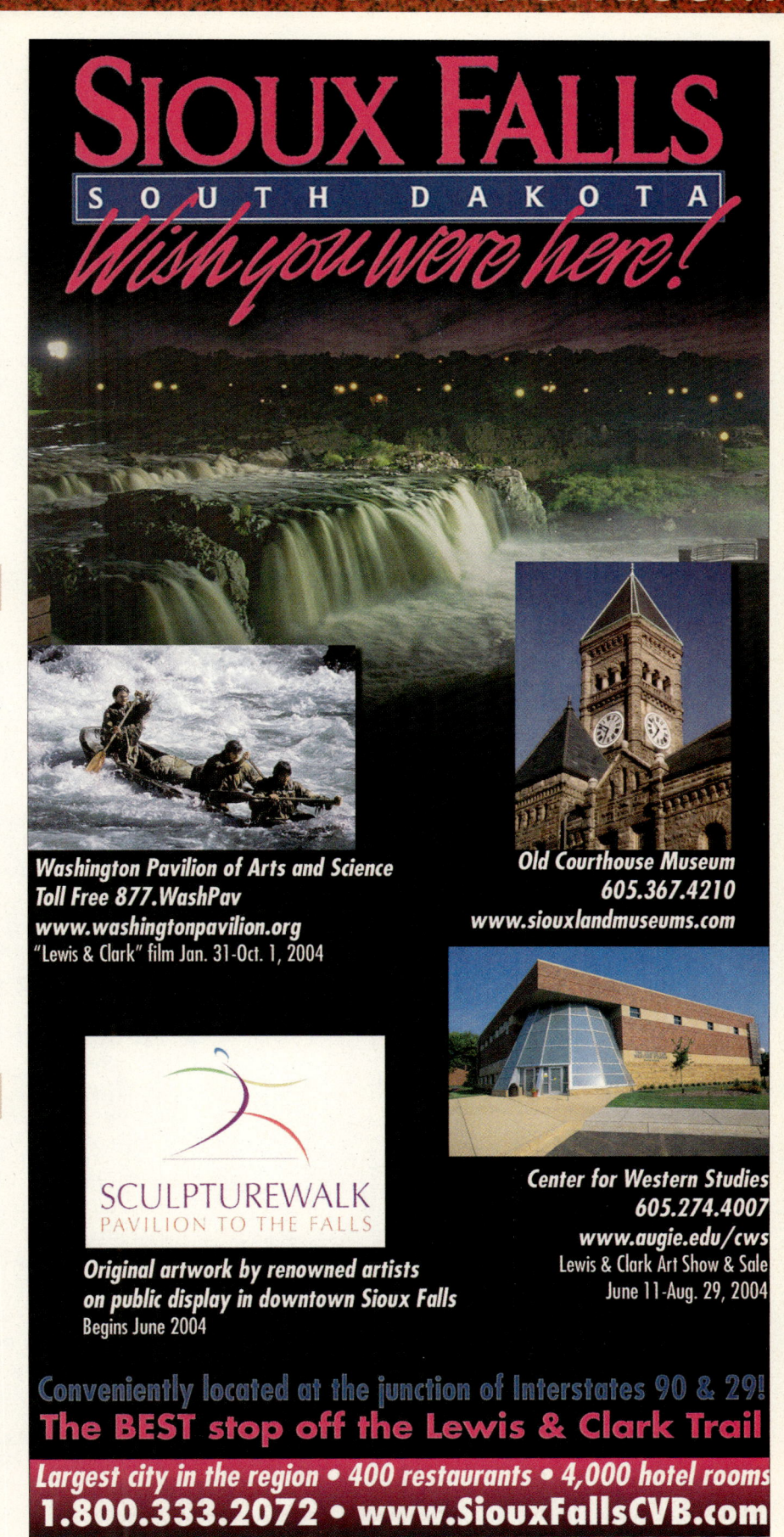

---

www.lewisandclark.com

SIOUX FALLS
SOUTH DAKOTA
Wish you were here!

Washington Pavilion of Arts and Science
Toll Free 877.WashPav
www.washingtonpavilion.org
"Lewis & Clark" film Jan. 31-Oct. 1, 2004

Old Courthouse Museum
605.367.4210
www.siouxlandmuseums.com

SCULPTUREWALK
PAVILION TO THE FALLS

Original artwork by renowned artists on public display in downtown Sioux Falls
Begins June 2004

Center for Western Studies
605.274.4007
www.augie.edu/cws
Lewis & Clark Art Show & Sale
June 11-Aug. 29, 2004

Conveniently located at the junction of Interstates 90 & 29!
The BEST stop off the Lewis & Clark Trail

Largest city in the region • 400 restaurants • 4,000 hotel rooms
1.800.333.2072 • www.SiouxFallsCVB.com

South Dakota

Lake Francis Case and Lewis & Clark Lake

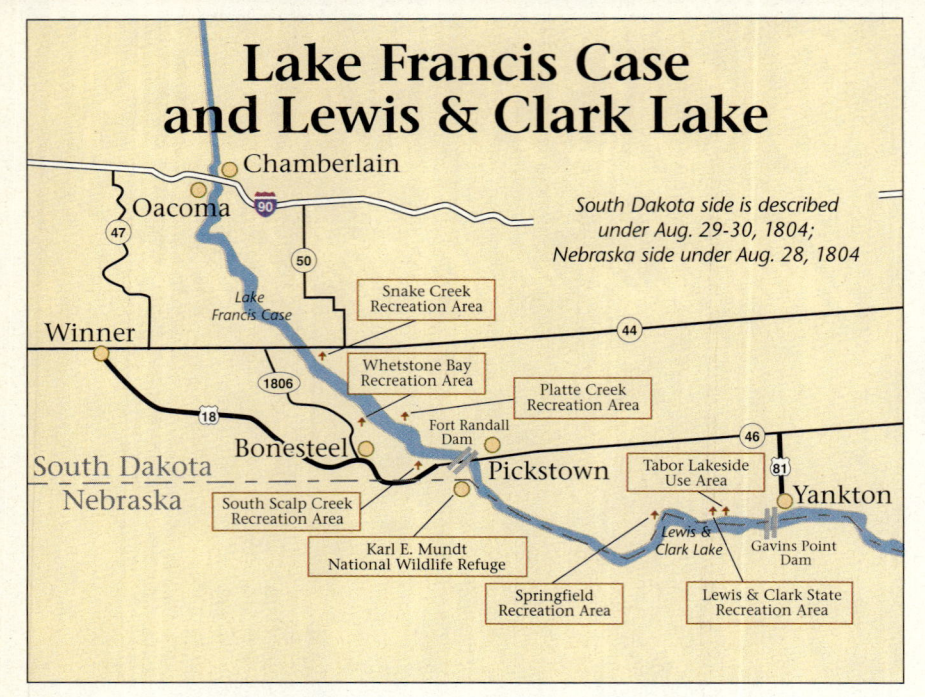

South Dakota side is described under Aug. 29-30, 1804; Nebraska side under Aug. 28, 1804

OLD WEST TRADING POST

12,600 sq. ft. of Antiques, Collectibles, and the Unusual Huge Selection of Lewis & Clark Information including Authentic Trade Beads, Candles, Books, Prints, and Dried Flowers just like Lewis & Clark collected. **FLEA MARKET DURING THE SD SIGNATURE EVENT. VENDOR SPACE STILL AVAILABLE - CALL FOR DETAILS.**

I-90 Exit 260 · Chamberlain/Oacoma, SD
605-734-0770

Today's Yankton remembers its term as Dakota Territory capital, beginning in 1861 when the town was only three years old, the heyday of steamboating on the Upper Missouri, and frontier development. Pick up a brochure for the self-guiding architectural tour of Yankton, which includes Victorian mansions.

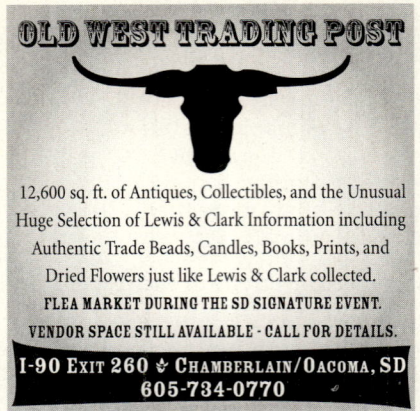

Yankton Area Chamber of Commerce
218 W. Fourth St., Box 588
Yankton, SD 57078; 800-888-1460

Dakota Territorial Museum
8th & Summit in West Side Park; 605-665-3898
Walk through frontier life in restored homes and shops filled with artifacts, including a schoolhouse, train depot, and blacksmith shop.

Cramer-Kenyon Heritage Home
509 Pine St.; 705-665-7470
In its setting of gardens, this 1886 Queen Anne house exhibits original furnishings and fine detail work.

FORT RANDALL CASINO • HOTEL

THE LAND OF THE FRIENDLY PEOPLE

We're Gonna Win You Over

OPEN 24 HOURS LOOSE SLOTS BLACKJACK
POKER BINGO GIFT SHOP RESTAURANT
LIVE ENTERTAINMENT LODGING TRAVEL PLAZA

Come visit The Yankton Sioux Tribe, "The Land of the Friendly People" and Gateway to the Great Sioux Nation. A place where Lewis and Clark made their first friends on their journey to the west. Located three miles east of the Missouri River on Highway 46, Fort Randall Casino and Hotel offers you the finest in dining, poker, slots and blackjack, along with pleasing hotel accommodations.

3 MILES EAST OF FORT RANDALL DAM ON HWY 46
605-487-7871 OR 800-362-6333 (TOLL FREE FOR HOTEL RESERVATIONS ONLY) · WWW.FORTRANDALLCASINO.COM

www.lewisandclark.com

Lewis and Clark Recreation Area

A hiking and biking trail—with great views of the bluffs—parallels Lewis and Clark Lake (Missouri River). The marina offers rentals of canoes, jet skis, and pontoons; accommodations run from camping to cabins to resort with beachfront.

Lewis and Clark Lake—North Shore & Downstream
605-668-2985

Nine units on the lake's South Dakota side offer hundreds of campsites (primitive, modern, RV), fishing, boat access, swimming, tennis, playgrounds, biking trails, horseback riding. (See also South Shore listing in Nebraska section, August 29-30, 1804.)

Gavins Point Dam, Lewis and Clark Lake Regional Visitor Center
on Nebraska side of Missouri across from Yankton
402-667-7873

The story of the Calumet Bluff council is among exhibits on Upper Missouri native peoples, later history, Gavins Point Dam construction, and Lewis and Clark Lake recreation.

September 7, 1804
PICKSTOWN — see map on page 46

The captains met "an animal the French call the prairie dog" and explored the prairie dog village of underground burrows by digging into it and pouring "a great quantity of water" (five barrels) down one hole to see if they could fill it. They captured a flushed-out prairie dog live, and wrote in detail about the little creatures previously unknown to science. The following spring, Lewis would ship several live prairie dogs from Fort Mandan to President Jefferson, and one would survive the journey.

13 Fort Randall Dam
US18/281, one mile W; 605-487-7845

Daily guided tours of the dam are offered during the summer; appointments needed other times. Marked trails lead to overlooks of the dam and Lake Francis Case. The lake, which extends for miles up the Missouri, is surrounded with recreation areas and campsites.

September 16-17, 1804
OACOMA 13

Time to dry out, and enjoy some fresh fruit! The men emptied their boats to dry trade goods and supplies at a campsite on a "beautiful plain…surrounded with timber…in which there is great quantities of fine plums." Gunpowder and replacement flannel shirts were distributed. The stop had to be extended a day for further drying, after a nighttime rain fell. The Missouri was growing shallower, and wet cargo weighed the boats down too much.

On the second day, Lewis noted the presence of "barking squirrels" (prairie dogs), "wolves of the small kind" (coyotes), and skunks, and he made the first written description of black-billed magpies, a subspecies of the bird familiar in Europe but not previously recorded in North America. That day, Clark killed a "curious" species of deer that the captains later named mule deer for its large ears.

return: August 28, 1806

The Corps reclaimed the same campsite, stopping at noon to send men hunting for meat and also for specimens of "barking squirrels" and magpies. Four deer, two bison, and two prairie dogs were bagged, and the men again raided the local plum crop.

Old West Museum
US 16 and I-90 Business Loop; 605-734-6157

Exhibits on Sioux and cattle-ranching history, including live bison and Texas longhorns.

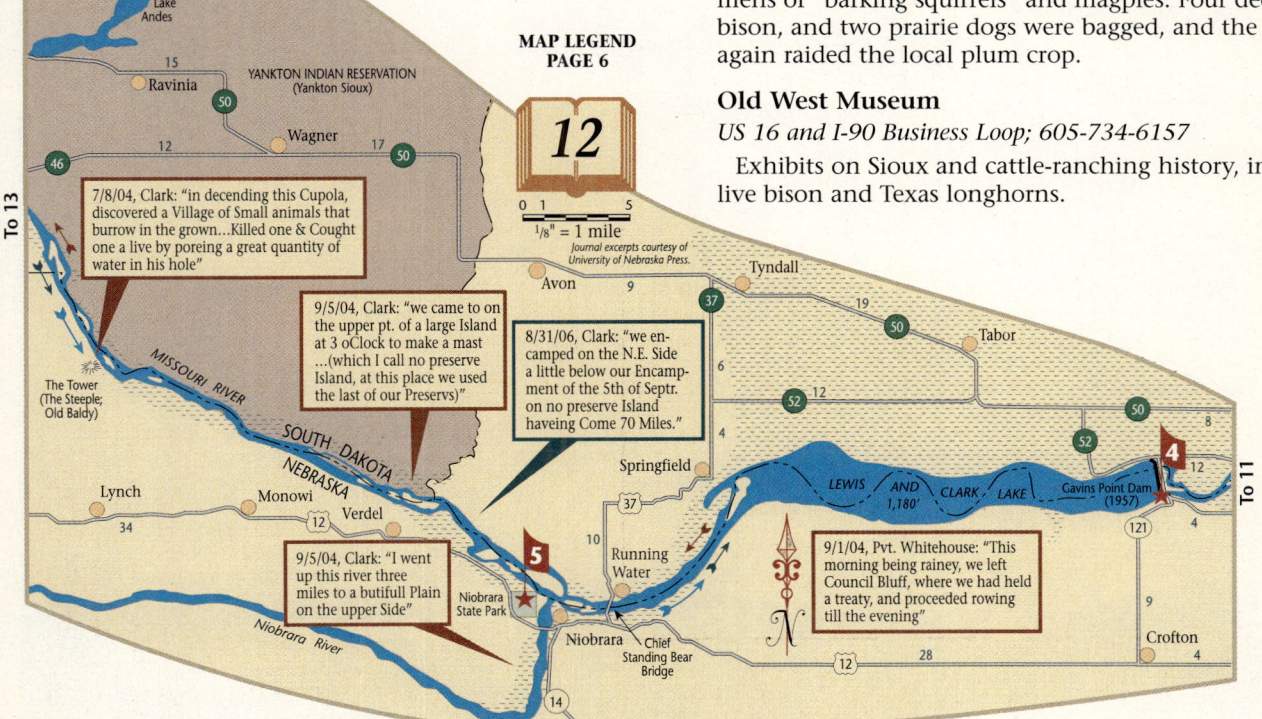

SOUTH DAKOTA

September 18, 1804

CHAMBERLAIN 13

"Proceeding on" against a headwind, the men slowly passed the site of future Chamberlain in the morning. Clark, walking on shore, observed pronghorn, elk, bison, deer, coyotes, wolves, porcupines, rabbits, and prairie dogs. More worrisome, Lewis noticed the first goose flying south for winter—when the Corps had to be safely at the Mandan villages. Camp was set up on the Missouri's west shore after only seven miles of fighting the wind.

Chamberlain developed in the late 19th century as the freight transfer point between western South Dakota's ranch and mine products and eastern South Dakota's farm produce. Today the town also is an access point to recreation on Lake Francis Case.

Lewis and Clark Information Center
I-90 just E of town; 705-734-6719

On a grassy bluff overlooking the Missouri River through a 30-foot glass wall. Exhibits include reproductions of gear and trade goods and tell of the Expedition's adventures in future South Dakota.

Akta Lakota Museum and Cultural Center
on the campus of St. Joseph's Indian School, I-90, exit 263

Exhibits on Yankton and Teton Lakota (Sioux) culture and lifestyles.

Native American Scenic Byway
This highway follows the Lewis and Clark route from Chamberlain to Pierre, through two Sioux reservations. Obtain self-guiding tour maps at:

Chamberlain–Oacoma Chamber of Commerce
115 W. Lawler Ave., Chamberlain, SD 57325
605-734-4416; www.chamberlainsd.org

east of Chamberlain

MITCHELL

East of Chamberlain 83 miles on I-90, Mitchell is a hub to farming communities and a mecca for commerce and shopping in the James River Valley.

Mitchell Chamber of Commerce
601 N. Main St., P.O. Box 206, Mitchell, SD 57301
866-273-CORN

Corn Palace
Sixth and Main; 800-257-2676

Every year, new murals made of corn, seeds, and grasses are applied to the exterior (and some interior) of this hall, which also boasts Oscar Howe–designed decoration. Guided tours during summer.

Middle Border Museum & Oscar Howe Art Center
I-90, Exit 330 to 1300 E. University Ave. on campus of Dakota Wesleyan University; 605-996-2122; www.oscarhowe.com

---

Discover Chamberlain/Oacoma South Dakota

The newly constructed Lewis & Clark Interpretive Center and Scenic Overlook gives an in-depth look at Lewis & Clark's adventures throughout South Dakota. Step out on the deck of the Corps' keelboat and experience the best kept secret along the trail.

Cedar Shore Resort
888-697-6363 www.cedarshore.com
We're Makin' Every Day Count!
Kick back and relax along the Lewis and Clark Trail at this beautiful full service resort on the banks of the Missouri River. There is something for everyone whether you stay at the hotel, dine in the restaurant, camp along the river or rent a pontoon boat. Enjoy swimming, fishing, golfing, outdoor dining or relaxing on your own private deck overlooking the Missouri River.

Akta Lakota Museum
800-798-3452 www.stjo.org/museum
The Akta Lakota Museum offers a rare combination of authentic Native American artifact displays, contemporary Sioux artworks and various traditional art forms. Located on the banks of the Missouri, the Akta Lakota preserves the Sioux culture through the arts and history of the people.

Al's Oasis
605-734-6054 www.alsoasis.com
Al's Oasis, a South Dakota Tradition since 1919, is located where Lewis and Clark looked south to the Missouri River in 1804. Al's Oasis offers a AAA rated restaurant with seating for 325. Famous for buffalo burgers, prime rib, home-made pies, salad bar, and 5¢ coffee! Visit the Last Chance Saloon, expanded clothing and gift shop and large supermarket, Oasis Inn, Conoco convenience store, and riverside cabins.

Chamberlain – Oacoma Area CHAMBER OF COMMERCE
605-734-4416
115 West Lawler
Chamberlain, SD 57325
chamber@chamberlainsd.org
www.chamberlainsd.org
I-90 Exits 260, 263 & 265

Cultural center exhibits "Lewis and Clark: Discovering Dakota," Native American history and early homesteading, art of Oscar Howe, Charles Hargens, Harvey Dunn, and others. Restored historic church, school, depot, and 1886 Italiante home.

Prehistoric Indian Village
Indian Village Rd.; 605-996-5473
Reconstructed lodge, ongoing archaeological excavation, audio-visual presentation, and museum show life in a fortified village of about 1,000 years before present, and before the Sioux and Mandan.

September 19, 1804
A crisp early-autumn day allowed the men to move along well, up to the beginning of the Missouri's Big Bend. With no Big Bend Dam and no Lake Sharpe, the river was narrow and low. Hunting separately, Clark, York, and a party of four enlisted men brought in a bison, two elk, and four deer. Men in the boats shot two bison that were swimming across the Missouri. In his journal, Clark described the surrounding prairie as "handsome" and "beautiful."

Big Bend Dam & Lake Sharpe 14

SD 47 on the Missouri; 605-245-2331 (powerhouse): 605-245-2255 (lake)
Completed in 1966 for irrigation, electricity, and flood control, Big Bend Dam created Lake Sharpe on the Missouri. Powerhouse lobby has exhibits, and complete powerhouse tours are offered during summer months. North Shore area has primitive camping, picnicking, swimming, boat access. West Bend area offers cabins, campsites (tent and RV), swimming, hiking trails.

September 25-28, 1804
The expedition met in council with the Teton Sioux at the mouth of the Bad River. Both Indians and whites had warned the captains that the Tetons were warlike; the Tetons were used to traders rather than visitors who wanted to give a few presents and go on with full boats. Also, no member of the Corps spoke their language. Pvt. Pierre Cruzatte spoke Omaha to a prisoner of the Tetons, who translated to his captors. Twice hostilities almost began when the two sides misunderstood each other and suspected attack. Feasting and dancing accompanied the talks, but the groups parted with neither great friendliness nor serious trouble.

return: August 26, 1806
Lewis, recovering from his gunshot (See North Dakota, Aug. 11, 1806), was able to walk, but the next day he'd take too energetic a walk and suffer for it. Everyone was alert for the Teton Sioux, but they were out hunting bison.

PIERRE 15

Be sure to pronounce its name "peer" when visiting South Dakota's capital. Missouri steamboat traffic serving Black Hills gold rushers helped shape the frontier town, and early railroads helped it win capital status upon statehood in 1889.

Pierre Area Chamber of Commerce
800 W. Dakota Ave., Pierre, SD 57501; 800-962-2034; www.pierrechamber.com

15 South Dakota Cultural Heritage Center
900 Governor's Dr.; 605-773-3458
Exhibits on Sioux life and culture include a walk-through tipi, and European-American exhibits go back as far as an 18th-century plate marking France's claim on this land, and include a replica Jefferson peace medal such as Lewis and Clark presented Native Americans.

River Place Inn
Bed & Breakfast

Majestically situated along the Lewis & Clark trail, on the river bluffs overlooking the Missouri River.

Four rooms with queen or king beds and two private baths. Private water access with dock—kayaks for rent.

Reservations:
ph: 605-224-8589
e: upland@dakota2k.net
w: www.bbonline.com
109 River Place • Pierre, SD 57401

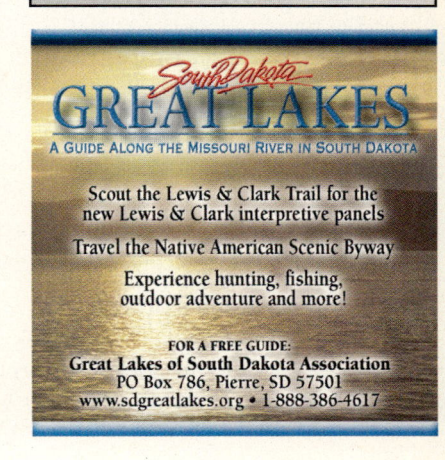

South Dakota GREAT LAKES
A GUIDE ALONG THE MISSOURI RIVER IN SOUTH DAKOTA

Scout the Lewis & Clark Trail for the new Lewis & Clark interpretive panels
Travel the Native American Scenic Byway
Experience hunting, fishing, outdoor adventure and more!

FOR A FREE GUIDE:
Great Lakes of South Dakota Association
PO Box 786, Pierre, SD 57501
www.sdgreatlakes.org • 1-888-386-4617

South Dakota

Fort Pierre 15

The American Fur Company traded with the Arikara from its post built by the mouth of the Bad River, from 1817 until the army bought it in 1855. A second Fort Pierre arose north of town but lasted only five years (1858-63). The 1870s gold rush brought a booming steamboat trad

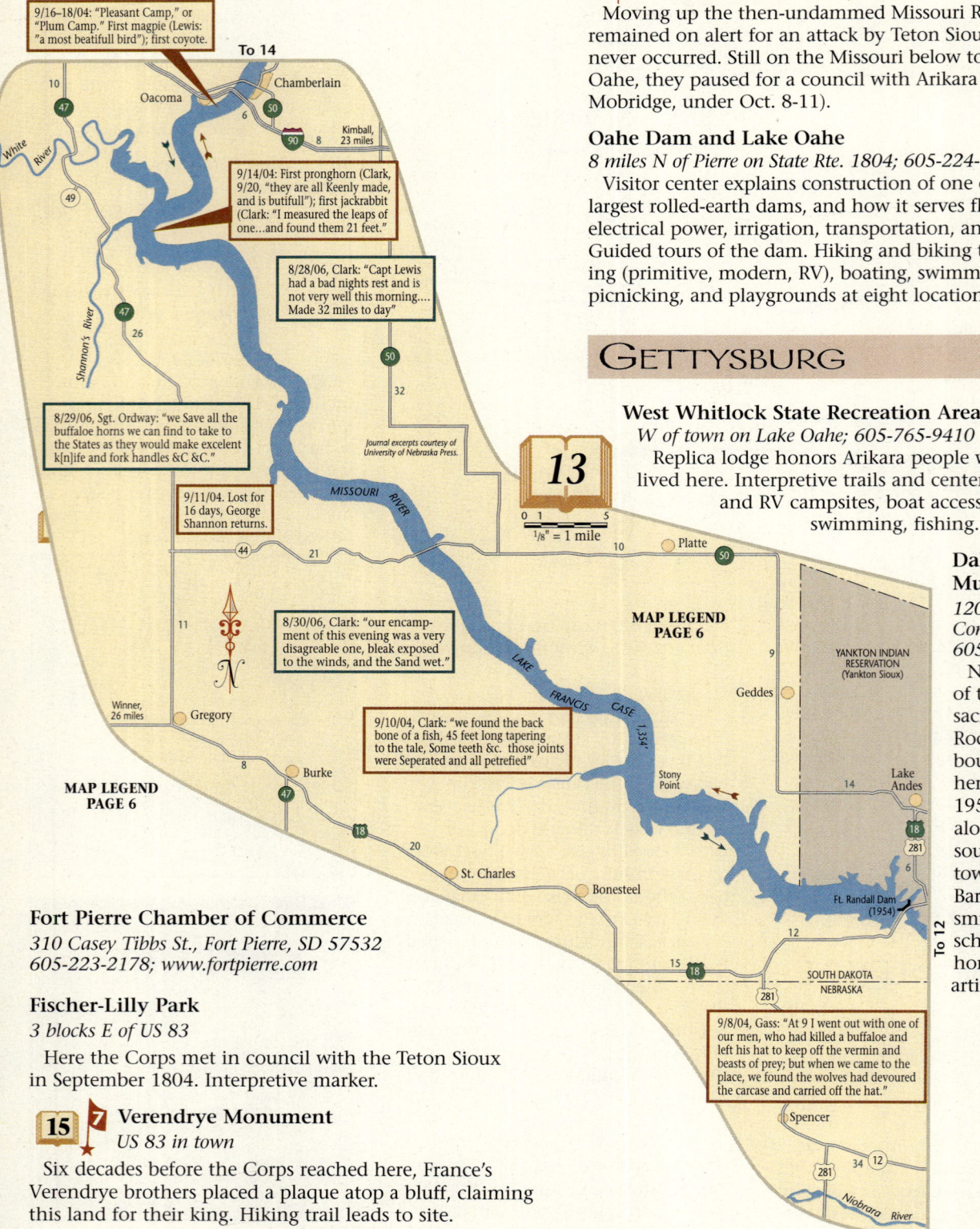

Fort Pierre Chamber of Commerce
310 Casey Tibbs St., Fort Pierre, SD 57532
605-223-2178; www.fortpierre.com

Fischer-Lilly Park
3 blocks E of US 83
Here the Corps met in council with the Teton Sioux in September 1804. Interpretive marker.

15 7 Verendrye Monument
US 83 in town
Six decades before the Corps reached here, France's Verendrye brothers placed a plaque atop a bluff, claiming this land for their king. Hiking trail leads to site.

16 8 Fort Pierre National Grassland
5 miles S US 83
Administered by U.S. Forest Service. More than 100,000 acres of prairie make excellent habitat for pronghorn, sharptailed grouse, and prairie chicken. Primitive camping, birding, and fishing. Hunting season Sept.-Nov.

September 29-October 13, 1804
Moving up the then-undammed Missouri River, the men remained on alert for an attack by Teton Sioux—which never occurred. Still on the Missouri below today's Lake Oahe, they paused for a council with Arikara (see Mobridge, under Oct. 8-11).

Oahe Dam and Lake Oahe
8 miles N of Pierre on State Rte. 1804; 605-224-5862
Visitor center explains construction of one of the world's largest rolled-earth dams, and how it serves flood control, electrical power, irrigation, transportation, and recreation. Guided tours of the dam. Hiking and biking trails, camping (primitive, modern, RV), boating, swimming, fishing, picnicking, and playgrounds at eight locations.

Gettysburg

West Whitlock State Recreation Area
W of town on Lake Oahe; 605-765-9410
Replica lodge honors Arikara people who once lived here. Interpretive trails and center. Cabins, tent and RV campsites, boat access, hiking, swimming, fishing.

Dakota Sunset Museum
1205 W. Commercial Ave; 605-765-9480
Now the home of the Lakotas' sacred Medicine Rock, a 40 foot boulder moved here in the 1950s from along the Missouri, where it towered in 1804. Barber & blacksmith shops, schoolhouse, & homesteader artifacts.

Journal excerpts (map callouts):

- 9/16-18/04: "Pleasant Camp," or "Plum Camp." First magpie (Lewis: "a most beatifull bird"); first coyote.
- 9/14/04: First pronghorn (Clark, 9/20, "they are all Keenly made, and is butifull"); first jackrabbit (Clark: "I measured the leaps of one…and found them 21 feet."
- 8/28/06, Clark: "Capt Lewis had a bad nights rest and is not very well this morning…. Made 32 miles to day"
- 8/29/06, Sgt. Ordway: "we Save all the buffalo horns we can find to take to the States as they would make excelent k[n]ife and fork handles &C &C."
- 9/11/04. Lost for 16 days, George Shannon returns.
- 8/30/06, Clark: "our encampment of this evening was a very disagreable one, bleak exposed to the winds, and the Sand wet."
- 9/10/04, Clark: "we found the back bone of a fish, 45 feet long tapering to the tale, Some teeth &c. those joints were Seperated and all petrefied"
- 9/8/04, Gass: "At 9 I went out with one of our men, who had killed a buffaloe and left his hat to keep off the vermin and beasts of prey; but when we came to the place, we found the wolves had devoured the carcase and carried off the hat."

Journal excerpts courtesy of University of Nebraska Press.

www.lewisandclark.com

east of Mobridge
ABERDEEN

Ninety-two miles east of Mobridge on US 12, Aberdeen was home during 1888-1891 to L. Frank Baum, creator of the Wizard of Oz (who used Dakota plains experiences in some of the 14 Oz books), and to Hamlin Garland, author of realistic 19th-century novels about homesteading life & his autobiography, *A Son of the Middle Border.*

Aberdeen Convention & Visitors Bureau
516 S. Main, P.O. Box 1179
Aberdeen, SD 57402;
800-645-3851

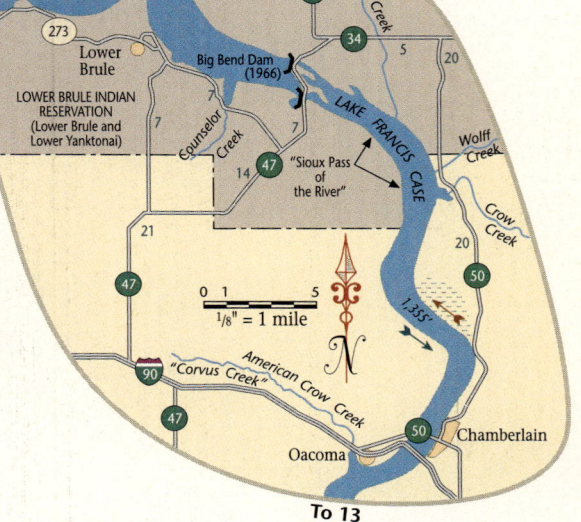

October 8-11, 1804
MOBRIDGE

The Corps met in friendly council with Arikaras in this area. Two French traders interpreted. The Indians were fascinated with York's black skin, and York told them he'd been a cannibal before Clark "caught" him and especially enjoyed eating small children. Clark felt York's joke went a bit too far.

Sakakawea Monument
6 miles W on US 12, then 4 miles S on SD 1806
At the fur-trade post of Fort Manuel near here, in 1812, Sacagawea died and was buried. Today a monument honors the young Shoshone interpreter who carried her new baby on the trip and was the Corps' sole woman member from April 1805 to August 1806.

Klein Museum
West US 12; 605-845-7243
Open daily except Tuesday from April through October. On exhibit are Indian beadwork, headdresses, clothing, tools, and early photographs. Many artifacts from early white settlers are displayed in room settings.

Sitting Bull Monument
6 miles W on US 12, then 4 miles S on SD 1806
The great Ogalala Sioux medicine man of the last years before reservation life was killed in 1890, fourteen years after he fought in the Battle of the Little Big Horn (see North Dakota, October 15, 1804). He was reburied here in the 1950s; the granite bust weighs seven tons.

Standing Rock Indian Reservation
The reservation extends into North Dakota; see information in North Dakota section, Oct. 15, 1804.

Oscar Howe Indian Murals
Scherr-Howe Arena, 212 Main St.;
605-845-3700
Ten murals by the Sioux artist (1915-1983) and University of South Dakota art professor show Sioux life and culture. Howe finished them in 1942 in a burst of 20-hour days after receiving his World War II call-up.

Dacotah Prairie Museum; *First and Main;*
605-626-7117
Period rooms and homesteader and Sioux artifacts tell the story of the Dakota Midlands.

October 13, 1804
POLLOCK

John Newman was court martialed near here and convicted of mutinous talk and undermining the cap-

---

EXPLORE POLLOCK, SOUTH DAKOTA
Lewis & Clark did in 1804!
The Lewis & Clark trail travels right through Pollock, SD on Hwy 1804. Here you'll find:
- Lewis & Clark nature trails
- the site of the Court Martial of Private Neuman
- Veteran's Memorial
- Home of the Stone Idols
- Exceptional fishing and hunting

"A City Built on a Hill Cannot Be Hid"
Town of Pollock • PO Box 57 • Pollock, SD 57648
PH: 605-889-2490 • www.pollocksouthdakota.com • www.pollockschool.com

SOUTH DAKOTA 51

SOUTH DAKOTA

tains' command. Lewis dismissed him from the army and assigned him to the crew of Frenchmen in the red pirogue. Newman also received 75 lashes.

Five miles away is Langelier Bay (see North Dakota; section, October 14, 1804).

Pollock was founded in 1901 as a Soo Line spur railhead. When Oahe Dam was being built in the 1950s, residents voted to move the townsite south. By 1962 new Pollock existed, and the waters of causeway-created Lake Pocasse covered the remains of the old town. On State Highway 1804, it is a hunting and walleye fishing center.

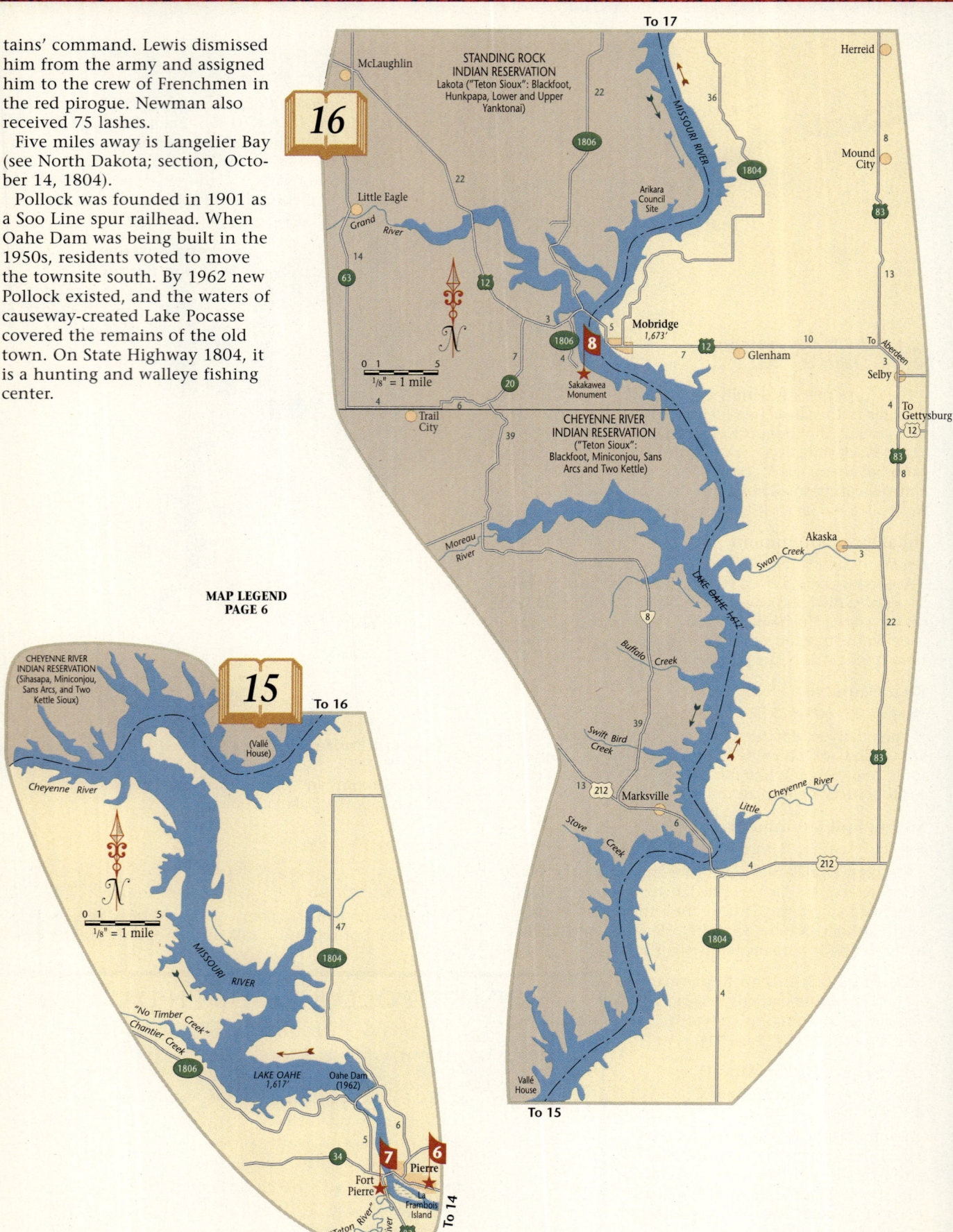

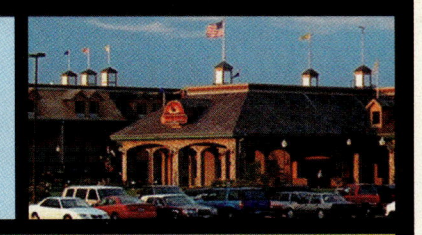

Chart a path to game and fortune.

The Lewis & Clark Trail travels through the middle of the Standing Rock Sioux territory. Here you'll find Prairie Knights Casino and Resort and Grand River Casino and Resort. They're located 64 miles apart on the vast and beautiful Dakota prairie.

Prairie Knights offers 600 reel and video slots, blackjack, Three Card Poker and Let It Ride. Its Pavilion event center hosts big name entertainers and conferences.

Grand River offers 250 reel and video slots as well as blackjack and poker. The Sage Bar & Grill is being renovated and a buffet and Lodge is also being added. The expansion is planned to be complete summer 2004.

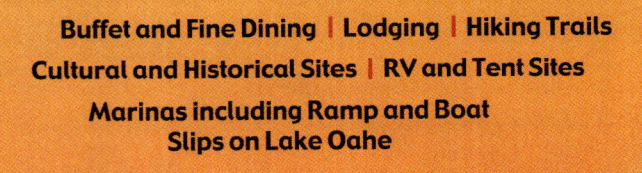

Buffet and Fine Dining | Lodging | Hiking Trails
Cultural and Historical Sites | RV and Tent Sites
Marinas including Ramp and Boat Slips on Lake Oahe

PRAIRIE KNIGHTS CASINO AND RESORT
Off I-94 at Mandan, 46 miles south on Hwy 1806
prairieknights.com • 1-800-425-8277

GRAND RIVER CASINO AND RESORT
West Hwy 12, Mobridge
grandrivercasino.com • 1-800-475-3321
The Bay • 605-845-7106

Legendary

In North Dakota, you can follow the trail of legends like Lewis and Clark, Sakakawea, Custer, Sitting Bull and Teddy Roosevelt, or blaze your own trail! Whether your trail takes you biking in the Badlands or hiking through the mall, fishing for walleye or hunting for antiques, you'll find legendary adventure in North Dakota.

North Dakota LEGENDARY

LEWIS & CLARK
A North Dakota Legend

Contact us for a Free Travel Guide.
1-800-HELLO-ND (435-5663)
www.ndtourism.com

NORTH DAKOTA

When the expedition crossed into today's North Dakota in mid-October 1804, they were nearing their goal: the Mandan-Hidatsa villages. There they planned to winter, finding safety in numbers, plus assistance and information from these plains dwellers. At their winter camp they enjoyed friendship and learned as much as they could about the path ahead. They also added the final members to the Corps of Discovery—a family of three.

Fort Mandan replica, Washburn. CHUCK HANEY

Statewide resources on North Dakota

North Dakota Tourism
400 E. Broadway, Suite 50, Bismarck, ND 58501
800-HELLO-ND; www.ndtourism.com

National Park Service Midwest Region
1709 Jackson St. Omaha, NE 65102-2571
402-221-3471; www.nps.gov

October 14, 1804
Langelier Bay Recreation Area
US 83, 32 miles from Linton

The Corps' first camp in North Dakota is now under the waters of Lake Oahe, and this nearby lakeshore site offers primitive camping, fishing, and boating access.

October 15, 1804
FORT YATES 17

The Corps camped among 10 Arikara lodges south of present Fort Yates on a rainy night.

Headquarters for the Standing Rock Indian Reservation (home to Sioux), the village offers water recreation on the upper Oahe Reservoir, and tribally owned Prairie Knights Casino. The public is welcomed to powwows and other Standing Rock events.

Standing Rock Sioux Tribal Office
P.O. Box D, Fort Yates, ND 58538; 701-854-7291

17 1 Fort Yates Historic Site
Off ND 24; 701-854-7231

Sitting Bull lived on Standing Rock reservation from 1883 to 1890 (leaving to tour with Buffalo Bill's Wild West Show in 1885) and continued to be an influential Sioux leader. When the Ghost Dance movement reached Standing Rock in 1890, the Indian agent feared Sitting Bull's support of it and sent Indian police to arrest the medicine man. In the attempt, Sitting Bull, his son, and six policemen were killed.

Standing Rock
across from Standing Rock Agency Headquarters

Sacred to both the Arikaras and the Dakota Sioux, the rock resembles a seated woman. Legend says that she remained behind when her village moved, because she was jealous of her husband's attention to his second wife. Those who went back seeking the woman found her seated, wearing a shawl—and turned to stone.

October 20, 1804
MANDAN 17

Clark walked on the Missouri's west side this day and viewed the remains of On-a-Slant Village just south of the Heart River. After crossing Apple Creek, Clark ran across the first grizzly bear the expedition had seen (although they'd been warned about the fearsome animal). His shot only wounded it. Elsewhere, Private Pierre Cruzatte also wounded a grizzly and dropped his precious tomahawk and gun in running from it; when the bear fled, Cruzatte reclaimed his gear. (The Corps wouldn't get a grizzly specimen until the following April 29, when Lewis killed one; see Montana section.) Camp that night was inside today's Fort Abraham Lincoln State Park.

Across the Missouri from Bismarck, its smaller twin of Mandan is a North Dakota shipping and trade center that calls itself "Where the West Begins" and celebrates its frontier heritage during Rodeo Days around the Fourth of July.

Bismarck-Mandan Convention & Visitors Bureau
1600 Burnt Boat Dr., Bismarck, ND 58503
800-767-3555; www.bismarckmandancvb.com

On-a-Slant Indian Village
in Fort Abraham Lincoln State Park, 7 miles S on ND 1806
701-667-6343; 800-807-4723

Reconstructed earth lodges show life in this Mandan village of 1675-1781, home to a thousand residents and birthplace of Chief Shehek but abandoned before the expedition passed by. Third-person interpreters.

17 2 Fort Abraham Lincoln State Park
7 miles S of Mandan on Highway 1806

For three years, ending in 1876, Colonel George Custer and the Seventh Cavalry were stationed here, until marching out to the Little Bighorn. Today there is an interpretive center housing exhibits on area

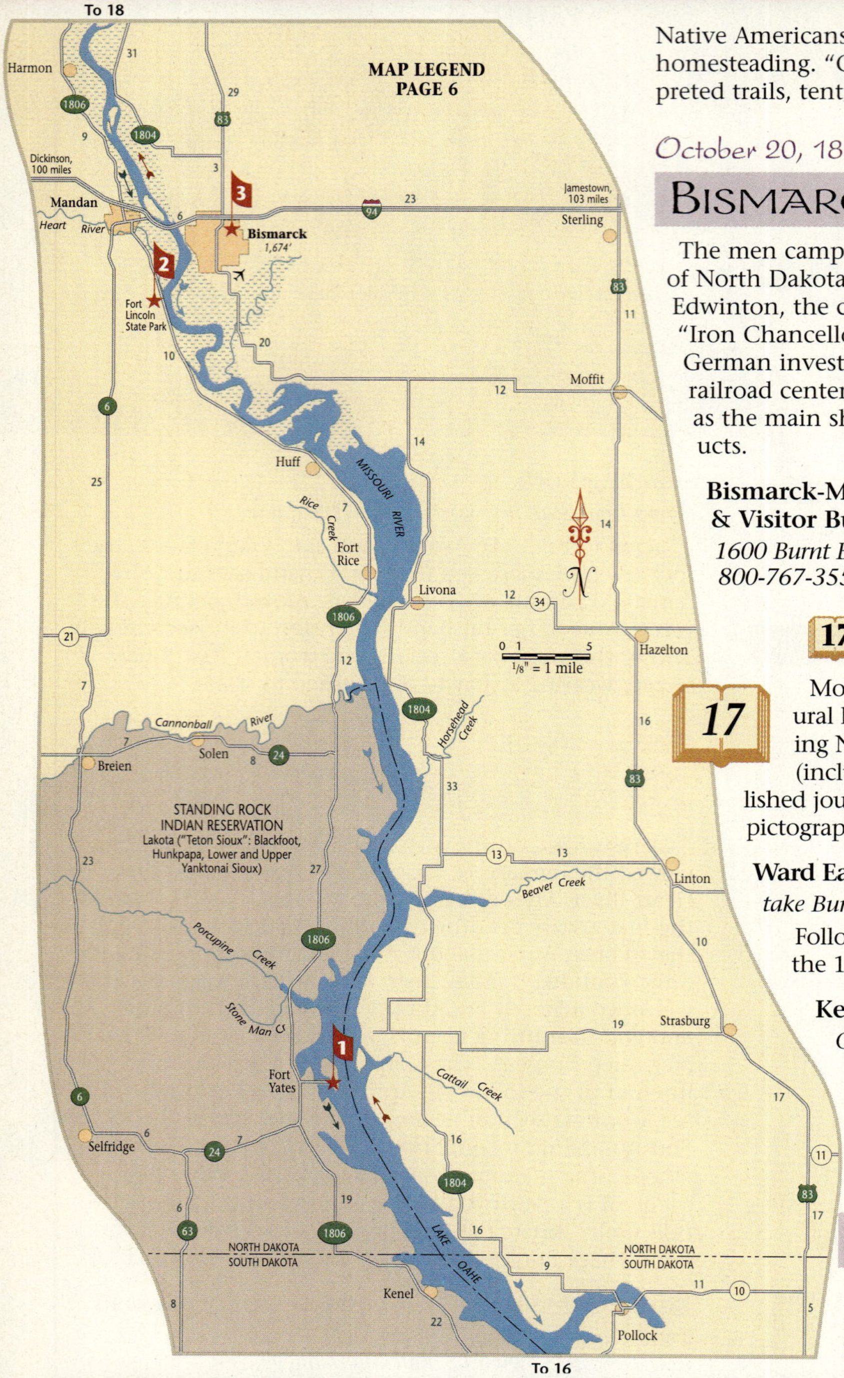

NORTH DAKOTA

Native Americans, the military, the fur trade, railroad building, and homesteading. "Custer House" has first-person interpreters. Interpreted trails, tent/RV campsites.

October 20, 1804
BISMARCK 17

The men camped across the Missouri River from the future site of North Dakota's territorial and state capital. Founded in 1872 as Edwinton, the city's name was later changed to honor Germany's "Iron Chancellor," Otto von Bismarck, in hopes of attracting German investors. The Black Hills gold rush made Bismarck a railroad center in 1873, and the city, with Mandan, continues as the main shipping point for agricultural and mining products.

Bismarck-Mandan Convention & Visitor Bureau
1600 Burnt Boat Dr., Bismarck, ND 58503, 800-767-3555; www.bismarckmandancvb.com

17 North Dakota Heritage Center
on the Capitol Grounds; 701-223-2666
Modern building houses fine presentation of state natural history, and human prehistory and history, including Native Americans, Lewis and Clark Expedition (including Peace Medal, 1807 edition of Sgt. Gass's published journal, Jefferson's 1806 report to Congress, pictographs of the Corps' visit), homesteading, and more.

Ward Earthlodge Village Historic Site
take Burnt Boat Rd. to N. Grandview Rd.
Follow the trail through remains of a Mandan village of the 1700s; interpretive signs.

Keelboat Park
Grant Marsh Bridge on the Missouri
Walk up and look over the full-size replica of the expedition's keelboat, "drydocked" here in Autumn 2003.

west of Bismarck
DICKINSON

Dickinson is the business and services center of southwestern North Dakota, proud of its German, Scandinavian, and Ukrainian ethnic heritages, cowboy history, and outdoor recreational opportunities.

Come See the Animals Lewis and Clark Saw...

Open daily: 10 am - 8 pm, May-Sept.
Fri, Sat, Sun: 1-5 pm, Oct.-April
Weather Permitting

DAKOTA ZOO
Sertoma Park
Riverside Park Road
Bismarck, ND 58504
701-223-7543
www.dakotazoo.org

Expressway Inn & Suites
Conveniently located near shopping!

Bismarck Inn (800) 456-6388
Bismarck Suites (888) 774-5566
Fargo Inn (800) 437-0044

Advanced reservations required. Not valid during conventions, tournaments or special events. Excludes economy singles. No other discounts apply. Expires 1-31-05

$8 OFF $8 OFF

Journey to the Heart of the Lewis & Clark Trail

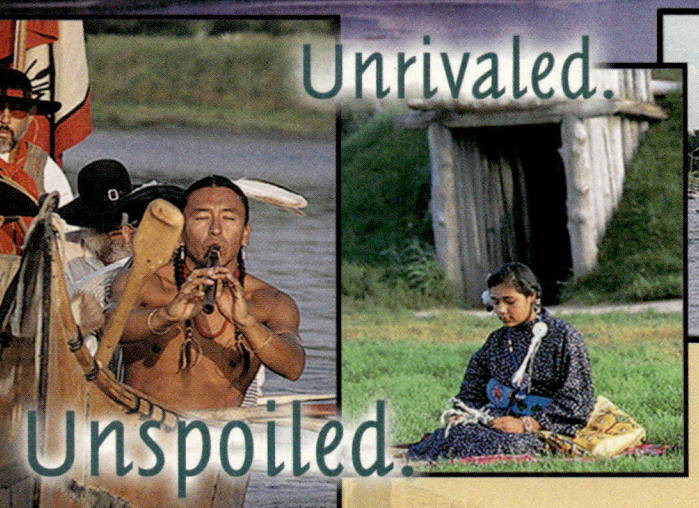

Bismarck-Mandan
Genuine Dakota

Unrivaled.

Undeniable.

Unspoiled.

Unexpected.

Lewis & Clark National Signature Event October 22-31, 2004

Renew the bonds of friendship and cooperation forged by the Corps of Discovery during the winter of 1804-05. Experience authentic Native American interpretations and demonstrations accenting their living history.

Groups register free. ★ Experience history through the eyes of reenactors and scholars.
Explore a virtual reality Mandan Village. Taste what they tasted. See what they saw. Hear what they heard.
Be entertained with flute music and drum presentations. ★ Discover reconstructed earthlodges.

For travel, lodging and dining info, journey to **bismarckmandancvb.com**

Bismarck–Mandan Convention and Visitors Bureau   Exit 157 off I-94, Bismarck, North Dakota ★ 1-800-767-3555

NORTH DAKOTA

Dickinson Convention & Visitors Center
72 Museum Drive; (800) 279-7391;
www.dickinsoncvb.com

Dakota Dinosaur Museum
I-94, Exit 61, 200 Museum Dr.
701-225-DINO; www.dakotadino.com

A fossil-lover's paradise with an actual Triceratops skeleton, ten full-scale dinosaur models, and thousands of rock, mineral and fossil specimens.

Joachim Regional Museum
200 Museum Dr.; 701-456-6225

Included in Dakota Dinosaur Museum admission. Historical artifacts from around southwestern North Dakota, with a new theme-exhibit each summer.

Prairie Outpost Park
in Museums complex

Historic buildings from around southwestern North Dakota include a schoolhouse, church, train depot, general store, railroad caboose, replica German stone house, and Scandinavian stubbar. Open Memorial Day through Labor Day.

east of Bismarck

JAMESTOWN

Jamestown, the Buffalo City, is the hometown of westerns author Louis L'Amour and singer Peggy Lee. Overlooking the city is the world's largest buffalo, a 26'-high, 46'-long, 60-ton concrete monument.

Jamestown Promotion & Tourism Center
800-22-BISON; www.jamestownnd.com

National Buffalo Museum
Louis L'Amour St., (701) 252-8648;
800-22-BISON

Presents the American bison in a 27-minute video, art, artifacts, and related Native American items. Outdoor bison herd includes White Cloud, the albino bison born in Michigan in 1996.

Frontier Village
Louis L'Amour St., 701-252-6307

Reconstructed Old West town, open May to October, offering pony and stagecoach rides from Memorial Day to Labor Day.

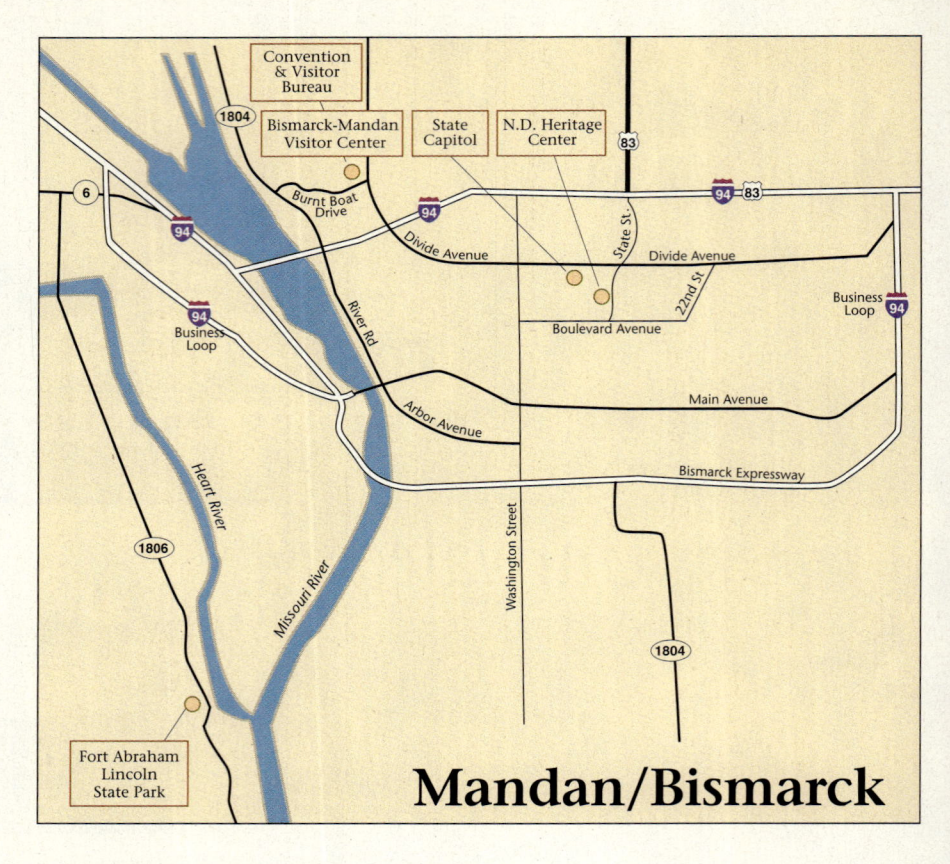

Mandan/Bismarck

October 24, 1804–April 7, 1805

WASHBURN 18

The Corps finally reached the first of two Mandan villages on October 24 and continued upriver to the other Mandan village and to the mouth of Knife River, site of one of three Hidatsa villages. These farming and trading peoples, reduced by smallpox, had joined forces for protection from enemies. Their trade network extended far and wide, and the captains met English and French traders and other Indian visitors while wintering here.

After looking upriver for a suitable site, the Corps returned downstream of the first Mandan village. On November 2, the captains selected a site across the river, on the Missouri's east side, for their winter encampment. It was about 14 miles west of today's Washburn, and the site is now under the Missouri River.

Two days later a Frenchman who had married into the Hidatsas arrived and offered his services as interpreter on the journey ahead. His two wives were Shoshones captured by the Hidatsas, whose language would be useful when the Corps met the

DICKINSON
THE WESTERN EDGE

EXPLORE THE WESTERN EDGE

History meets adventure when you pick up the trail of the great legends, Sitting Bull, Custer and Theodore Roosevelt's National Park. Visit the Dakota Dinosaur Museum next to the North Dakota Badlands.

Dickinson Convention & Visitors Bureau
72 E. Museum Dr., Dickinson, ND 58601
(701) 483-4988 or (800) 279-7391
www.dickinsoncvb.com
E-mail cvb@dickinsoncvb.com

www.lewisandclark.com

Some of "Our Neighbors"

People of the five Mandan and Hidatsa villages near where the Corps built their Fort Mandan were friendly during the winter of 1804-1805, visiting the "fort" and welcoming officers and enlisted men to their own towns. Their leaders included:

Sheheke ("Coyote"), chief of the lower Mandan village, the one nearest to Fort Mandan. White traders called him "Big White" because he was fat and fair-skinned. He was also adventurous enough to return to Washington, D.C., with the captains in 1806, to visit the president and U.S. cities. Arikara and Sioux warfare blocked his 1807 return escort, led by Sgt. Nathaniel Pryor of the expedition. The chief finally reached home in 1809. After his people wouldn't believe the tales Sheheke told about how Americans lived in their home country, traders heard that he wished to go live among whites. He never did, and died at the hands of Sioux enemies in 1832.

Black Cat ("Posecopsahe" in Mandan), thought by Lewis and Clark to be the sole chief of the upper Mandan village. Both captains remarked on his intelligence and friendliness. He was a good host to British fur traders in 1806 but made a point of displaying the American flag that the captains had given him.

Black Moccasin, chief of the second Hidatsa village, where Sacagawea lived. As an elder, he sat for a portrait by painter George Catlin in 1833 and asked Catlin to remember him to his old friend William Clark.

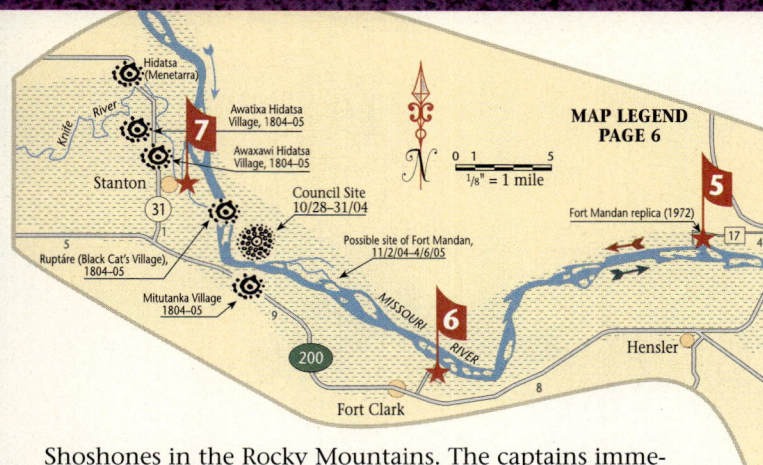

Shoshones in the Rocky Mountains. The captains immediately hired Toussaint Charbonneau and wives as interpreters. Although Lewis noted that one of Charbonneau's wives gave birth to her first child on February 11, 1805, it wasn't until Clark's journal entry of April 7, 1805, that her name was recorded: "Sah-kah-gar we a" in his spelling.

Washburn developed as a frontier trading post site and served Missouri river steamboats of the 19th century. Today it's part of a regional power-production area that uses Upper Plains coal to make electricity distributed in the Central Plains. Coal Creek Electrical Generating Station, six miles north on US 83, gives guided tours of one such plant.

Lewis & Clark Fort Mandan Foundation
P.O. Box 607, Washburn, ND 58577-0607
701-462-8535, 877-462-8535; www.fortmandan.com

North Dakota Lewis and Clark Interpretive Center
US 83 & ND 200A; 701-462-8535, 877-462-8535
www.fortmandan.com

Excellent exhibits emphasize the Corps' winter at Fort Mandan but cover the entire trip. View one of four complete sets of Karl Bodmer prints of paintings he made on an 1833 trip up the Missouri. He met some natives who had known Lewis and Clark.

The enlarged center now includes exhibits on Fort Clark (see Stanton listing, below), the American Fur Company post (1830-60) named for the captain that followed in the expedition's wake.

November 2, 1804-April 7, 1805

Fort Mandan Historic Site
4 miles W on CR 17; 701-462-8535,
877-462-8535; www.fortmandan.com

Ten miles from the now-flooded site of the original, this replica of the Corps' rough fort includes a comfortable visitor center, open year-round. Living history interpretation and other programs are offered.

The men set to work on November 2, 1804, building a crude, triangular, log stockade with huts snugged against its palisades, which they grandly named "Fort Mandan in honor of our neighbors." The fort was completed on November 25.

Winter at Fort Mandan consisted of preparing botanical and biological specimens, drawing maps, and writing reports to send to President Jefferson in the spring. The captains treated illnesses and injuries among their own men

North Dakota

and also their neighbors. Hunting parties went out regularly, and the Corps also traded with the Mandans and Hidatsas for preserved vegetables, so they ate well all winter. Lewis and Clark visited with white and Indian traders who came through, quizzing each about what lay upriver on the Missouri, what the Rocky Mountains were like, and what to expect beyond. They got both helpful and incorrect information.

Eagerly watching the Missouri's ice break up in spring, the men began preparing to "proceed on" and were able to leave on April 7. The keelboat and its "return party" headed downriver for St. Louis, and the two pirogues and six canoes turned upstream into what was for most of them the great unknown.

At the last minute, one of Charbonneau's wives decided not to go, and so the Corps of Discovery's only woman member was teenaged Sacagawea. She carried the couple's 55-day-old son, Jean Baptiste.

return: August 14–17, 1806

Upon reaching the villages on the return trip, the Corps of Discovery paused to visit friends from the winter of 1804. They paid Charbonneau for "his services": $500.33⅓.

The captains urged some of the chiefs to accompany them to Washington, D.C., and meet the "great father," President Jefferson. Finally, Mandan Chief Sheheke agreed, provided they would also take his wife and son, and trader/interpreter Rene Jusseaume, with his wife and children. The captains agreed. After the visit, the Corps' Sgt. Nathaniel Pryor led an Army escort taking Sheheke home. It took three tries (in 1807, 1808, and 1809) to get through the warring Arikaras. George Shannon, another former Corps member in the escort, lost a leg in an 1807 Arikara battle. Sheheke's group finally reached home in 1809.

Part of the reason for the trip was to show the Mandans how these dirty white army men lived in their home country, but it backfired. When Sheheke told his people about the cities he'd seen, their common sense wouldn't let them believe him, and he lost face.

On April 17, 1806, as they left for the second and last time, the Corps paused at "the old works," as Clark now called Fort Mandan, which had accidentally burned down.

Cross Ranch State Park
ND 1806, eight miles SW; 701-794-3731

Hiking trails, summertime educational programs, cabins and primitive campsites.

Cross Ranch Nature Preserve
ND 1806, eight miles SW; 701-794-8741

Take a self-guided trail hike through thousands of acres of protected natural prairie.

Winter of 1804–1805

STANTON 19

Mercer–Oliver Counties Visitor Bureau
P.O. Box 730, Beulah, ND 58523; 800-441-2649

18 6 Fort Clark State Historic Site
ND 200A, 7 miles SE at Fort Clark; 701-328-3567

After the Corps passed by, a fur trading post and Mandan village were built here, but residents died during a subsequent smallpox epidemic. Settlement in the 1850s led to the fort's reopening. Take a self-guided tour among foundations of the lodges and post; informative programs are offered in summer.

18 7 Knife River Indian Villages National Historic Site
just N on CR 37; 701-745-3309

At the mouth of the Knife River on the Missouri, artifacts dating back 11,000 years have been found, and non-Hidatsa people lived here from 8,000 years ago. The expedition first visited here in October 1804, while seeking a site to winter. The Hidatsa then inhabited villages in use since 3,500 years before present. Sacagawea lived in the middle village, now called the Sakakawea Site.

Today, visitors walk interpreted trails to the remains of three villages and view a reconstructed, furnished lodge. Visitor center explores Hidatsa and Mandan culture.

North Dakota

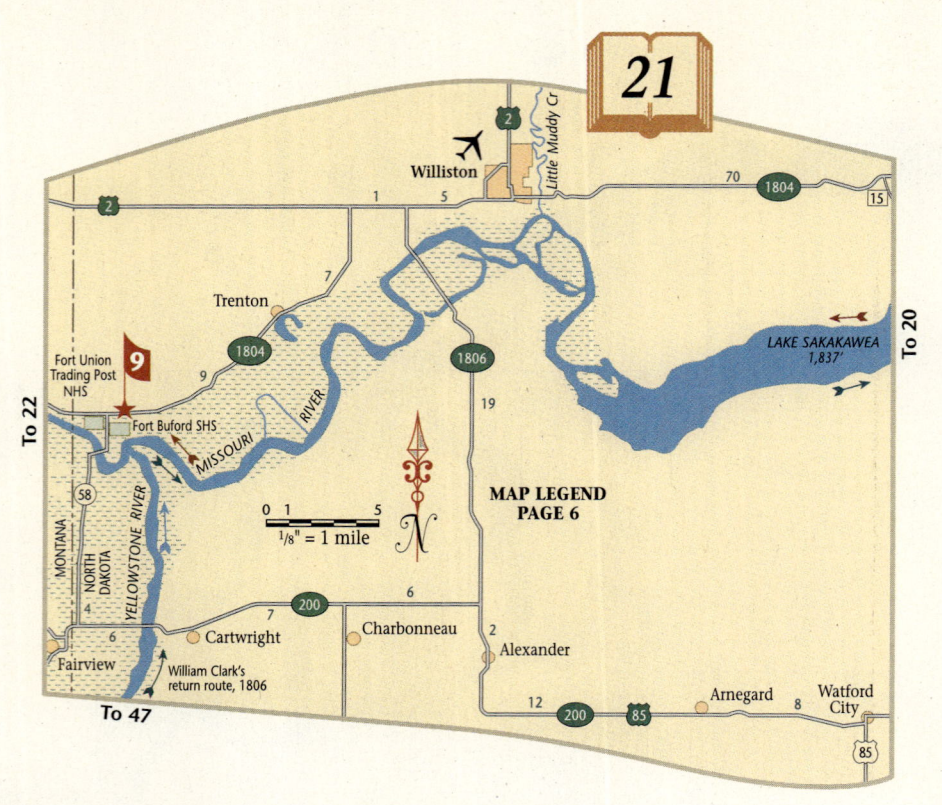

April 9, 1805

Pick City & Riverdale 19

When the Corps passed the future site of Garrison Dam, Clark noted the extensive layers of coal along the river banks, coal that would shape this area's future.

Garrison Dam
On the Missouri River; 701-654-7441
Guided tours of the dam are offered during the summer months. The National Fish Hatchery—where several game species are raised—has a visitor center with dioramas and an aquarium; an intriguing species is the paddlefish, six-foot-long primitive fish with fins like sharks' and long flattened noses that look like canoe paddles.

Fort Stevenson State Park
3 miles S of Garrison off ND 37; 701-337-5576
Exhibits on the expedition, along with camping (tent and RV), showers, barbecue grills. Swimming, fishing, marina, boat rentals. Full operation is May through September.

Minot

Thirty-six miles north of Lake Sakakawea on US 83 is Minot, home to the North Dakota State Fair in late July, and the Norsk Høstfest in mid-October, North America's largest celebration of Scandinavian heritage.

Ward County Pioneer Village and Museum
State fairgrounds on US Hwy. 2; 701-839-0785
Pioneer home, shops, church, and school are furnished with artifacts of 19th-century homesteading; museum houses antique vehicles and farming equipment.

April 12, 1805

Killdeer 20

At the mouth of the Little Missouri River (now widened into a bay by Lake Sakakawea), the Corps stopped early in order to make celestial observations. These were used to figure longitude and latitude, necessary for the captains' mapping the Missouri River's route.

Little Missouri State Park
17 miles N on ND 22; 701-794-3262
On the Missouri's south side. Seventy-five miles of hiking/horseback trails; horse rentals. Campsites (tent and RV), picnic sites.

April 14, 1805

New Town 20

Passing the mouth of Bear Den Creek, Captain Lewis wrote that now they were in country where no whites had gone before.
Today the headquarters for Fort Berthold Indian Reservation (home of the Hidatsa, Mandan, and Arikara), New Town was created by the U.S. Army Corps of Engineers in 1952 after Lake Sakakawea flooded existing area towns.

Three Tribes Museum; *ND 23; 701-627-447*
Exhibits, including an earthlodge, show culture and history of Fort Berthold's Three Affiliated Tribes (Mandan, Hidatsa, and Arikara), including that winter visit from the Corps of Discovery, and how the then-enemies later became allies.

www.lewisandclark.com

return: August 11, 1806

His return party still not reunited with Clark's, Lewis was hunting elk on a willow-covered sandbar, along with the one-eyed Pvt. Pierre Cruzatte. Both men were dressed in leather clothing the same color as elk. After downing two elk together, they separated to go after more. As Lewis aimed again, a bullet passed through his left thigh and grazed his right side. As doctor for the group, Lewis had to dress his own wounds. Cruzatte protested his innocence, and Lewis believed the private was too embarrassed to admit the accident.

Lewis and Clark State Park
16 miles E of Williston on ND 1804, on Missouri River 701-859-3071

The island where Lewis was shot is now under the waters of Lake Sakakawea in this area. Hiking trails give birding and wildlife-watching opportunities, tent/RV campsites, picnic sites, showers, swimming, fishing, boating. In full operation May through September, but open year-round.

return: August 12, 1806

Crow Flies High Butte Historic Site
ND 23, two miles W of New Town; 701-859-3071

Near here the Corps of Discovery was reunited on the return from the Pacific, after splitting into four parties to cross Montana. The meeting point was to be at the mouth of the Yellowstone River, but mosquitoes there had driven Clark's group downstream. Ordway's party

International Inn — MINOT

1505 North Broadway • Minot, ND 58703 • 701-852-3161

CALL TOLL FREE FOR RESERVATIONS
1-800-735-4493

www.internationalinn.com

- 270 Comfortable Rooms
- Minot's Largest Indoor Pool & Jacuzzi
- Primo Dining Room and Coffee Shop
- Reflections Lounge & Casino featuring standup comedians Thursday, Friday & Saturday evenings
- Fitness Center
- Business Center
- HBO
- High Speed Internet

MINOT — NORTH DAKOTA

Minot—Your portal to the Lewis & Clark Trail!

Whether you are starting your journey, or want to venture off the trail– with easy access from the West and South–Minot will welcome you with it's unique history and many fun things to do!

More information about Minot, call 800-264-2626 or visit us on the web: www.visitminot.org.

Skandinavian Heratige Park • Souris River Golf Course • The Roosvevelt Park and Zoo • Much More!

Start Your Lewis & Clark Journey With Minot!

North Dakota

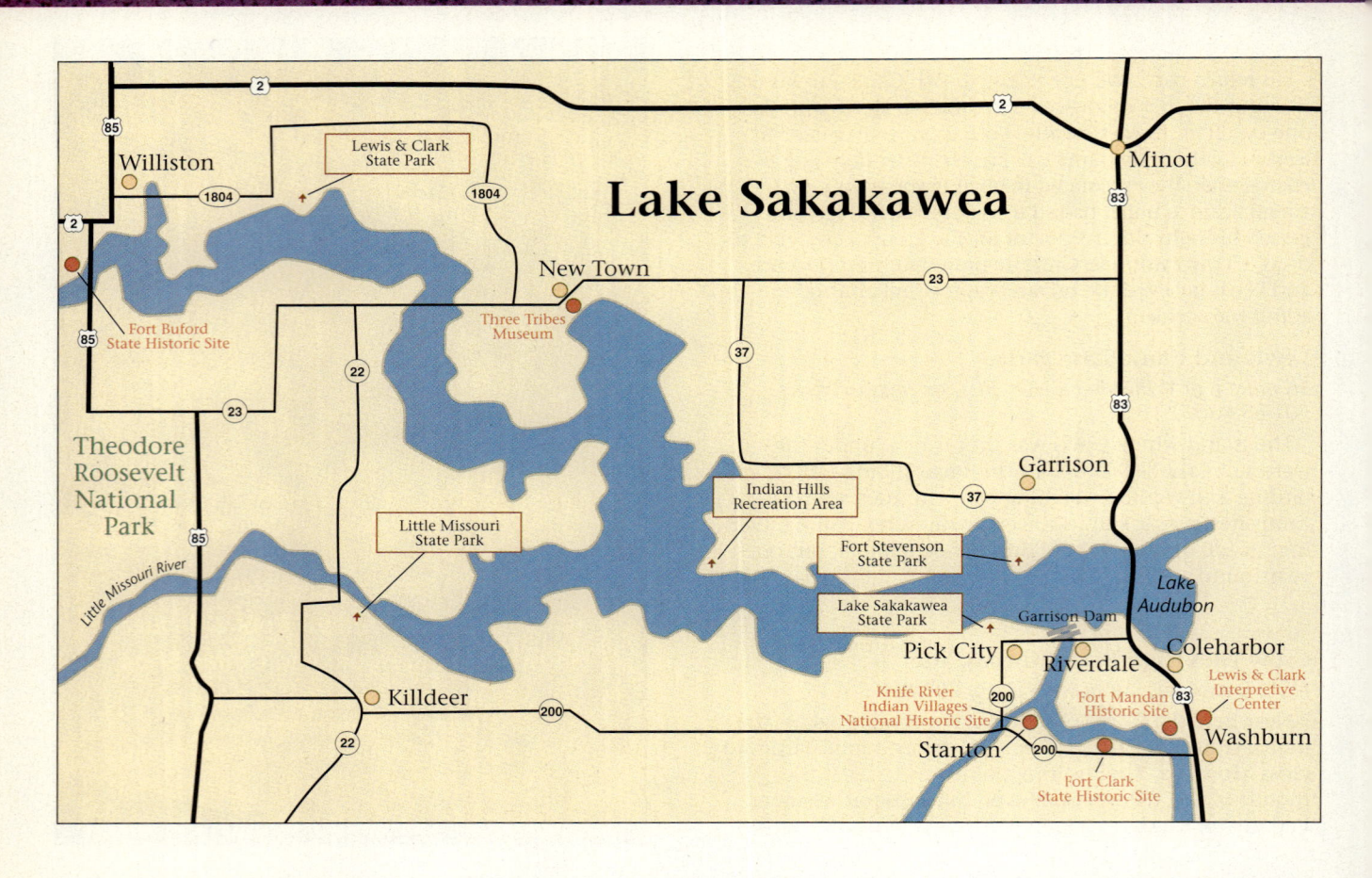

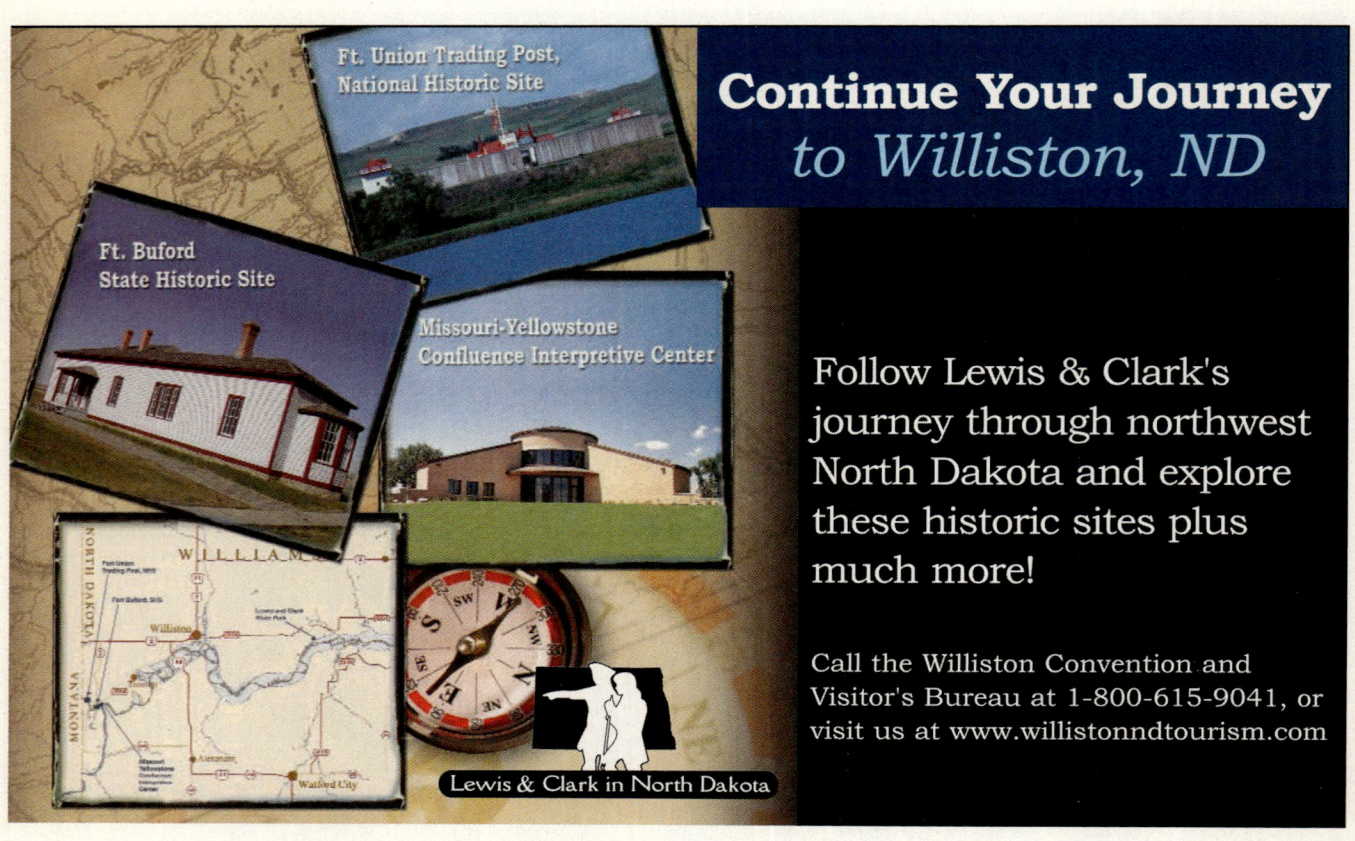

Continue Your Journey to Williston, ND

Follow Lewis & Clark's journey through northwest North Dakota and explore these historic sites plus much more!

Call the Williston Convention and Visitor's Bureau at 1-800-615-9041, or visit us at www.willistonndtourism.com

www.lewisandclark.com

caught up with Clark's on August 8. Lewis and Ordway's groups had joined on the Missouri and reached the others in this area four days later.

April 18, 1805
WATFORD CITY 21

During the morning, men had to tow the boats, then a severe afternoon wind from the north began swamping the canoes. The expedition waited out the wind from 1:00 to 5:00 before "proceeding on."

Tobacco Garden Bay
ND 1806, 26 miles N; 701-842-6931

On the Missouri's south side. Campsites with hookups are open May through October, showers; barbecue grills, fishing, boat access and rentals.

Pioneer Museum
104 Park Ave. W.; 701-842-2990

Reconstructed homestead kitchen, mercantile, schoolroom, and horse stall, clothing and other artifacts show how early white settlers lived.

Theodore Roosevelt National Park
North Unit entrance: 14 miles S on US 85; Visitor Center, 701-842-2333. Information requests: Superintendent, Theodore Roosevelt National Park, Medora, ND 58645; 701-623-4466, or visit www.nps.gov/

North Unit Visitor Center has exhibits about the park's wildlife, plants, and geology. Campsites are nearby.

The entire park's 70,000 acres extend far to the south and include badlands and early ranches, among them the Maltese Cross, where future president Theodore Roosevelt retreated in 1883 after the death of his first wife.

April 25-26, 1805
WILLISTON 21

Arriving at the mouth of the Yellowstone River was cause for celebration, so the captains issued whiskey, the Corps dined on buffalo calf, Cruzatte brought out his fiddle, and singing and dancing followed into the evening.

Whether the Yellowstone was navigable was an important question, so Clark made careful measurements of its channel and width. On the expedition's return trip from the Pacific, Clark would lead a group exploring downstream on the Yellowstone.

21 Williston Convention and Visitors Bureau
10 Main St., Williston, ND 58801; 800-615-9041; www.willistonndtourism.com

Fort Union Trading Post National Historic Site
US 2 and ND 1804, 24 miles SW; 701-572-9083

The American Fur Company built this post in 1828 and ran it for more than three decades. (The fort was at the mouth of the Yellowstone River, which since has shifted east.) This reconstruction, featuring costumed guides, includes wayside exhibits on the Corps of Discovery and the Plains Indian tribes and Europeans who traded here.

21 Fort Buford State Historic Site
Drive 2 miles W to US 2 and US 85, then 17 miles N on ND 1804; 701-572-9034

This military post, built in 1866, served U.S. army troops who fought in the Sioux Wars and is where Sitting Bull and his band surrendered in 1881. Original buildings open to the public are the stone powder magazine and the officers' quarters that now house a museum. Birding and small-animal watching can be enjoyed.

Missouri-Yellowstone Confluence Center
Hwys 58 &1804, 22 miles SW of Williston; 701-572-9034

Permanent and changing exhibits on area geography and geology, prehistoric life, and the impact of people arriving by "Trails, Tracks, Rivers and Roads," Lewis and Clark Expedition, fur trade era, Fort Buford, and modern irrigation and energy industries. Artifacts include replica of Clark's compass, frontier army transport wagon, steamboat pilot's navigating wheel, 1903 Cadillac. Video "Splendid Isolation: Fort Buford" chronicles the frontier army post of 1866-1895.

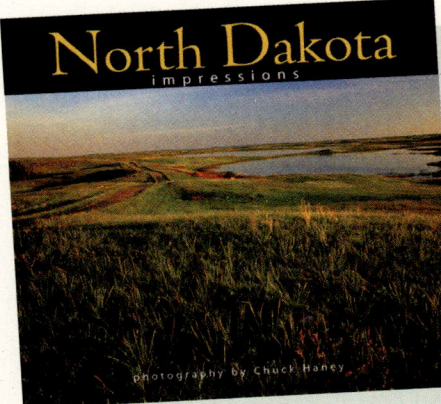

North Dakota: Impressions
By Chuck Haney.

Wide open prairies, exotic badland formations, vast farm fields, rivers both gentle & rushing— here is North Dakota in rich color. 80 color photos. 80 pages, 9⅛" x 8⅛". Softbound. $9.95

Theodore Roosevelt National Park Impressions
By Chuck Haney. Foreword by Bruce M. Kaye.

This beautiful collection of photographs pays tribute to the land Roosevelt sought to protect for our & future generations. 80 color photos. 80 pages, 9⅛" x 8⅛". Softbound. $9.95

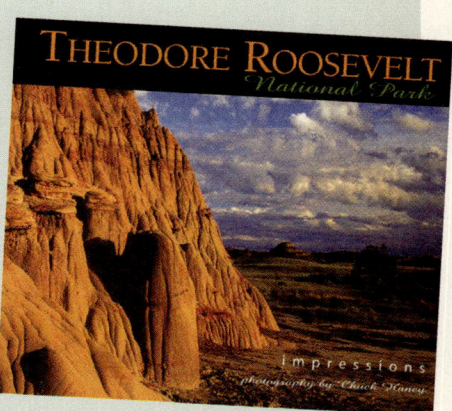

Order today!
1-800-821-3874
www.farcountrypress.com

Montana

The Lewis and Clark Expedition covered more miles in Montana than in any other future state, not just because of its size, but because the Corps split into four parties for the 1806 return trip, each with a different assignment and route. For that reason, the return trips are discussed separately at the end of this section.

The Gates of the Mountains near Helena. RICK & SUSIE GRAETZ

Statewide resources on Montana

Travel Montana
P.O. Box 200533, Helena, MT 59602
800-VISIT-MT; www.visitmt.com

Montana Fish, Wildlife & Parks
1420 E. 6th Ave., P.O. Box 200701, Helena, MT 59620-0701
406-444-2535; www.fwp.state.mt.us

Bureau of Land Management, Montana State Office
Box 36800, Billings, MT 59107; 406-255-2888
www.mt.blm.gov

National Park Service, Intermountain Region
P.O. Box 25287, Denver, CO 80225-0287
303-969-2000; www.nps.gov

Missouri River Overlook
3 miles S of Culbertson at Missouri River bridge, 406-787-6320

Signage interprets the Corps of Discovery's first days in future Montana and the area's geography.

Medicine Lake National Wildlife Refuge
24 miles N of Culbertson on MT 16; 406-789-2305

The refuge's 31,000 acres offer a car tour and both hiking and canoe trails among wildlife and waterfowl.

May 9-10, 1805
FORT PECK 24

A windy day allowed the men some relief; they put up sails and made 24 miles progress today (it had been 14-18 miles upstream on a good day recently). But the next day the wind was too strong for them to proceed.

Important note: Fort Peck Lake is wide and exposed to winds, so it frequently develops waves. It's not the river the Corps paddled, and there are no shoreline towns to put in to. Those who want to float the Missouri as the Corps saw it should look to the Wild & Scenic Missouri. (See June 10, 1805, right.)

The town of Fort Peck was created to house workers building Fort Peck Dam on the Missouri during the Depression.

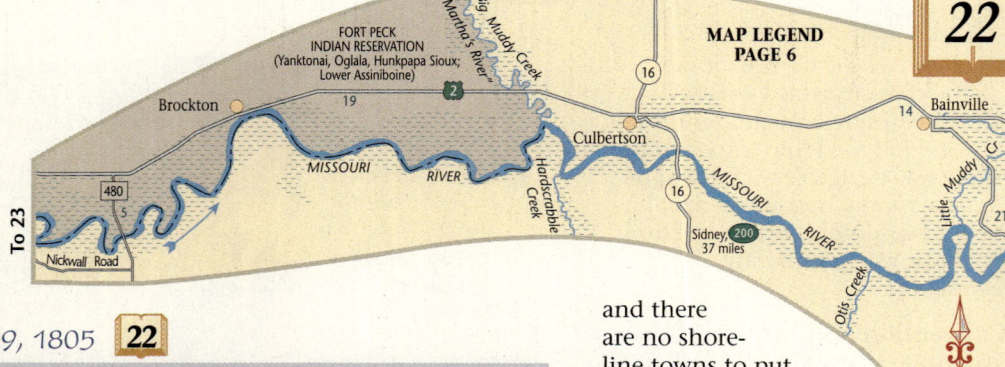

April 29, 1805 22
BAINVILLE & CULBERTSON

Walking just west of Little Muddy Creek with an enlisted man, Captain Lewis met two grizzly bears. Both men fired, wounding both bears. One bear fled, but the other charged Lewis for 70 yards or so. Lewis and his partner reloaded their flintlocks and together brought the bear down. Lewis left the encounter thinking that, with guns, they need not fear grizzlies.

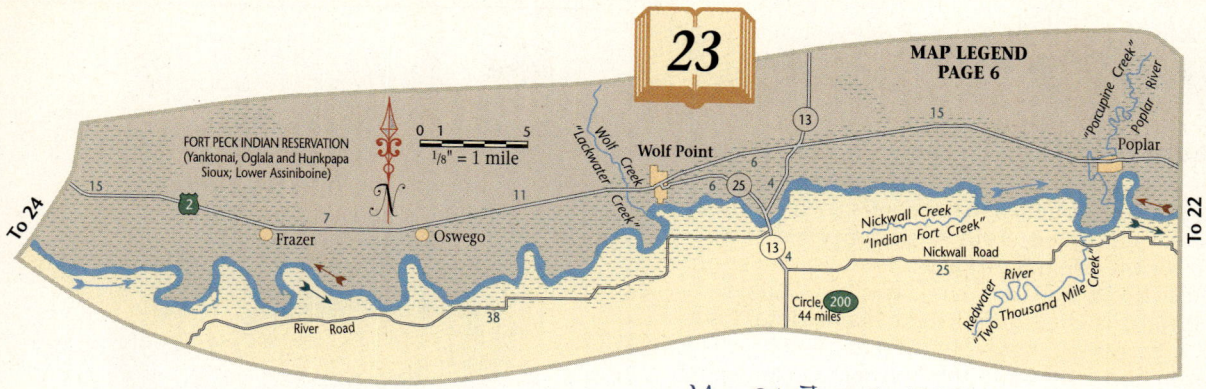

www.lewisandclark.com

23

FORT PECK INDIAN RESERVATION (Yanktonai, Oglala and Hunkpapa Sioux; Lower Assiniboine)

MAP LEGEND PAGE 6

Frazer • Oswego • Wolf Point • Poplar

"Lockwater Creek" • Wolf Creek • "Porcupine Creek" • Poplar River

Nickwall Creek "Indian Fort Creek" • Nickwall Road • Redwater River • "Two Thousand Mile Creek"

Circle 44 miles

To 24 / To 22

Lewis and Clark Overlook
0.5 mile E of Fort Peck Dam on Montana Hwy 24; 406-526-3411

Overlooks three expedition campsites. Interpretive sign on the Corps' travel in northeastern Montana, picnic area.

Milk River Observation Point
4 miles E of Fort Peck Dam; turn left on Tower Rd after crossing spillway; 406-526-3411

Quarter-mile hiking trail to where Clark saw the Mandan-named "River That Scolds All Others," today called Milk River. Interpretive signage at parking area.

Fort Peck Museum/Dam
MT 24; 406-526-3411

Completed in 1937, this is one of the world's largest filled-earth dams, containing 1.25 billion cubic yards of earth and extending four miles. Guided tours of the powerhouse are offered June through September.

May 21–June 3, 1805

WINIFRED   26

26 Missouri Breaks National Back Country Byway

This 81-mile loop goes through wildlands largely unchanged since the Corps passed, including part of the Charles M. Russell National Wildlife Refuge. Signs interpret the Lewis and Clark Expedition and the Nez Perce National Historic Trail. Road is only for high-clearance vehicles in dry weather; rain here turns the surface to sticky "gumbo" mud.

MONTANA • RIVER • RANCH

Lewis & Clark History • Working Ranch Trips
Float Trips • Wildlife Photography

We would like to welcome you to our ranch that is in the heart of the Lewis & Clark expedition. With the Missouri River running alongside, our land is filled with history. We are located near the historic sites of Ft. Union, the confluence of the Missouri and Yellowstone Rivers, and Ft. Buford, the fort where Sitting Bull surrendered.

Visit us on the World Wide Web:
www.montanariverranch.com

HC 58 Box 9 • Bainville, MT 59212
Toll-Free 1-877-277-4084 • (406) 769-2404
fax: (406) 769-2200 • email: mtrivrch@nemontel.net

"THE JOURNEY"
8 Historic Lewis and Clark Expedition events rendered on the Official Library of Congress Trail Map

by [signature]

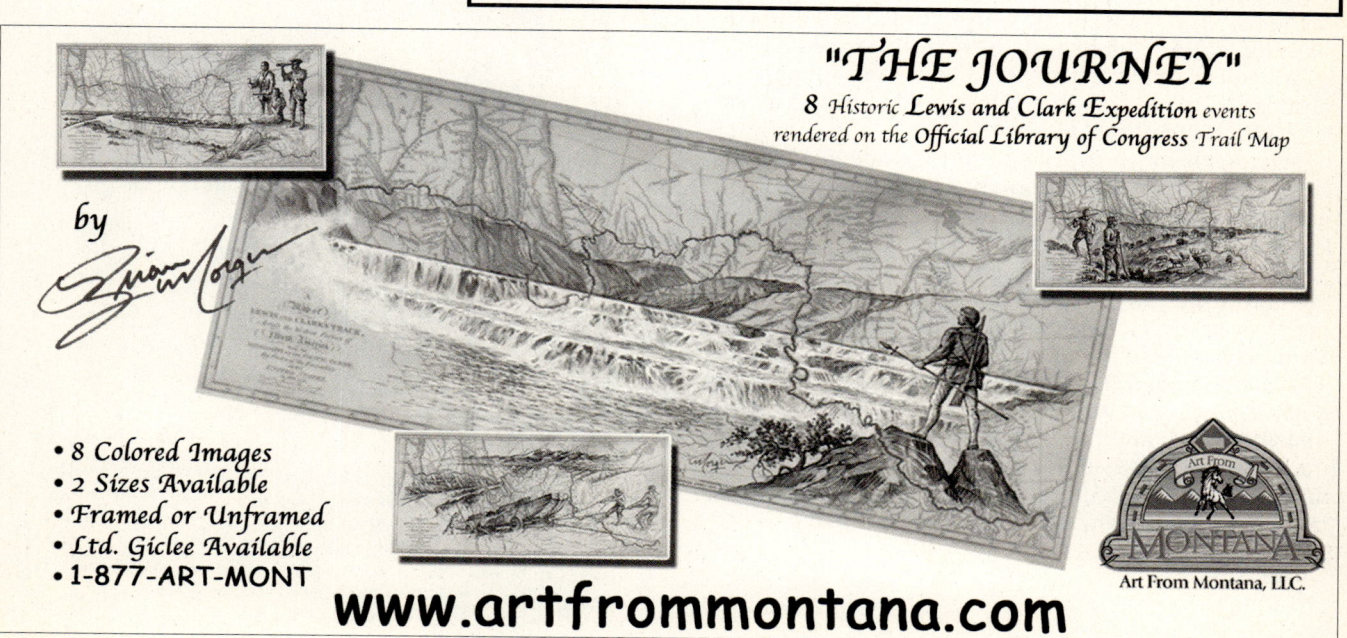

- 8 Colored Images
- 2 Sizes Available
- Framed or Unframed
- Ltd. Giclee Available
- 1-877-ART-MONT

Art From Montana, LLC.

www.artfrommontana.com

MONTANA

Montana

north of Winifred

Havre

Wahkpa Chu'gn Archaeological Site
U.S. Highway 2; 406-265-6417; www.buffalojump.org

Beginning 2,000 years ago, native peoples used atlatls to kill bison here. Later American Indians stampeded bison over the cliff for the kill and processed meat and hides on the site. Guides lead a walking tour at Wahkpa Chu'gn (pronounced walk-pa-chew-gun), where mannequins and exhibit houses reveal the most extensive and best preserved bison bone deposit in the northern Great Plains and how this site was used before the horse came along.

Havre Beneath the Streets
120 3rd Avenue; 406-265-8888
www.theheritagecenter.com/beneath

When fire destroyed most of Havre, business owners moved underground until the town could be rebuilt. Today guided historical walking tours (reservations required) visit the Sporting Eagle Saloon, an opium den, a Chinese laundry, an ethnic restaurant, and a bordello.

June 4, 1805

Loma 27

Here the Corps of Discovery may have come as close to mutiny as it ever did. As the boats came up the Missouri, they reached an unexpected split in the river, one that no informant had mentioned. From the north came a river just as wide and muddy as the Missouri they'd been traveling, while the southern "fork" was clearer. Everyone but the captains believed the northern fork was the main river. The captains argued that water coming from the Rocky Mountains would be clearer this close to the mountains, and that the northerly fork was muddy from crossing open plains. This logical argument didn't work.

The captains decided to encamp at the point between the forks. While most of the Corps hunted and dressed skins for clothing (their army-issue cloth garments were wearing out), each captain would take a small group upstream on one fork. They'd been told to expect a very large waterfall on the Missouri.

Lewis and six men struck out north, while William Clark and five others went south. They agreed to turn back after one and a half days (although Lewis stayed out longer, causing great concern).

Neither found a waterfall, but what Lewis observed of the north fork convinced him more fully that it was not the Missouri. In fact, he named it Marias (muh-rye-uss) for his cousin Maria Wood.

Back at the point, Pvt. Pierre Cruzatte, their experienced riverman, still held out for the north fork. So now Lewis took some men and headed south, planning to go farther than Clark's group had. He found the "waterfall" (See June 14–July 14, 1805, below) on the third day out, 10 miles farther upstream than Clark had reached.

Charlie Russell Manor
An Historic Bed and Breakfast

Offering Gracious Western Hospitality for All Special Occasions

The Heart of Montana! Located between Yellowstone and Glacier National Parks. Five spacious bedrooms equipped with luxurious linens and towels, private bath, telephone, television, data port & AC. The English Ballroom is ideal for parties, receptions, meetings or other special events.

825 4th Avenue North • Great Falls, Montana 59401
Toll Free 877-207-6131
www.charlie-russell.com

...where Entertaining is our Specialty.

Base Camp
At The Heritage Inn

Breakfast Shift at White Bear - Ron Ukrainetz ©2000

Kids Eat, Stay & Play Free — Restaurant & Bar & Casino
Pool, Hot Tub & Sauna — Complimentary Transportation
Conference Facilities & Tennis

Best Western
Best Western Heritage Inn
1700 Fox Farm Rd.
Great Falls, MT 59404
Tel: (406) 761-1900 ✱ 800 548-8256 ✱ Fax: (406) 761-0136
www.bestwestern.com/heritageinngreatfalls

27 **Lewis and Clark Decision Point**
0.5 mile W of Loma Bridge on US 87
Interpretive exhibit at an overlook of the mouth of Marias River and the Corps' campsite.

BIG SANDY 27

North of Loma, Big Sandy developed as a freighting point for steamboats that unloaded at Coal Banks Landing on the Missouri and then served as a center for homesteaders and the Great Northern Railroad.

Big Sandy Historical Museum
406-378-3102
Housed in the former Great Northern depot, this is home to a large collection of historical photographs of Chouteau County and tells the story of homesteading and "Golden Triangle" wheat farming.

June 10, 1805
Lewis return: July 28, 1806

FORT BENTON 28

Outward bound, first Clark passed by here looking for the Great Falls, then came Lewis, then the whole Corps. Fort Benton was the head of steamboat navigation on the Missouri from 1860 to 1887. Through here, goods flowed to serve Montana's gold rushers in the 1860s and their developing cities, until railroads arrived.

River Front Park
on the Missouri; 406-622-5494
Honors Fort Benton's place in history and includes a heroic-sized bronze commemorating the Lewis and Clark Expedition, a replica keelboat built for a 1950s movie, and a bronze statue of Shep, a dog that saw his master's body taken away by train and subsequently met every train until his own death.

Museum of the Upper Missouri
1801 Front St.; 406-622-5316
Next to Old Fort Benton, the 1846 blockhouse is Montana's oldest building. Museum exhibits tell the story of the Upper Missouri through the 19th century.

28 **Wild and Scenic Missouri River**
Starting point for a summer-only downstream float is at Fort Benton, and the full trip takes seven days of primitive camping. Information available from River Manager, P.O. Box 1160, Lewistown, MT 59457, 406-538-7461.

June 13–July 14, 1805
Lewis return: July 12-16, 1806

GREAT FALLS 29

When Meriwether Lewis's advance party reached a waterfall on the Missouri on June 13, he was relieved to identify the Missouri's course. But as he surveyed the falls for a portage route, he walked upstream and—heard another falls! No one at Fort Mandan had mentioned two falls, so Lewis

Montana

walked on to see the second one. And again, and again, and again—the "Great Falls" was actually a series of five. And the banks were high, with deep cuts from creeks, meaning the Corps couldn't walk along the river's edge. Just past the falls, the river turned south, almost at a right angle.

Past the falls, Lewis met a grizzly near the mouth of the Sun River west of today's city of Great Falls—when his flintlock was unloaded. The bear chased Lewis into the Missouri, then gave up the hunt and left. The explorer developed a new respect for these massive bears.

After the main party camped near the mouth of today's Belt Creek, Clark laid out an overland course that paralleled the river and met it upstream of its bend. The men built caissons with slices of cottonwood logs for wheels. A canoe filled with provisions and gear would be placed on a caisson and pulled uphill along Belt Creek, then across the prairie that was lumpy from bison hoofprints in dried mud and carpeted with prickly pear cactus. When rain fell, the men carried freight on their backs. Beginning on June 23, it took eight days just to get everything carried past the falls. The men worked from dawn to dusk and were so tired they fell asleep as soon as they paused in their labors.

Then they had to pack the canoes, including two dugouts—and finally set off four weeks after reaching the falls they'd been told would take "a day" to pass.

**BOOKS - EDUCATIONAL TOOLS - MAPS
NATIVE AMERICAN ART AND MORE!
(406) 453-6248**

Portage Cache Store
LEWIS & CLARK NATIONAL HISTORIC TRAIL INTERPRETIVE CENTER

4201 GIANT SPRINGS ROAD - GREAT FALLS, MT 59405
www.lewis-clarkstore.com

**Capture The Memory Of Montana
The Bitterroot**
14 kt Gold Pendant with Yogo Sapphire
$195

**Sutherland's
1-800-570-1440**
#18 4th St. No. Great Falls, MT 59401

See it. Right. Here.

Charles M. Russell, *The Exalted Ruler*, 1912, oil, 54" x 72"
Gift of Friends of The Exalted Ruler

Must Go to the Russell!

C.M. RUSSELL MUSEUM
400 13th Street North Great Falls, Montana 59401
TEL [406] 727-8787   FAX [406] 727-2402
www.cmrussell.org

The C.M. Russell Museum keeps the vanishing era of the Old West alive and interprets that period of American history through its permanent collection of artworks by Charles M. Russell. The Museum features the most complete collection of Russell artwork in the world. See it. Right. Here.

- Traveling Exhibitions
- Hands-on Children's Gallery
- Gallery Tours
- Education Programs
- The Museum Shop
- Meeting Rooms

Discover the Spirit of Lewis & Clark

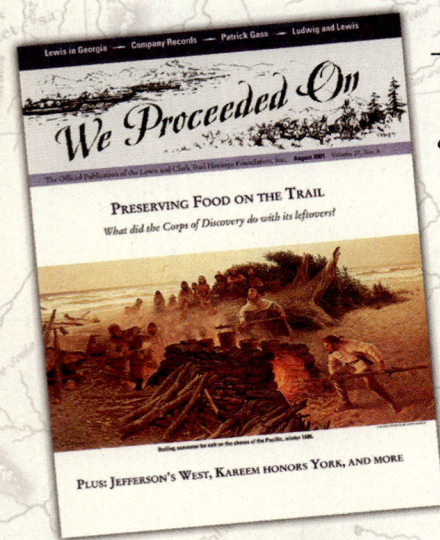

The Lewis and Clark Trail Heritage Foundation invites you to rediscover days gone past and relive the journey of two of America's greatest heros - the expedition of Meriwether Lewis and William Clark. Membership benefits include "We Proceed On," a historical quarterly packed with fascinating in-depth articles about the Corps of Discovery.

For more information contact the Foundation at:
P.O. Box 3434, Great Falls, MT 59403
email: discovery@lewisandclark.org
www.lewisandclark.org
1-888-701-3434

Join Us!

LEWIS & CLARK TRAIL HERITAGE FOUNDATION, INC.

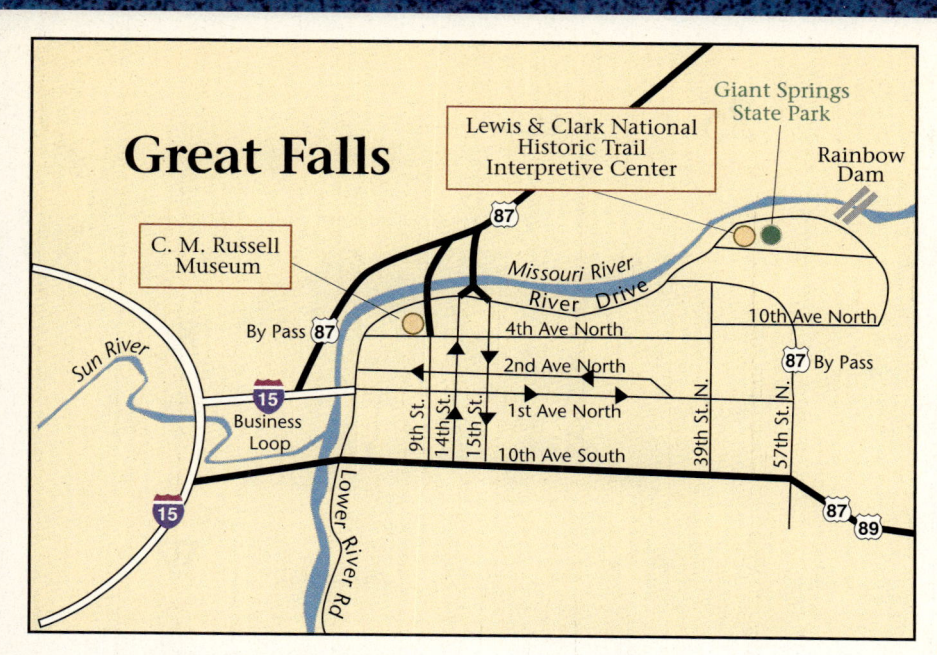

Great Falls

Great Falls Chamber of Commerce
926 Central Ave., Great Falls, MT 59403; 406-761-4434

William P. Sherman Library
in Lewis and Clark National Historic Trail Interpretive Center
Research and reference library welcomes expedition buffs and serious researchers alike. Open weekdays from Memorial Day to Labor Day, Tuesday–Friday and by appointment the rest of the year.

29 2 Ryan Dam
on River Dr. along Missouri River; 406-723-5454
Corps interpretation, hiking, picnic area, fishing.

29 3 Rainbow Scenic Overlook/Lewis & Clark Scenic Overlook
on Giant Springs Rd. at Missouri River.
Expedition intepretation, bicycling trails, picnic area.

29 Giant Springs State Park
River Drive, 3 miles E of US 87; 406-454-3441
The nation's largest freshwater spring, first seen by Lewis on June 18, 1805. Interpretive expedition trail, visitor center, fish hatchery (open to public), picnic and fishing.

29 1 Lewis and Clark National Historic Trail Interpretive Center
at Giant Spring State Park on River Dr.; 406-727-8733
On the south side of the Missouri, the museum overlooks the area where dams have tamed the falls. Exhibits cover the entire voyage, with special focus on Native American cultures and the Great Falls portage.

Your outlet for:
ART OF THE WEST

LIFE-SIZE EAGLE by Connie Tveten
for Fine Western Art:
www.artofthewest.biz
for "The Lewis and Clark Bicentennial Collection":
www.lewisandclarkproducts.com

JAKER'S
STEAK RIBS
FISH PASTA

Featuring absolutely the best choice and prime graded steaks and prime rib 100% guaranteed.

Great Bloody Mary's, Martini's and Margarita's.

Reservations accepted but never required and the dress is casual.

Kids Menu
Senior Menu
Lunch M-F
Dinner Daily

Great Falls
1500 10th Ave S
727-1033

Missoula
3515 Brooks St
721-1312

Visit Jaker's in Idaho Falls, Twin Falls and Boise.

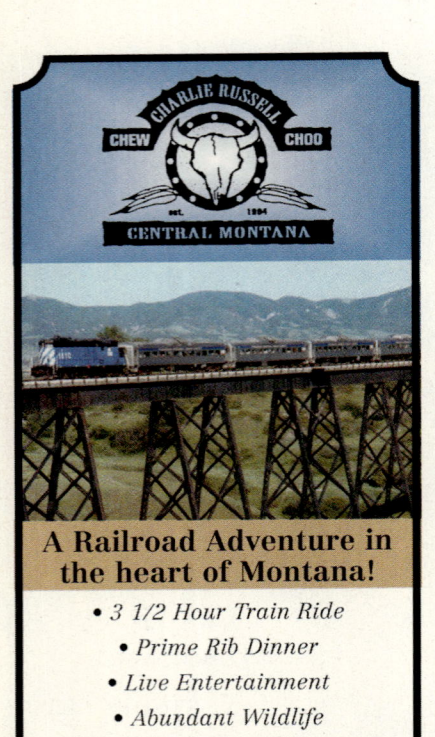

Montana

25

[Map of Fort Peck Lake area, Charles M. Russell National Wildlife Refuge, Missouri River, UL Bend Wilderness]

CHARLIE RUSSELL CHEW CHOO — CENTRAL MONTANA

A Railroad Adventure in the heart of Montana!
- 3 1/2 Hour Train Ride
- Prime Rib Dinner
- Live Entertainment
- Abundant Wildlife
- Trestles, Tunnels, Ghost Towns, Surprises

Yogo Inn of Lewistown, MT
Between Billings & Great Falls
1-800-216-5436

29-5 West Bank Park
17th Ave. N.E. & 3rd St. N.W.
At the mouth of the Sun River, where Lewis faced the grizzly (see Great Falls).

29-6 Broadwater Portage Overlook
10th Ave. S. & 2nd St.; 406-771-0885
Interpretive displays at a heroic bronze sculpture honoring the Corps; open summer.

C.M. Russell Museum
400 13th St. N.; 406-727-8787
Museum houses a large collection of realistic Western art by Russell (1864-1926) plus changing contemporary exhibits; also tour Russell's adjoining home and the log-cabin studio that looks just as he left it.

southeast of Great Falls
LEWISTOWN

About 99 miles southeast of Fort Benton, 66 miles southeast of Great Falls, Lewistown is at Montana's geographic center. City tap water flows directly from Big Springs, which is surrounded by a park; this is fossil country, and the park includes places to hunt for them.

Lewistown Chamber of Commerce
408 Northeast Main, Lewistown, MT 59457; 800-216-5436

Charles M. Russell National Wildlife Refuge
Headquarters: Airport Rd.; 406-538-8706
Protects 1.2 million acres bordering the Missouri River and Fort Peck Lake. Live bison are penned at the headquarters, from which a loop auto tour begins via MT 191. Sights include waterfowl, raptors, deer, and the world's largest remaining herd of prairie elk. In spring 1805, on future refuge land, Lewis shot an elk that stood 5'3" at the shoulder.

July 15, 1805
ULM 30

"Dinner" at mid-day was "just above…a beautifull river…which in honour of Mr. Robert Smith the Sec-

www.lewisandclark.com

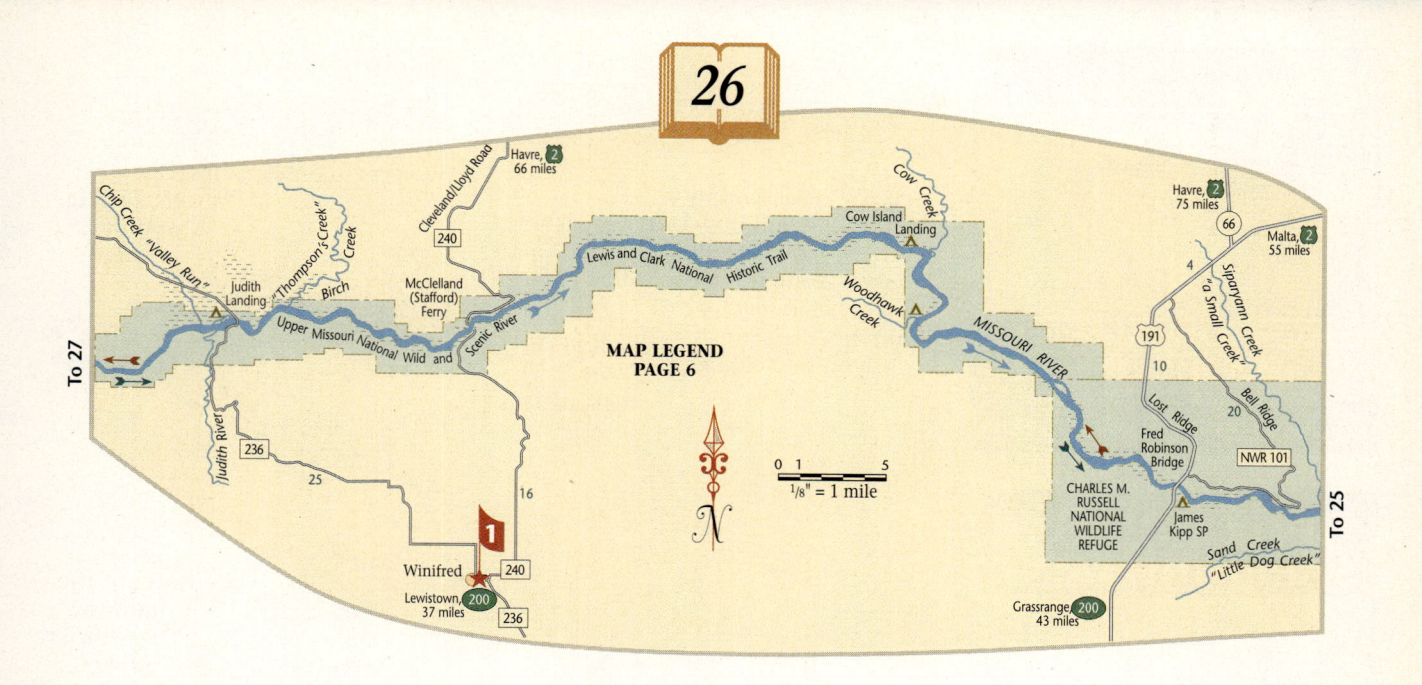

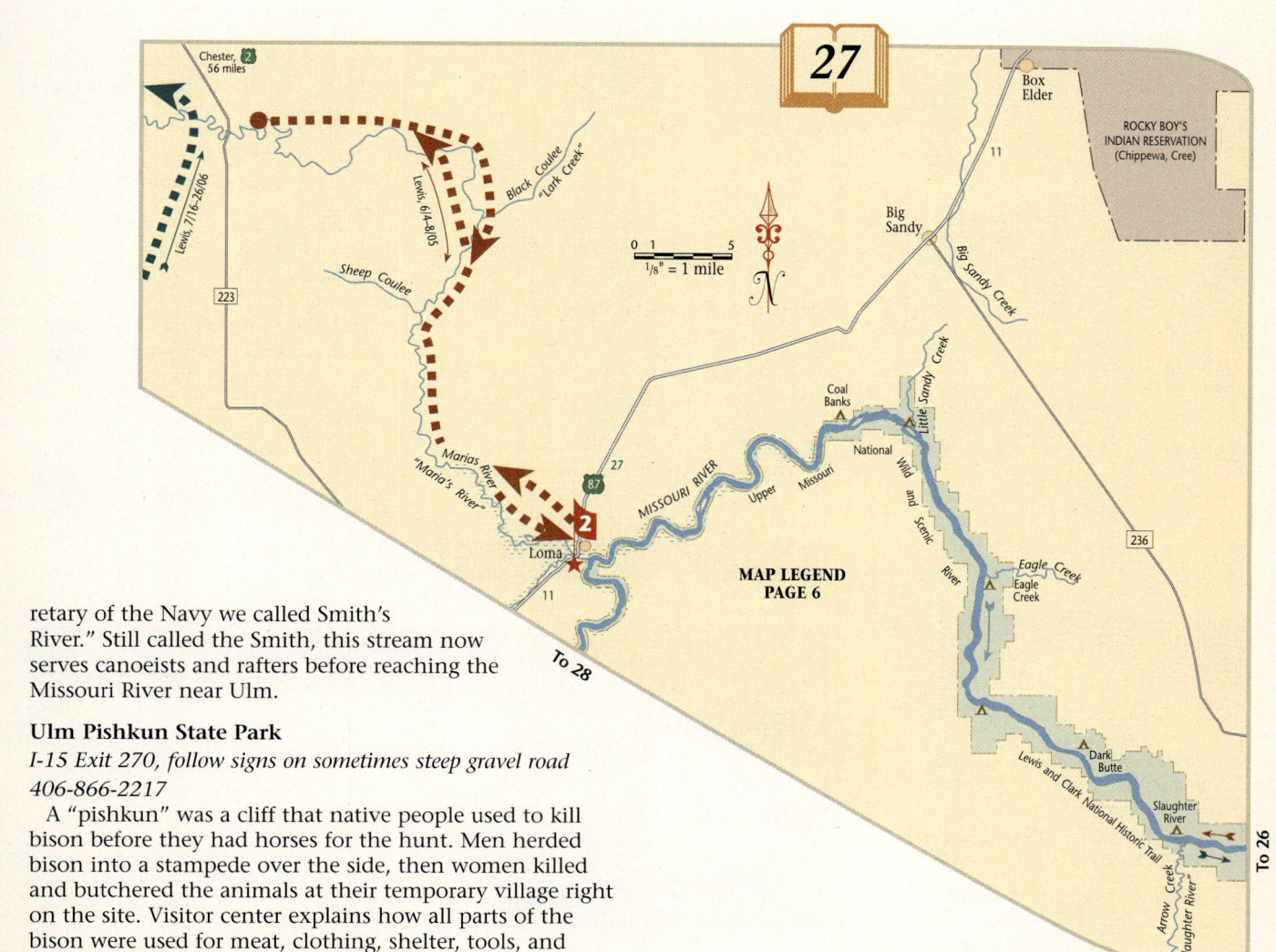

26

27

retary of the Navy we called Smith's River." Still called the Smith, this stream now serves canoeists and rafters before reaching the Missouri River near Ulm.

Ulm Pishkun State Park
I-15 Exit 270, follow signs on sometimes steep gravel road
406-866-2217

A "pishkun" was a cliff that native people used to kill bison before they had horses for the hunt. Men herded bison into a stampede over the side, then women killed and butchered the animals at their temporary village right on the site. Visitor center explains how all parts of the bison were used for meat, clothing, shelter, tools, and toys. Open mid-April to mid-October.

73 Montana

Montana

Wildlife Woodcarving

FOR VIEWING APPOINTMENT CALL:
406 442-1656
AFTERNOONS & EVENINGS
PO Box 6505 • Helena, MT 59604

Spokane Bar Sapphire Mine

CIRCA 1870s, MONTANA HISTORICAL SOCIETY

...the Clifts Contain flint a dark Stone & redish bron intermixed and no one Clift is Solid rock, all the rocks of everry description is in Small pices appears to have been broken by Some Convulsion... Capt. Clark, July 19, 1805

SPOKANE BAR 1999

ON THE LEWIS & CLARK TRAIL...
DIG SAPPHIRES FOR FUN AND FORTUNE
ON ANCIENT RIVER GRAVEL TERRACES.
A MONTANA ADVENTURE!

SPOKANE BAR SAPPHIRE MINE
AND GOLD FEVER ROCK SHOP
5360 CASTLES ROAD • HELENA, MT 59602
OPEN DAILY 9-5
1-877 DIGGEMS • 406-227-8989
WWW.SAPPHIREMINE.COM
SALES@SAPPHIREMINE.COM

Holton's of Helena — Montana Gift Gallery

A Premier Gift Gallery
Celebrating Montana's Heritage
Montana Gifts, Books, Art, Antler Decor,
Sapphire Jewelry
Authorized Big Sky Carvers Dealer
Lewis & Clark Commemoratives

1219 11th Avenue, Helena
406-442-3688
Three blocks north of Capitol
Closed Sunday and Monday

July 16, 1805
CRAIG 30

Recreation Road
Pull off I-15 at Craig exit to take a two-lane road that curves along the Missouri for 12 miles before rejoining the Interstate at Canyon interchange.

[Map: showing Lewis & Clark route along Missouri River, featuring Great Falls, Morony Dam (1930), Ryan Dam (1915) "Great Falls", Morony Dam Road, Highwood Creek "Shields River", Carter, Carter Ferry, Ferry Road, Fort Benton, Teton River "Tansy River", Lewistown 99 Miles, Lewis 7/27/06, Lewis 6/11-13/05, scale 1/8" = 1 mile, To 29, To 27]

Rocking Z Guest Ranch

Lewis & Clark Programs
Great Horseback Riding
8 New Luxurious Rooms
Excellent Ranch Meals

Enjoy the great Montana view from the top of the mountains
2020 Sieben Canyon Road
Wolf Creek, MT 59648

406-458-3890 • www.rockingz.com

July 19, 1805
WOLF CREEK

Access to public lands, camping, resorts, fishing, wildlife, and views.

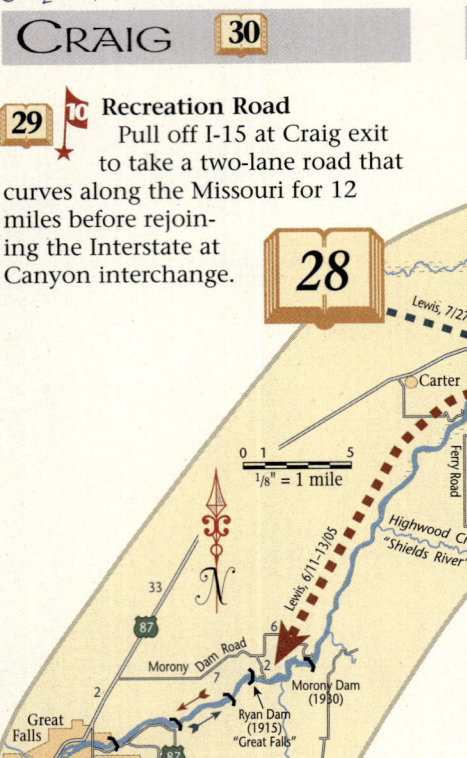

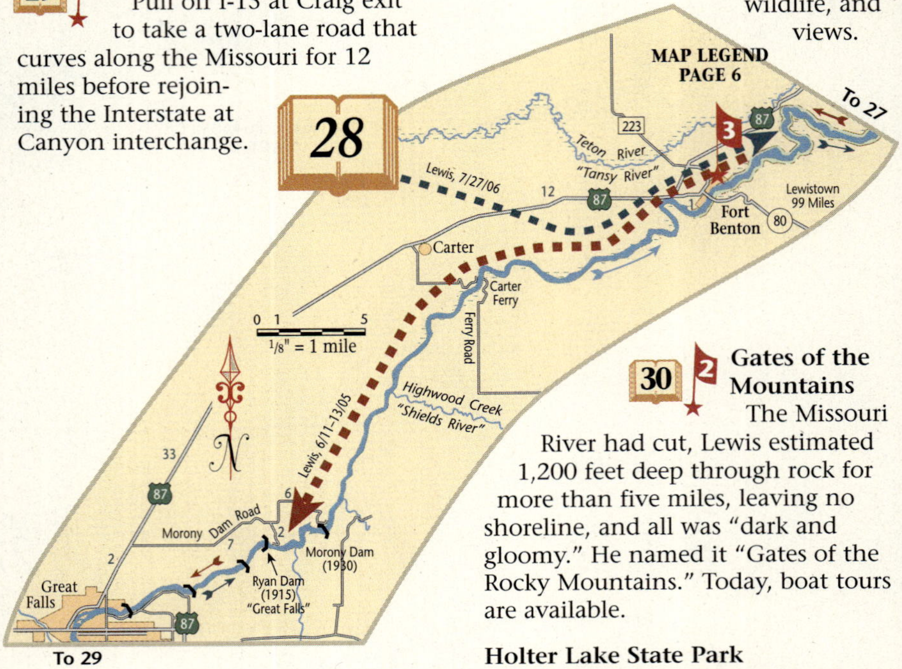

MAP LEGEND PAGE 6

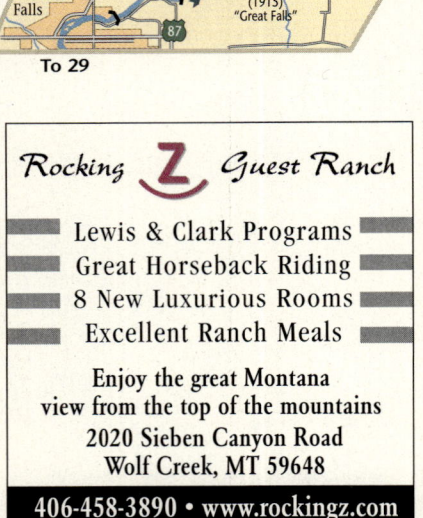

Gates of the Mountains
The Missouri River had cut, Lewis estimated 1,200 feet deep through rock for more than five miles, leaving no shoreline, and all was "dark and gloomy." He named it "Gates of the Rocky Mountains." Today, boat tours are available.

Holter Lake State Park
N of Helena on the Missouri River, I-15 exit 228

Hauser Lake
NE of Helena on the Missouri via County Rd 280
Created by river dams, these recreational lakes offer camping, fishing, guided boat tours, water sports, marinas, and dining.

July 21, 1805
HELENA 30

Because they were close to Shoshone lands and hoped to obtain

Helena's Grandest Hotel

149 spacious guest rooms and suites
Colonial Restaurant and Martini's Lounge & Casino
24-hour fitness center ■ 24-hour indoor swimming pool and hot tub
Seasonal outdoor swimming pool ■ Over 15,000 square feet of meeting and banquet space

Just minutes from the "Gates of the Mountain" Boat Tour
—Named by Lewis & Clark on their journey through Montana

redlion.com | 800-Red Lion

RED LION COLONIAL HOTEL
HELENA
2301 Colonial Drive • Helena, MT 59601 • (406) 443-2100
WestCoast Family of Hotels

Follow the Footsteps...
OF THE LEWIS & CLARK JOURNEY THROUGH MONTANA

Explore...

ATTRACTIONS
Great Northern Carousel
X-Ploration Works Science Museum

SHOPPING
Better Body Fitness
Boxwoods Funiture & Design
Cobblestone Clothing
Grand Junction Mercantile

FOOD & BEVERAGE
Brewhouse Pub and Grille
D&E Depot Deli
Insomnia Gourmet Coffee
Silver Star Steak Company

ACCOMMODATIONS
Best Western Helena Great Northern Hotel

SERVICES
Ahmann Brothers Realtors
AZ & Company
Great Northern Fitness Company
Information Technology Core
Montana Newspaper Association
Mosaic Architecture
Mountain West Bank
Office Business Center
Project Management

EXPLORE THE PAST
Retrace the footsteps of Lewis & Clark and see what they saw as they journeyed through Montana at a permanent outdoor exhibit at the Great Northern Town Center. Follow an etching of the Missouri River along one side of the pedestrian plaza and the Yellowstone along the other side, experiencing several of the journey's highlights along the way.

AT THE GREAT NORTHERN TOWN CENTER, HELENA, MONTANA

"Anticipated Opening Summer of 2004"

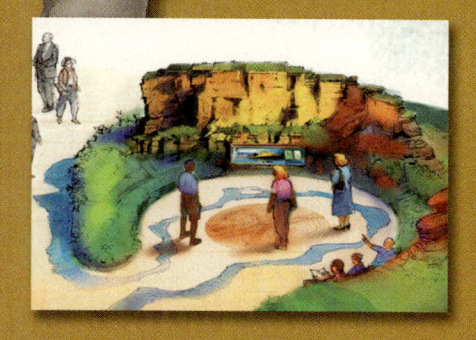

EXPLORE THE PRESENT
Modern day explorers can enjoy new adventures... ride a buffalo at the Great Northern Carousel, visit the Xploration Works Science Museum, enjoy homemade ice cream at the Painted Pony Ice Cream parlor, and see the outdoor Lewis & Clark exhibit. Features include the Great Falls of the Missouri, Pompey's Pillar, Gates of the Mountains, and more.

A replica of Pompey's Pillar, with Clark's signature and date, the only physical evidence of Lewis & Clark's journey!

A replica of the Great Falls of the Missouri River

For more information visit us at
www.gntowncenter.com

Great Things Are Happening!

Painted Pony ICE CREAM PARLOR & GIFT SHOP
Parties For All Occasions
- homemade fudge
- old fashioned sodas
- ice cream cake

457-5353
fun@gncarousel.com

GREAT NORTHERN CAROUSEL

Best Western Helena GREAT NORTHERN HOTEL
- 101 Oversized, Non-smoking Guest Rooms
- Indoor Pool, Jacuzzi, and Fitness Center
- FREE High-speed DSL in Every Room
- 8000 Square Feet of Meeting Space

(800) 829-4047
www.gnhotelhelena.com

SILVER STAR STEAK COMPANY
A CUT ABOVE
LUNCH • DINNER • CASINO • OUTDOOR DINING
Reservations 495-0677, located in the Great Northern Town Center

Get Ready!

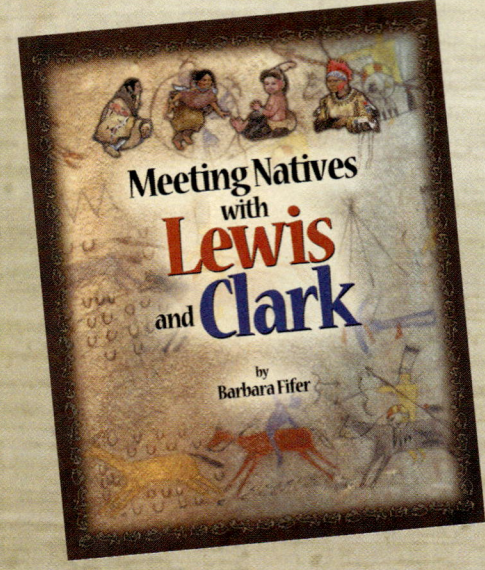

Meeting Natives with Lewis and Clark

By Barbara Fifer.

As the Lewis and Clark Expedition traveled west, white explorers and Native American peoples encountered each other for the first time. In picture and story, Barbara Fifer shows us lifestyles and customs of Sioux, Cheyenne, Nez Perce, Tillamook, and dozens more American Indian tribes and nations—all the residents of America from the Mississippi to the Pacific met by Lewis and Clark as they explored the continent. Learn how the natives lived, how they interacted, and what they thought of the explorers from the east.

56 full-color pages, 8½" x 11". Softbound. $12.95

Sheheke: Mandan Indian Diplomat
The Story of White Coyote, Thomas Jefferson, and Lewis and Clark

By Tracy Potter.

"Finally our great, great, great, great grandfather will be recognized for the great deeds he completed for the Corps of Discovery."—Diana Medicine Stone, Sheheke descendant. Potter eloquently tells the story of Sheheke, the Mandan Indian who traveled from North Dakota with Lewis and Clark to meet President Thomas Jefferson in Washington, D.C., in 1806. The story of Sheheke's life has been too long untold. Sheheke was an ambassador for the Mandan Nation, a consistent friend of the United States, and an important part of the Lewis and Clark Expedition. In sharing his story, his legacy of kindness, friendship, and courage lives on.

208 pages, 6" x 9". Softbound. $15.95
Hardbound. $21.95

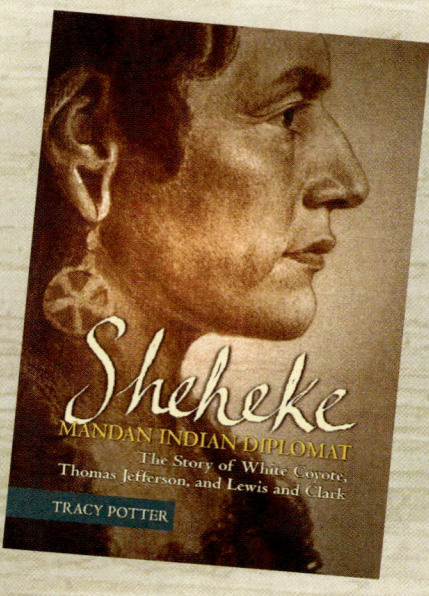

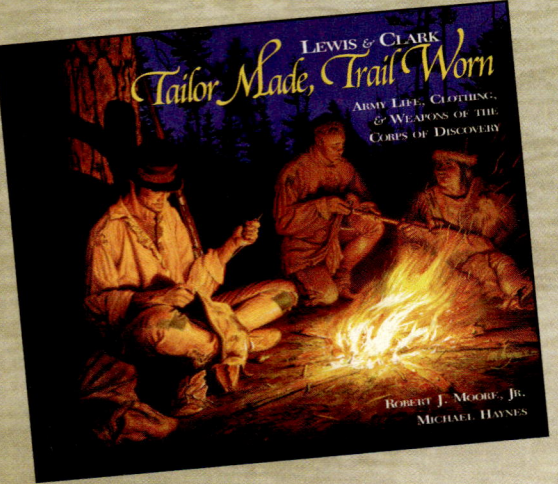

Lewis & Clark Tailor Made, Trail Worn
Army Life, Clothing, & Weapons of the Corps of Discovery

By Robert J. Moore, Jr. and Michael Haynes.

When the Lewis and Clark Expedition crossed the continent, they began in U.S. Army uniforms, which gradually were replaced with simple leather garments. Historian Moore and artist Haynes research archives and museums to determine what the men wore, and Haynes illustrates the clothing in scenes of the trip. Also included are Indian styles the men adopted and wardrobes of Creole interpreters and French boatmen. Weapons and accessories round out this complete record of what the expedition wore or carried—and why. A great reference for artists, living history performers, museums, and military historians.

Index. 288 pages, 10$^{3/8}$"x10". Hardbound. $39.95

Lewis and Clark's Green World:
The Expedition and Its Plants

By A. Scott Earle and James L. Reveal.

Botanist Reveal joins forces with devoted amateur Earle to follow the Corps of Discovery's trail, focusing on plant specimens Capt. Meriwether Lewis collected for President Jefferson and other scientists of the early 19th century. Earle's and Reveal's seasonal color photographs illustrate complete botanical descriptions of each plant, with quotes from Lewis's journal. Nominated for the Fifth Annual Literature Award by the Council on Botanical & Horticulture Libraries.

Index. 288 pages, 8½"x8½". Hardbound. $34.95

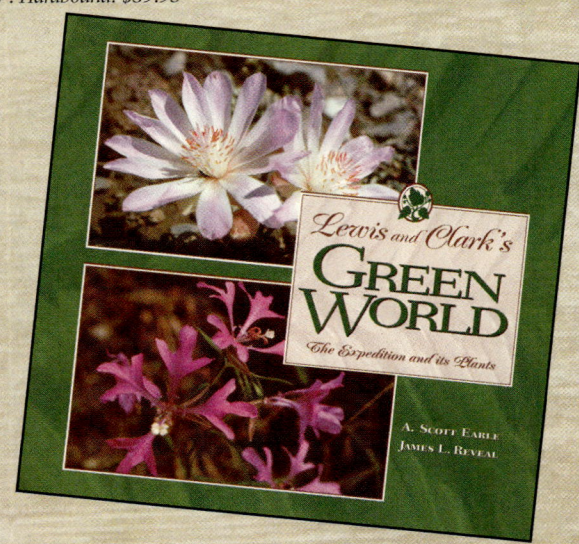

FARCOUNTRY PRESS

We are your best source for Lewis & Clark titles!

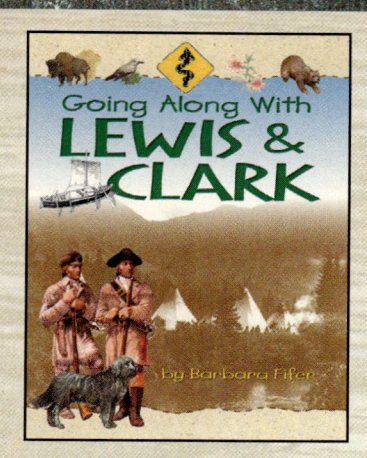

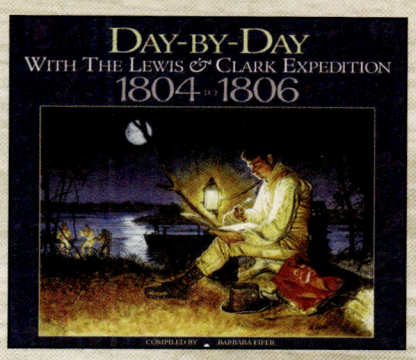

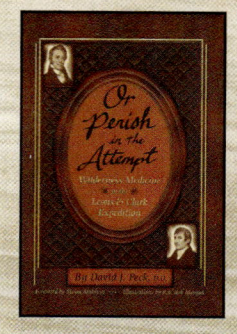

Going Along with Lewis & Clark
By Barbara Fifer.
For kids of all ages. Lighthearted, attention-grabbing design with dozens of color maps, sketches, paintings, and photographs covering "Who They Were," "People They Met," "What They Ate," and more.
48 pages. 8½"x11". Hardbound, $15.95; Softbound, $11.95

Day-by-Day with the Lewis & Clark Expedition, 1804–1806
By Barbara Fifer.
Not an appointment calendar, but an easy way to join the Lewis & Clark Expedition on each of their 862 days on the trail. Calendars for the years 1804 to 1806 are filled with brief notes telling what each new day brought: numbing cold, near-starvation, feast & surprising foods, triumph, wonders, fear, or new friendships. Color illustrations show people, gear, clothing, plants & animals, the boats, & more.
36 pages, 13¾"x12"(closed). Softbound. $12.95

Or Perish in the Attempt: Wilderness Medicine in the Lewis & Clark Expedition
By David J. Peck, D.O.
The medical challenges Lewis & Clark encountered and treated using the primitive medicine and theories of 1803.
Index. 352 pages, 6"x9". Hardbound, $24.95; Softbound, $18.95

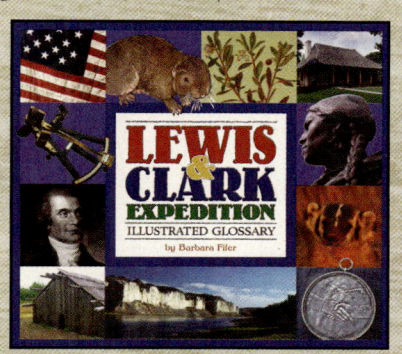

Lewis & Clark Expedition Illustrated Glossary
By Barbara Fifer.
Did the Lewis and Clark expedition really feast on anchovies and pheasants? How many beads were in a brace? What kinds of rifles did the men use? Who are the Pahkee Indians? And whatever is an espontoon or a circumferentor? This is a quick alphabetical aid to enjoying the journals kept during 1803 to 1806, with text and illustrations.
80 pages, 9½" x 8⅜". Softbound. $11.95

POSTER: Along the Trail with Lewis and Clark
Full-color poster outlines the trip from St. Louis to the Pacific & back, showing land & water routes, 53 sites to visit, 44 landmark or intriguing events. 36"x24" individually shrink-wrapped. *$9.95*

Along the Trail with Lewis and Clark Second Edition
By Barbara Fifer and Vicky Soderberg with maps by Joseph Mussulman.
The whole story of the Expedition, beginning east of the Mississippi River as Thomas Jefferson and Meriwether Lewis planned. Follows the expedition to the Pacific and back to St. Louis. Accessible history text combines with tourism information, and maps combine both then and now. No advertising.
Extensive index. 216 pages, 8½"x7". Softbound, Stitched. $19.95

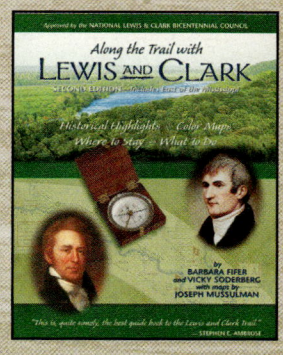

SEND TO: FARCOUNTRY PRESS • P.O. BOX 5630 • HELENA, MT 59604
OR CALL TOLL FREE 1-800-821-3874 • FAX: 406-443-5480

LCTP

SHIPPING CHARGES
- $6.00 for first item
- $2.00 for each additional item
- Free shipping on all orders $75.00 and over
- Avoid shipping delays... add postage/shipping fee!

NAME _____
ADDRESS _____
CITY _____ STATE _____ ZIP _____ PHONE _____
PAYMENT: ☐ CHECK ENCLOSED CHARGE TO: ☐ VISA ☐ MASTERCARD ☐ AMERICAN EXPRESS ☐ DISCOVER
SIGNATURE _____
ACCT. NO. _____ EXP. DATE _____

QTY	TITLE	PRICE	TOTAL
	ALONG THE TRAIL WITH LEWIS & CLARK SECOND EDITION (SOFTBOUND)	$19.95	
	DAY-BY-DAY WITH LEWIS AND CLARK (SOFTBOUND)	$12.95	
	GOING ALONG WITH LEWIS AND CLARK (SOFTBOUND)	$11.95	
	GOING ALONG WITH LEWIS AND CLARK (HARDBOUND)	$15.95	
	LEWIS & CLARK EXPEDITION ILLUSTRATED GLOSSARY (SOFTBOUND)	$11.95	
	LEWIS AND CLARK GREEN WORLD: THE EXPEDITION AND ITS PLANTS (HARDBOUND)	$34.95	
	LEWIS & CLARK TAILOR MADE, TRAIL WORN (HARDBOUND)	$39.95	
	MEETING NATIVES WITH LEWIS AND CLARK (SOFTBOUND)	$12.95	
	OR PERISH IN THE ATTEMPT: (HARDBOUND)	$24.95	
	OR PERISH IN THE ATTEMPT: (SOFTBOUND)	$18.95	
	POSTER: ALONG THE TRAIL WITH LEWIS & CLARK	$9.95	
	SHEHEKE: MANDAN INDIAN DIPLOMAT (SOFTBOUND)	$15.95	
	SHEHEKE: MANDAN INDIAN DIPLOMAT (HARDBOUND)	$21.95	
	POSTAGE/SHIPPING FOR FIRST ITEM	$6.00*	$6.00
	POSTAGE/SHIPPING FOR EACH ADDITIONAL ITEM	$2.00 EA	
	ALL ITEMS ARE SHIPPED EITHER 1ST CLASS MAIL OR VIA UPS *FOREIGN ORDERS: PLEASE ADD $5.00	TOTAL DUE	

Montana

Shoshone horses and aid to cross the Rockies, Captain Clark and four men went ahead hoping to find Sacagawea's people. Sacagawea had told the captains that the Shoshones would be wary of Blackfeet raiding parties, so when Clark's group needed to hunt he walked three miles ahead, then back four miles, before allowing shooting. The men found the river here a mile wide, shallow enough to pole the boats, and "crowded with islands." Today this stretch is under Canyon Ferry Lake.

Chamber of Commerce of Helena
225 Cruse Ave., Helena, MT 59601
406-442-4120;
www.helenachamber.com

Canyon Ferry Lake
Missouri River E of Helena
Visitor Center: US 12 nine miles SE, then 10 miles NE on Hwy. 284; 406-475-3310

Year-round recreation on 76 miles of shoreline. Six campgrounds offer tent/RV sites, picnic areas, fishing, boating access. Visitor center interprets the expedition, Canyon Ferry Dam construction, and area wildlife.

Montana Historical Society Museum
225 N. Roberts; 406-444-2694

C. M. Russell paintings and bronzes, F. J. Haynes photography of Yellowstone National Park's early days (and his photo-studio railroad car), and state history from Native Americans to the Corps to the 20th century.

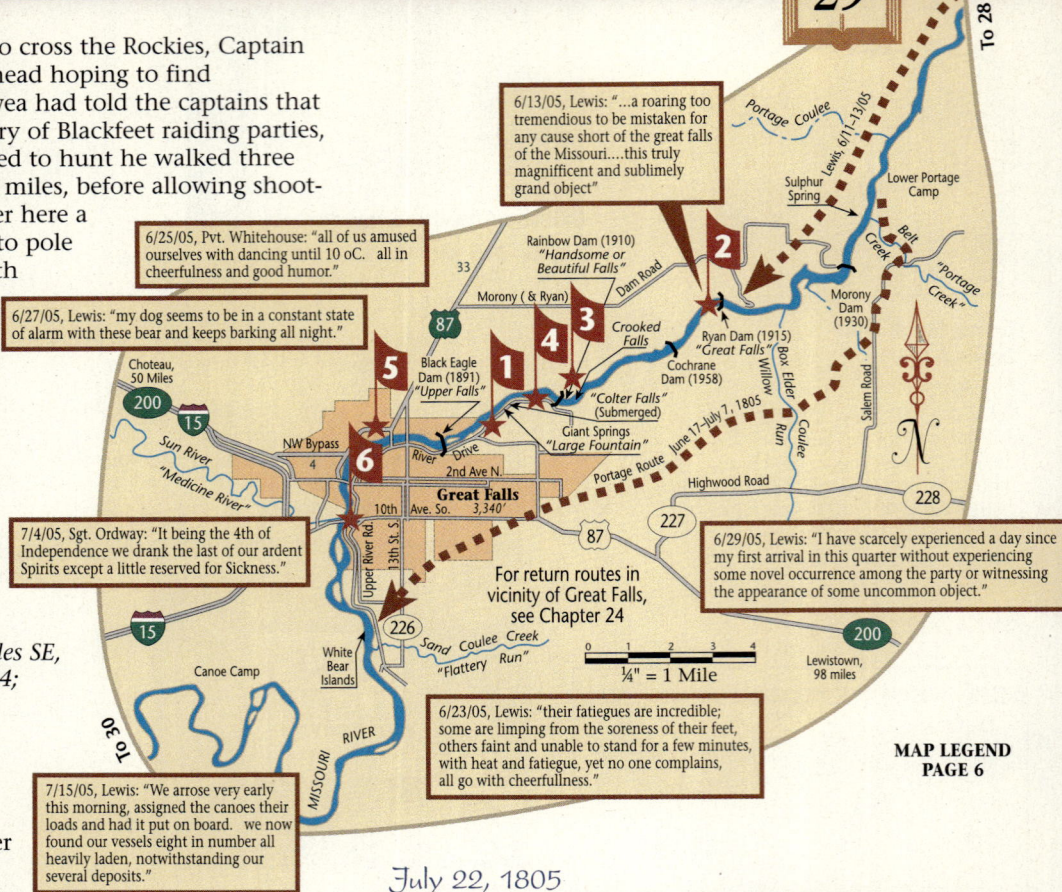

Map callouts

- 6/13/05, Lewis: "...a roaring too tremendious to be mistaken for any cause short of the great falls of the Missouri....this truly magnifficent and sublimely grand object"
- 6/25/05, Pvt. Whitehouse: "all of us amused ourselves with dancing until 10 oC. all in cheerfulness and good humor."
- 6/27/05, Lewis: "my dog seems to be in a constant state of alarm with these bear and keeps barking all night."
- 7/4/05, Sgt. Ordway: "It being the 4th of Independence we drank the last of our ardent Spirits except a little reserved for Sickness."
- 6/29/05, Lewis: "I have scarcely experienced a day since my first arrival in this quarter without experiencing some novel occurrence among the party or witnessing the appearance of some uncommon object."
- 6/23/05, Lewis: "their fatiegues are incredible; some are limping from the soreness of their feet, others faint and unable to stand for a few minutes, with heat and fatiegue, yet no one complains, all go with cheerfullness."
- 7/15/05, Lewis: "We arrose very early this morning, assigned the canoes their loads and had it put on board. we now found our vessels eight in number all heavily laden, notwithstanding our several deposits."

For return routes in vicinity of Great Falls, see Chapter 24

MAP LEGEND PAGE 6

July 22, 1805
Montana City 30

East of here the Missouri River was divided into "a number of channels by both large and small islands," and Lewis said it was hard to guess where its main channel was. Today the river waters backed up in Canyon Ferry Lake totally cover the area where the men struggled to pull their boats.

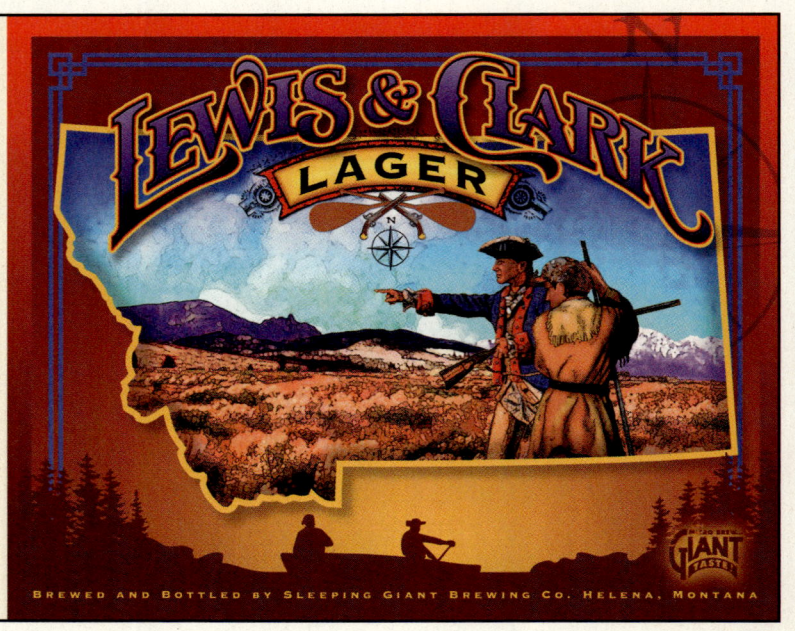

Join the Adventure...
Pick up a 6-pack of Lewis & Clark Lager as you journey along the trail!

For commemorative Pint Glasses, T-shirts, Hats & all sorts of great Lewis & Clark Lager gifts visit:
www.LewisandClarkLager.com or Stop by and see us while in Helena. We are located behind the Carousel in the Great Northern Town Center.

Sleeping Giant Brewing Co. Helena, MT

www.lewisandclark.com

July 23, 1805
TOWNSEND [31]

Clark's advance party traveled ahead, followed a day later by the rest of the Corps, who worked hard poling their boats against the shallow but swift Missouri, their poles slipping on the river bottom's smooth stones. North of Townsend with the main group, Sacagawea began to recognize landmarks and assured Captain Lewis that her home country, and the Missouri's headwaters, was not far now.

Yorks Islands
US 287 4 miles S, 1 mile W on county road
Primitive campsites, fishing and boating access on the shore with a view of privately owned islands in the Missouri, which the captains named for Clark's slave.

Broadwater County Museum
133 N. Walnut; 406-266-5252
Open May through September. Includes Indian artifacts, room exhibits of whites' frontier life, and a large collection of barbed wire.

BUTTE

Fifty miles west of Three Forks on I-90 at I-15, Butte sits atop "the richest hill on earth" and below the defunct Berkeley open-pit copper mine. Butte mixes ethnic neigh- borhoods, mining-baron mansions, and grand buildings of the late 19th and early 20th centuries.

World Museum of Mining
West Park and Granite St.; 406-723-7211
Twelve acres of indoor and outdoor exhibits interpret hard-rock mining of the 19th and 20th cent- uries, including the "Hell Roarin' Gulch" recreated mining town and antique and modern mining equipment.

Mai Wah
17 W. Mercury; 406-735-6814
Former Chinese-owned general store & noodle parlor today tells the story of Butte's many Asian immigrants. Open summers.

Our Lady of the Rockies
Visitor center: 434 N. Main; 406-494-2656
This 90-foot metal sculpture of St. Mary overlooks the mile-high city from 8,500 feet high on a mountainside. Tours available summer and fall.

VIRGINIA CITY

60 miles S of Three Forks on US 287
Half county seat and half historic site, Virginia City began with a gold rush in 1864, attracted highway robbers and vigilantes, became the territorial capital, and then turned into a quiet county seat after the streams' placer gold played out. Montana Historical Society manages restored, furnished buildings dating from the early years, open during summer.

Virginia City Chamber of Commerce
P.O. Box 218, Virginia City, MT 59755
406-843-5555; www.virginiacity.chamber.com

July 25-30, 1805; Clark's return: July 13, 1806
THREE FORKS [31]

Westward bound in 1805 Clark's party reached the Missouri's headwaters. The captains expected that the main feeder stream would guide them to the top of the Rockies, and they would climb over a single range to streams flowing into the Columbia River system to the Pacific. But which fork was the main stream?

79 MONTANA

Montana

Style Charm Heritage

Sacajawea Hotel
LODGING • STEAKHOUSE • SPIRITS
5 N. Main, Three Forks, Montana 59752
888-722-2529 www.sacajaweahotel.com

Clark first explored today's Jefferson River (his "north fork," which flows from the southwest). Fifteen miles upstream, they camped for the night. On the 26th, Clark took Pvts. Field and Frazier farther up the Jefferson, returned to collect Charbonneau and Pvt. Field, and crossed overland to the middle fork, the Madison River. Downstream on the Madison they reached the Three Forks in the afternoon, finding the rest of the Corps. Sacagawea said this camp was exactly where her people were staying five years before when they first saw the Hidatsa raiders who captured her. Some men tanned deerskins while others explored the three headwaters. On the sixth day they set off now believing—correctly—that the Jefferson River was the stream to follow.

Three Forks Chamber of Commerce
P.O. Box 1103, Three Forks, MT 59752
406-285-4753; www.threeforksmontana.com

31 Missouri Headwaters State Park
I-90 N of town; 406-994-4042

Interpretive exhibits, paved trails, picnic area, and a small primitive campground today mark this field where Missouri River waters quietly begin their 4,368-mile journey to the Gulf of Mexico.

Headwaters Heritage Museum
406-285-4778

Open from May to September, with exhibits on Missouri headwaters terrain and area history.

August 1, 1805   32
CARDWELL & WHITEHALL

Clark was exhausted, had been ill at the three forks (possibly from a tick bite), and one of his ankles swelled with an infection. Now Lewis went ahead with Sgt. Patrick Gass, Charbonneau, and interpreter George Drouillard to look for the Shoshones. Not knowing when they'd find them, how long the Rockies crossing would take, and when winter weather would hit these high-elevation mountains, all were anxious to connect with the horse-owners. That night Lewis's advance party camped west of Cardwell, and the main group to the east, both on the Jefferson, which looks today pretty much as it did then.

Lewis and Clark Caverns State Park
Exit 256 from I-90, then 7 miles E on MT 2;
406-287-3541

The Corps of Discovery passed nearby, but the caverns weren't found by whites until 1892; sixteen years later, President Theodore Roosevelt named them for the explorers. Two-hour guided underground tours (available May through October) include hundreds of stairs, but mobility-impaired people can make advance reservations for tours of one large "room" of stalactites and stalagmites. Campground includes three small cabins and tent/RV sites.

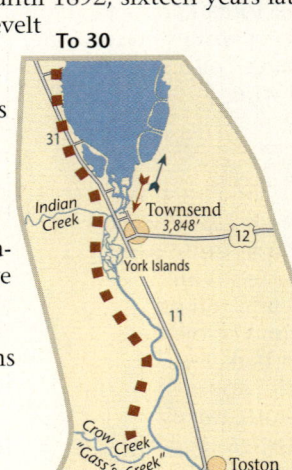

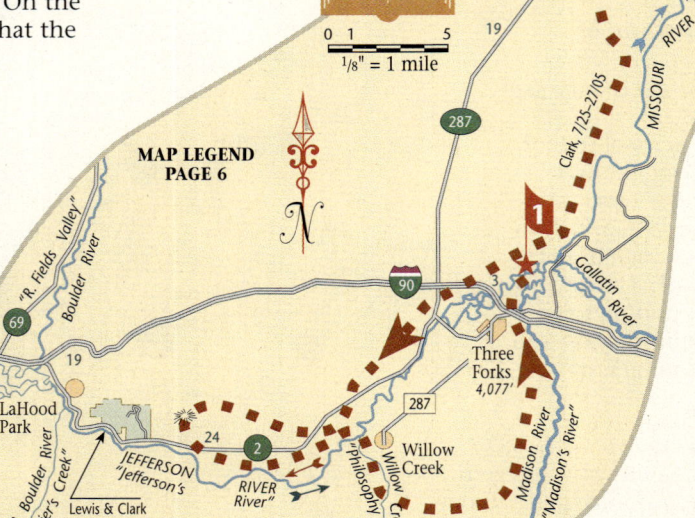

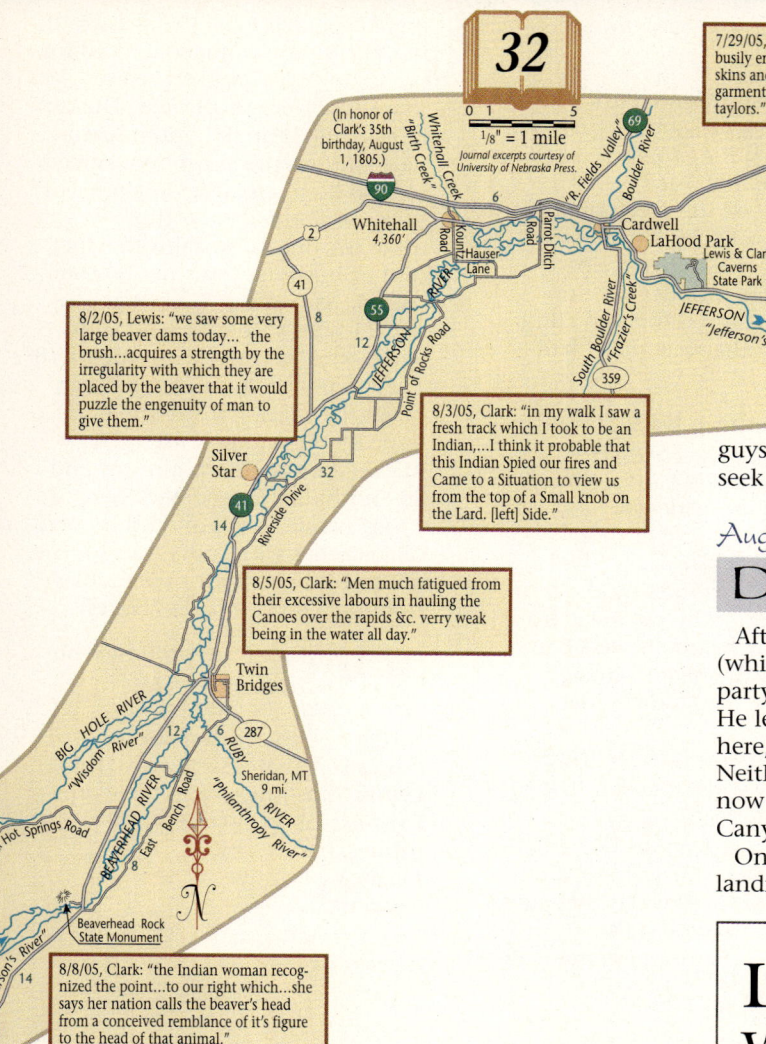

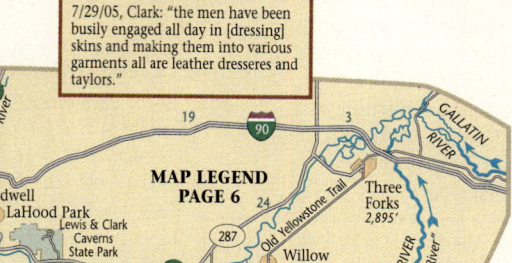

www.lewisandclark.com

32

1/8" = 1 mile
Journal excerpts courtesy of University of Nebraska Press.

7/29/05, Clark: "the men have been busily engaged all day in [dressing] skins and making them into various garments all are leather dresseres and taylors."

(In honor of Clark's 35th birthday, August 1, 1805.)

MAP LEGEND PAGE 6

8/2/05, Lewis: "we saw some very large beaver dams today... the brush...acquires a strength by the irregularity with which they are placed by the beaver that it would puzzle the engenuity of man to give them."

8/3/05, Clark: "in my walk I saw a fresh track which I took to be an Indian,...I think it probable that this Indian Spied our fires and Came to a Situation to view us from the top of a Small knob on the Lard. [left] Side."

8/5/05, Clark: "Men much fatigued from their excessive labours in hauling the Canoes over the rapids &c. verry weak being in the water all day."

8/8/05, Clark: "the Indian woman recognized the point...to our right which...she says her nation calls the beaver's head from a conceived remblance of it's figure to the head of that animal."

camp in the 1860s, one of the many centered on Virginia City. Today the vigilantes and the bad guys are gone, and Sheridan hosts anglers and others who seek peaceful relaxation.

August 9, 1805: Lewis; August 13, 1805: Clark

DILLON

After camping near here on the Beaverhead River (which feeds into the Jefferson), Lewis and his advance party decided to travel until they found the Shoshones. He left a note for Clark and the others to wait for him here, where two streams joined to form the Beaverhead. Neither small stream would allow the canoes to pass, so now was the time for horses. Today the site is under Clark Canyon Reservoir.

On August 8, Sacagawea had recognized the Shoshone landmark "The Beaver's Head," a massive rock, in the dis-

August 4-7, 1805

TWIN BRIDGES 32

Lewis's advance party came to a split in the Jefferson River; he correctly chose the left fork, today's Beaverhead River, as the main branch and continued upstream. He left a note for Clark, stuck on a willow pole, telling him which fork to follow. The next day Clark's party reached the fork, and Clark chose the other (today's Big Hole River) and proceeded upstream. Unfortunately, Lewis's note was on a green pole that a beaver must have carried away. Ten miles up, they met Drouillard, whom Lewis had sent out to hunt. Reunited, the entire Corps of Discovery camped at the fork to rest and dry out provisions.

Twin Bridges Historical Association Museum
202 S. Main; 406-684-5121
Open summers with exhibits on mining, agriculture, and family history in the Twin Bridges and Sheridan area.

SHERIDAN 32

Nine miles southeast of Twin Bridges, Sheridan sits in the Ruby River valley. The village began life as a gold rush

Look! We missed Virginia City!

We would have seen . . .
- Operating 1910 steam locomotive
- Two live theaters - Opera House & Brewery Follies
- Living history demonstrations
- Unique shopping, old-time saloons
- Historic accommodations & fine dining
- Stagecoach, fire engine & historic walking tours
- Ghost walk and special interest tours
- Frontier House Museum
- Nearby Nevada City, 100 historic buildings with artifacts

Lewis & Clark missed the excitement . . . Don't you!

1-800-829-2969
virginiacitychamber.com
virginiacitymt.com

Montana

tance. Having to tow their canoes up the shallow Beaverhead River, the main party moved slowly toward the welcome sight, at last passing it on the 13th. Scholars debate whether today's Beaverhead Rock, northwest of Dillon, is the exact one that heartened the Corps of Discovery, but the public claims it as Sacagawea's marker.

Clark's Lookout State Park
1 mile N on Old Hwy. 91; or, I-15 exit 41, 0.5 mile S, then 1 mile N on Old Hwy. 91; 406-834-3413

Clark climbed this steep hill on August 13, looking ahead to find Lewis's advance party. The site is under development, but visitors can climb up for the view that Clark had.

Beaverhead Rock State Park
13 miles N on MT 41; 406-944-4042; Interpretive pullout at the landmark.

August 12, 1805
Having seen an Indian riding "an elegant horse," who ran away from them the day before, Lewis's party followed his tracks and crossed Lemhi Pass into today's Idaho.

August 17–19, 22, 1805
Clark's return: July 8–10, 1806
Sacagawea and Charbonneau were walking ahead of Clark when they saw Lewis and the Shoshones approaching. Recognizing her people's clothing, the young woman "danced for the joyful sight" and signed to Clark that these were Shoshones. The captains named the site Camp Fortunate because the Shoshones agreed to help them cross the Rockies. For Sacagawea, the good fortune was more personal: Cameahwait, chief of the Shoshones, was her brother.

Clark, Sacagawea, Charbonneau, and 11 men with axes left camp with some Shoshones on August 18. They hoped to make canoes to go down the Salmon River and also to trade for Shoshone horses. On August 22, the Charbonneaus and 50 Shoshones arrived back here.

Meanwhile, Lewis and other men filled caches with provisions for the return trip, and built pack saddles from the empty wooden boxes.

33 Clark Canyon Reservoir
20 miles S on I-15; 406-683-6472

Interpretative information on Camp Fortunate, Sacagawea, the Lemhi Shoshones, and the Corps. Park also offers hiking, fishing, birding, picnic area, primitive camping.

The Expedition Crosses the Continental Divide:
- August 12, Westbound — Captain Lewis and 3 companions
- August 15, Eastbound — Lewis and 3 men plus about 60 Indians and horses
- August 19, Westbound — Captain Clark, 11 men, Sacagawea, Charbonneau, five Indians
- August 21, Eastbound — Sacagawea, Charbonneau, 50 Indian men plus some women and children, with many horses
- August 26, Westbound — Lewis and the rest of the Corps of Discovery, plus Cameahwait and other Indians. Baggage carried by 11 horses, 1 mule, and some Indian women. Sacagawea rode a horse.

www.lewisandclark.com

September 4-6, 1805
SULA [34]

Having gone west and then north through a corner of future Idaho, the Corps crossed later-named Lost Trail Pass back into future Montana and descended into the broad valley called Ross's Hole. (Later mountain men called mountain-ringed broad valleys "holes.") Here they met the Salish and Kootenai Indians, who had never seen whites and "received us friendly." The council, all day on the 5th, was slow because translations went through several languages between captains and chiefs.

September 6-8, 1805
The Corps of Discovery moved north through the Bitterroot Valley in dark, drizzly, windy September weather. Clark recorded that all were cold and wet.

HAMILTON [34]

Today a county seat and arts and outdoor recreation center, Hamilton was founded by "copper king" Marcus Daly in the late 1800s.

Bitterroot Valley Chamber of Commerce
105 E. Main St., Hamilton, MT 59840; 406-363-2400

Daly Mansion
251 Eastside Hwy.; 406-363-6004
Mid-May to mid-October, guided tours of Georgian mansion on Marcus Daly's thoroughbred farm, home to Daly's 1889 Kentucky Derby winner, Spokane.

Ravalli County Museum
205 Bedford; 406-363-3338
History exhibits include Flathead Indian artifacts, the Lewis and Clark Room on the Corps in this area, the story of research on Rocky Mountain spotted fever done nearby, and homesteaders.

VICTOR & STEVENSVILLE [34]

Fort Owen State Park/St. Mary's Mission
0.5 mile E of US 93–CR 269 junction; 406-542-5500
Fort Owen was originally the Catholic St. Mary's Mission to the Flathead Indians. It was founded in 1841 by Father Pierre-Jean DeSmet after several groups of Flatheads traveled to St. Louis to request missionaries. His emphasis on farming & other new ways, plus later ministering to the Blackfeet, traditional enemies of the Flatheads, lessened Flathead interest. In 1850, John Owen purchased the buildings from DeSmet to open a trading post among the Salish & Kootenai. Self-guided tour of original buildings include church, priest's house/pharmacy, Chief Victor's house, & indoor exhibits of artifacts found in on-site archaeological digs.

September 9-11, 1805
return June 29, 1806
LOLO

After moving north on the same route as today's US 93, the Corps rested here at Lolo Creek (which they named Travelers' Rest Creek), gathering strength for what proved to be the

Any Season...It's Fun At Lolo Hot Springs
Horseback Riding • Soak In The Pool • Bumper Boats • Restaurant • Snowmobiling
Cross-Country Skiing • Hiking • Bar and Casino • Soak in Hot Springs • Campsites and Cabins
38500 W. Highway 12, Lolo, Montana 59847
406-273-2290
1-800-273-2290
stoen@lolohotsprings.com
www.lolohotsprings.com

Lost Horse Creek Lodge
1000 Lost Horse Road
Hamilton, MT 59840
406-363-1460
www.losthorsecreeklodge.com
Just 8 miles South of Hamilton on Hwy 93 and 3.8 miles West
Enjoy an Authentic Lodging Experience on the Lewis and Clark Trail

• Luxury Jacuzzi Log Cabins
• Townhouses & Authentic 1800 Log Cabins
• Gourmet Dining
• Full Service Saloon & Casino
• Trail Rides
• Guided Fly Fishing
• River Rafting
• Hiking
• Meetings, Weddings and Reunions
Near the Clark Party's Lunch Site July 4, 1806
Open 7 Days a Week 8:00 am to 10:00 pm
Memorial Day to Labor Day

BITTERROOT RIVER INN & Conference Center
Holiday Inn EXPRESS HOTEL & SUITES
• 65 Lodge-Style Sleeping Rooms
• In-Room Coffee Makers
• Irons & Ironing Boards
• Hair Dryers • 25-inch Color TV's
• Free Local Calls & HBO
Suites Are Equipped With:
• Sitting Area W/Pull-out Sofa Bed
• Microwave Oven • Mini-Fridge
• 2 Deluxe Suites with Garden Whirlpool Tubs and Fireplaces
Conference Center Features:
• Grand Ballroom 2,908 Sq. ft.
No pets please
Indoor Pool • Sun Deck • Sauna • Hot Tub
Deluxe Complimentary Continental Breakfast
(406) 375-2525
139 Bitterroot Plaza Dr. • Hamilton, MT 59840

Montana Bed & Breakfasts and Guest Houses

A SPECIAL ADVERTISING SECTION

BOULDER

Boulder Hot Springs
P.O. Box 930 • Boulder, MT 59632
(406) 225-4339 • www.boulderhotsprings.com

Nestled in the foothills of Montana's Elkhorn Mountains, Boulder Hot Springs is an historic inn which offers theme B&B and guest rooms, geothermal pools and tasty, organic food. A relaxing and rejuvating place to stay!

THE RANCH BED & BREAKFAST
Box 47 • Boulder, MT 59632 • (406) 287-5835

In the mountains, near Headwaters. Working ranch. 1870's 2-story home. 3 rooms shared bath-1 private. Hearty ranch breakfast. Hunting, fishing, bird watching, and nature walks.

Open year-round.

EMIGRANT

Johnstad's
BED & BREAKFAST AND LOG CABIN

JOHNSTAD'S BED & BREAKFAST AND LOG CABIN
03 Paradise Lane • PO Box 981
Emigrant, MT 59027
1-800-340-4993 • (406) 333-9003
www.johnstadsbb.com

In Paradise Valley near north entrance to Yellowstone Park. Spacious B&B rooms, spectacular views, ensuite baths. Beautiful log cabin accomodates six. Private access to Yellowstone River.

Paradise GATEWAY
B&B & GUEST CABINS
PO Box 84 • Emigrant, MT 59027
1-800-541-4113 • (406) 333-4063
www.wtp.net/go/paradise

Near the North entrance to Yellowstone National Park, bordering the River. Charming rooms in the Inn, private baths. Irresitable log cabins with acreage. Gourmet breakfasts.

FORT BENTON

D & S RV PARK
316 Franklin • Fort Benton, MT 59442
(406) 622-3779 • (406) 622-5104

Quiet and rural setting in historical Fort Benton. Full hookups, daily and monthly rates. Call for reservations or just stop by.

GRAND UNION HOTEL
1 Grand Union Square
PO Box 1119
Fort Benton, MT 59442 USA
1-888-838-1882 • (406) 622-1882
www.grandunionhotel.com

Listed on the National Register of Historic Places and elegantly restored in 1999 to its original grandeur. Montana's oldest operating hotel provides 27 luxury historic guestrooms, a riverside restaurant, and conference facilities in Historic Fort Benton. AAA 3-diamond rated.

PIONEER LODGE MOTEL
1700 Front Street • P.O. Box 68
Fort Benton, MT 59442
1-800-622-6088 • (406) 622-5441
www.pioneerlodgemt.com

Located in the Historic 1916 T.C. Power Building along the Missouri River on the Lewis & Clark Trail. Tasefully decorated, spacious and affordable guest rooms have private baths, cable TV and complimentary continental breakfast.

GARDINER

YELLOWSTONE SUITES
Gardiner, MT • 1-800-948-7937
www.yellowstonesuites.com

Stay in a beautiful stone-built Victorian-era B&B, the closest B&B to Yellowstone National Park, with spacious rooms, a charming suite with kitchen, private bathrooms, verandas, shaded gardens, hot tub, and friendly innkeepers. Gourmet breakfast. MTBBA member.

GREAT FALLS

COLLINS MANSION
BED & BREAKFAST • CATERING
1003 Second Ave. NW • Great Falls, MT 59404
1-877-452-6798 • (406) 452-6798
www.collinsmansion.com

This beautiful mansion, listed on the National Register of Historic Places, boasts five beautifully appointed guest rooms with private baths. A graceful veranda recalls elegant Victorian sensibilities. Gourmet breakfasts. Ideal for small catered dinners, lunches, weddings, and just about any get-together. MTBBA Member.

HARDIN

HISTORIC HOTEL BECKER B&B
200 North Center • Hardin, MT 59034
(406) 665-2707

Located in downtown Hardin, the facility offers seven rooms, breakfast featuring local wild berry jellies, meeting room, and a hostess/owner with a half-century of knowledge about Hardin and the surrounding area.

HELENA

The Sanders
HELENA'S BED & BREAKFAST
328 North Ewing • Helena, MT 59601
(406) 442-3309 • www.sandersbb.com

Stay in Helena's finest bed and breakfast - one of the 100 best in the United States. History abounds, along with original furnishings, elegant rooms, great breakfasts, afternoon refreshments and plenty of luxuries. The Northwest Passage? Not quite, but a grand discovery!

LIVINGSTON

Mission Creek Ranch
Bed & Breakfast and Fishery

B&B & GUEST HOUSE
10 Mission Creek Rd • Livingston, MT 59047
1-800-320-5007 • (406) 222-8290
www.missioncreekbandb.com

Walk in the footsteps of William Clark along the majestic Yellowstone River! Mission Creek Ranch B&B, found at the heart of the historic 4,500 acre Mission Ranch, is tucked into a secluded bend along Mission Creek with an Absaroka Mountain back drop. Also featured: historic Fort Parker, miles of blue ribbon trout streams, meadows teeming with wildlife and tepees available.

THE PLEASANT PHEASANT
BED & BREAKFAST

PLEASANT PHEASANT B&B
126 Elbow Creek Rd • Paradise Valley
Livingston, MT 59047
(406) 333-4659

Close to the Yellowstone River and Yellowstone National Park. The 3-bedroom and 2-bath Barn, 3-bedroom and bath Bunkhouse, and 1-bedroom and bath Outhouse, each with kitchen and do-it-yourself breakfasts, make great places for family gatherings.

SEELEY LAKE

EMILY A B&B
P.O. Box 350 • Seeley Lake, MT 59868
(406) 677-FISH • www.TheEmilyA.com
11,000-square-foot log lodge overlooking Clearwater River. Five guest rooms, family suite, original homestead cabin. Hike, fish, or explore our big backyard. Visit the Prairie of the Knobs—Meriwether Lewis did! Full breakfast. MTBBA member.

SULA

A LI'L BIT OF HEAVEN
7987 Hwy 93 S • Sula, MT 59871
(406) 821-3433 • www.alilbitofheaven.com
Located on the Lewis and Clark Trail at the base of Lost Trail Pass. Two beautifully furnished log cabins in the Bitterroot mountains await you.

VIRGINIA CITY

BENNETT HOUSE COUNTRY INN
115 E Idaho St • Virginia City, MT 59755
1-877-843-5220 (toll-free)
www.bennetthouseinn.com
Enjoy casual elegance at the Bennett House in historic Virginia City. Six unique bedrooms, and a log cabin. Sumptuous full breakfast included. Open year-round.

---

worst overland part of the trip. On the return trip, they again enjoyed "the bath" at the nearby hot springs.

Travelers Rest State Park
0.5 mile W of Hwy. 93 at 6550 Mormon Creek Rd.; 406-273-4253; www.travelersrest.org
   Open daily Memorial Day to Labor Day, this is the confirmed location of the campsite where the Corps fortified themselves for the trip west over the Bitterroot Mountains in 1805 and relaxed after their return the next year.

34 **Howard Creek**
US 12, 18.5 miles W; 406-329-3962
   Exhibit on the Corps of Discovery and hiking trails along the route they followed.

35 **Lolo Hot Springs**
35 miles S of Missoula on US12: 406-273-2201
   Although the hot springs is on private, developed land, visitors can view the exact site of the Corps' soothing plunges at no charge.

35 *September 13, 1805*
Lee Creek
US 12, 26 miles W; 406-329-3962
Hike 2.5 miles along the Corps' probable path, view interpretation, go fishing, or enjoy primitive camping.

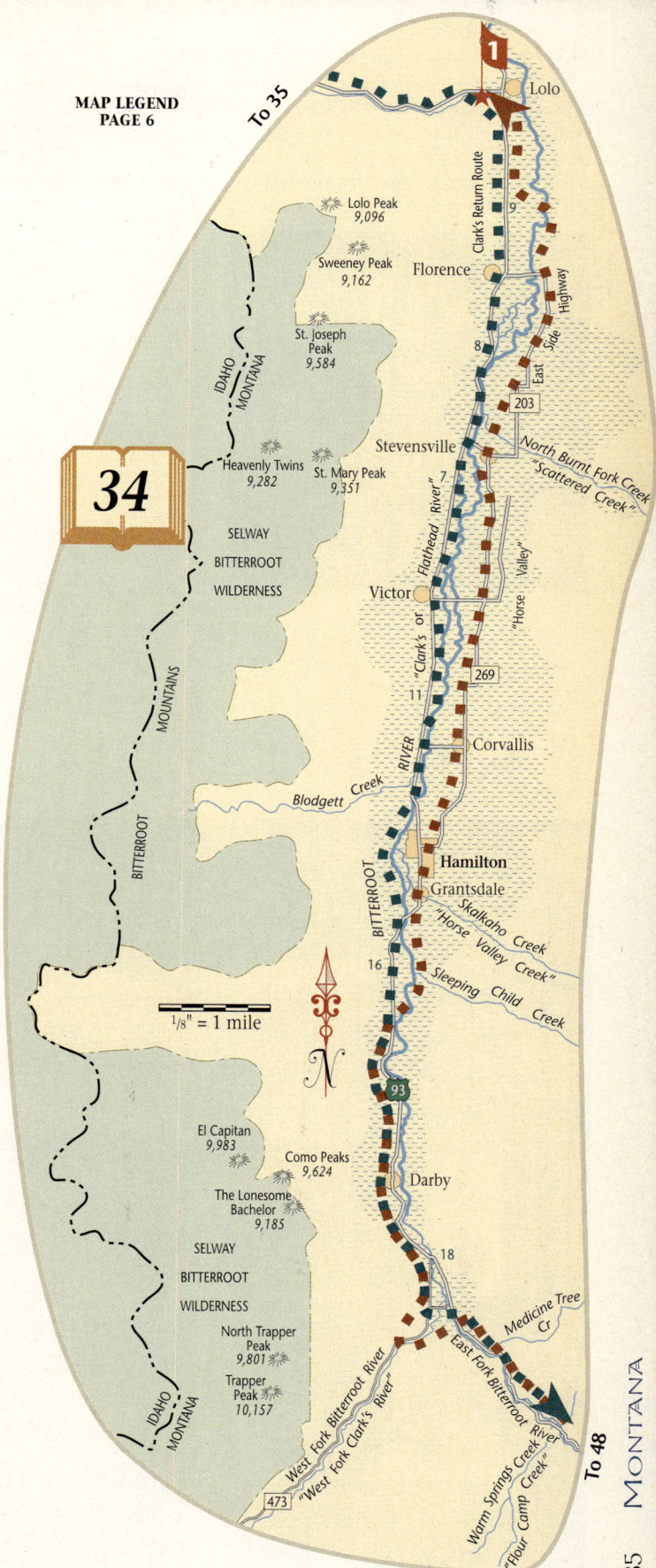

Montana

35 **2** **Lolo Pass**
28 miles W on US 12; 406-942-3113

Nez Perce guide Toby led the Corps to this 5,260-foot pass along a Nez Perce ("nez purse") Indian trail through thick woods; to Clark the trail was "most intolerable on the sides of the steep Stony Mountains." Visitor center is open summers only and has exhibits on the Corps' crossing of the Bitterroot Range.

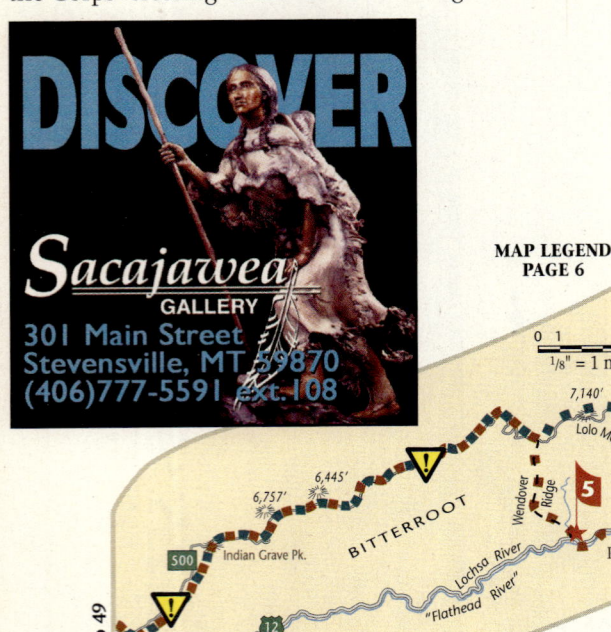

DRIVING THE BITTEROOTS

Follow US 12 into Idaho. This two-lane highway parallels the Lewis and Clark Trail slightly to the south but passes through occasional towns.

Between July 15 and October 1, permits are required to travel the Lolo Motorway (US Forest Service Road 500), which is closer to the trail. A lottery for permits is held in December and January. Entering the lottery costs $6.00 (nonrefundable), and permits are $25 or $55 depending on group size. For information or application packet, see www.fs.fed.us/r1/clearwater or call Lochsa Ranger District in Kooskia, ID, at 208-926-4274.

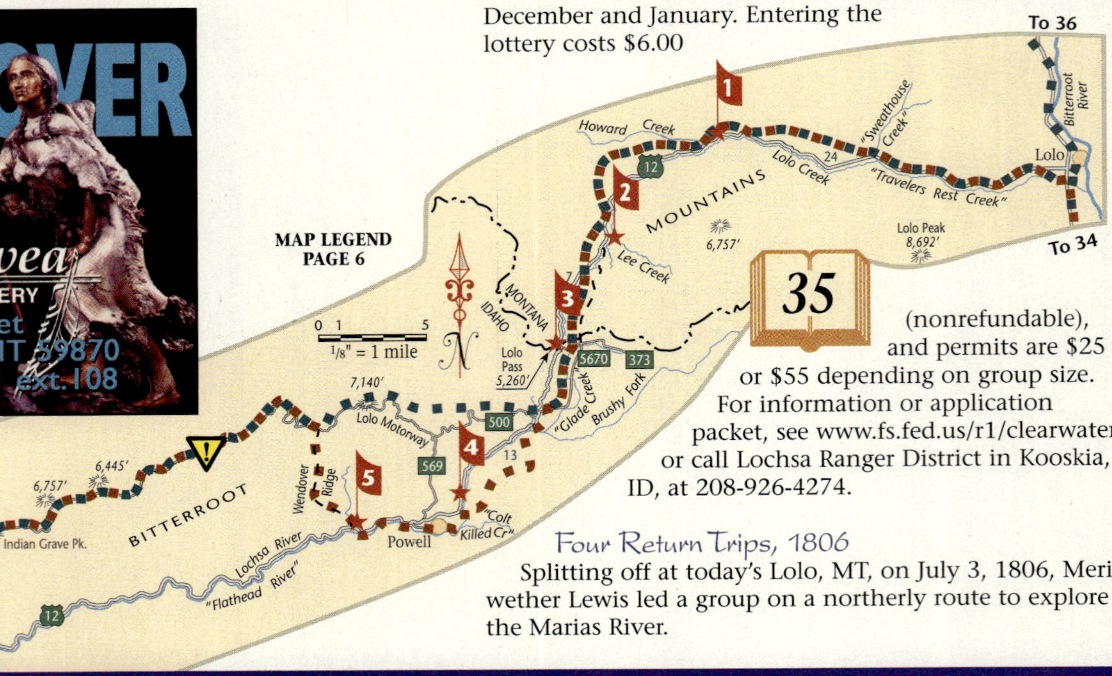

Four Return Trips, 1806

Splitting off at today's Lolo, MT, on July 3, 1806, Meriwether Lewis led a group on a northerly route to explore the Marias River.

DISCOVER Sacajawea GALLERY
301 Main Street
Stevensville, MT 59870
(406) 777-5591 ext. 108

The Lolo Trail Center

Lewis and Clark history comes alive! ON THE TRAIL next to Lolo Hot Springs on Hwy. 12, about 33 miles west-southwest of Missoula, Montana

SALISH & KOOTENAI MUSEUM DISPLAY

- Lodging (1 or 2 queen beds)
- $100,000 Art Display (Bronzes and limited editions)
- Fun for the Kids
- Lewis & Clark Information
- $100,000 in Collectibles ($200,000 by 2006)
- Dinner Theatre (seats 50)

RESERVATIONS: (406) 273-2201
E-MAIL: nhansen@lolotrailcenter.com • WEBSITE: www.lolotrailcenter.com

www.lewisandclark.com

William Clark and the rest went overland to the Missouri headwaters, then split into three parties. Clark's group, which included Sacagawea, went east to the Yellowstone River and explored it downstream to its mouth on the Missouri, in today's North Dakota. Sergeant John Ordway led men in canoes down the Missouri to retrieve supplies cached at the Great Falls, retracing the Corps' route of the previous year. Sergeant Nathaniel Pryor and a couple of men drove the horses overland, intending to go into southern Canada to trade them for supplies. After Indians stole the herd, Pryor's men ended up floating down the Yellowstone River after making two Mandan-style skin boats. They caught up with the Corps in North Dakota.

Lewis's Return, west of Missoula

HUSON

Ninemile Historic Remount Depot
20325 Remount Rd.; 406-626-5201
Visitor center, open from Memorial Day through Labor Day, tells about this site's service as source of pack horses and mules for Forest Service firefighters from the 1920s to 1953, when transportation changed to trucks and airplanes.

Lewis's return: July 4, 1806

MISSOULA 36

On July 3, Meriwether Lewis headed north from Traveler's Rest (Lolo, MT) with six men, five Nez Perce guides, and 17 horses. After pointing the way across the future townsite of Missoula, the Nez Perce left to return home. Lewis would travel overland to the Sun River, which entered the Missouri River just west of the Great Falls. Missoula developed as a lumber and paper-products town spreading out along five river valleys and became home to the University of Montana. U.S. Forest Service Region One offices were located here when the service was founded.

Missoula Convention & Visitors Bureau
825 E. Front St.; P.O. Box 7577-Z
Missoula, MT 59807; 800-526-3465

Missoula County Courthouse
220 W. Broadway; 406-721-5700
Decor includes eight murals of Montana history, including Lewis and Clark Expedition, by Edgar S. Paxson, whose work is also in the Montana Capitol at Helena.

Art Museum of Missoula
335 N. Pattee; 406-728-0447; www.artmissoula.org
Changing exhibitions of contemporary art in three galleries, including focus on Native American artists of Montana. As caretaker of the Edgar S. Paxon Missoula County Courthouse Murals, the museum offers group tours there by reservation.

7/8/06, Lewis: "much rejoiced at finding ourselves in the plains of the Missouri which aboud with game."

7/8/06, Lewis: "...runs a mear torrant tearing up the trees by the roots which stand in it's bottom hense the name we have given it."

7/7/06, Lewis: "saw some sighn of buffaloe early this morning...from which it appears that the buffalo do sometimes penetrate these mountains a few miles."

7/6/06, Lewis: "to our encampment ...through a beautiful plain on the border of which we passed the remains of 32 old lodges."

MAP LEGEND PAGE 6

Journal excerpts courtesy of University of Nebraska Press.

87 MONTANA

Montana

Fort Missoula
Fort Missoula Rd.; 406-728-3476

Permanent and changing exhibits, indoors and out, at a restored 1870s military fort cover area history, including the 1877 Flight of the Nez Perce, who passed nearby while attempting to outrun the army.

Smokejumper Visitor Center and Aerial Fire Depot
US 93 at I-90; 406-329-4934

Base tours (daily, May-September) are led by smokejumpers, who explain the complex training for and dangerous work of parachuting into wildfires.

east of Missoula
CLINTON [36]

About 25 miles east of Missoula on I-90, Clinton is a gateway to U.S. Forest Service and Bureau of Land Management lands in the Sapphire Mountains.

north of Missoula
POLSON

On Flathead Lake and at the foot of the Mission Mountain Wilderness, Polson serves recreationists who enjoy whitewater rafting, waterskiing, lake boat tours, mountain biking, and just plain relaxing.

Polson Chamber of Commerce
P.O. Box 677, Polson, MT 59860; 406-883-5969
www.polsonchamber.com

north of Missoula
SEELEY LAKE

Take MT 200 east and then MT 83 north (a total of about 60 miles) to detour from the expedition's trail and visit this small and friendly mecca for water sports. The town and lake enjoy a mild Pacific Northwest climate on the west side of the Continental Divide.

Lewis's return: July 6, 1806
OVANDO [36]

Following the Cokalahiskit Trail along the Blackfoot River, Lewis came to the mouth of a stream just southwest of future Ovando. He named it "Seaman's Creek" for his big Newfoundland dog, but it's now known as Monture Creek.

Streams and lakes have made Ovando the center for fishing, windsurfing, and birding (including eagles, loons, herons, & pelicans).

Lewis's return: July 7, 1806
LINCOLN [37]

Lewis's party camped on Beaver Creek two miles west of future Lin-

We Stack 'em Deep and Sell 'em Cheap!

NO SALES TAX IN MONTANA!

BRANDS AVAILABLE
Dutch Star • Discovery • Bounder
Kountry Star • Flair • Pace Arrow
Monaco • Southwind • Scottsdale
Dutchmen • Horizon • Itasca
Mountain Aire • Day Break • Alfa
Scottsdale • Intruder • Jamboree

BRETZ RV & MARINE
AMERICA'S RV DEALER OF THE YEAR

Reserve Street Exit at I-90
4800 Grant Creek Road
Missoula, MT
OPEN 7 DAYS A WEEK
www.bretzrv.com

541-4800
1-888 MONT RVS

HISTORICAL MUSEUM AT FORT MISSOULA

- Open year-round
- 13 historic structures
- Over 22,000 objects
- Indoor galleries
- Outdoor interpretive areas
- Located on 32 acres at Historic Fort Missoula
- Accredited by the American Association of Museums

SPECIAL EXHIBIT:
"Following in the Footsteps– Before and After Lewis & Clark"

Memorial Day–Labor Day
Mon-Sat, 10am-5pm; Sun, noon-5pm
Rest of the year, Tues-Sun, noon-5pm

406-728-3476
www.fortmissoulamuseum.org

–Keeping Missoula's History Alive–

www.lewisandclark.com

coln on the night of July 6, and the next morning they passed north of the townsite following the established Indian trail. They went north along Alice Creek and crossed the Continental Divide at today's Lewis and Clark Pass (which Clark never saw).

Lincoln's motels, restaurants, and stores form a welcoming year-round recreation center for camping, guided pack tours, fishing, hunting, and snowmobiling. An annual highlight is the Fourth of July rodeo.

Lewis's return: July 22-27, 1806

CUT BANK 38

Lewis left Sgt. Gass and Pvts. Frazier, Werner, and McNeal at the Great Falls to await Ordway's Missouri River canoe party and assist the portage. He then took Drouillard and brothers Joseph and Reubin Field and six horses northeast until they reached the Marias River. Since the Louisiana Purchase covered all lands drained by the Missouri system, knowing how far north the Marias began was significant.

On July 21, Lewis came to a fork in the Marias and chose the north fork, today's Cut Bank Creek. The next day took them past the future townsite of Cut Bank before the creek turned to the southeast, dashing Lewis's hopes of extending the Purchase into rich Canadian fur country. His camp, in sight of mountains in today's Glacier National Park, he named Camp Disappointment. Bad weather made it impossible for him to take celestial measurements, to determine the precise location, for three days.

On the 26th, a party of eight Pie-

KWATAQNUK RESORT AT FLATHEAD BAY
Best Western

Lewis & Clark originally met the Salish Indians at Travelers Rest South of Missoula where they were grateful to receive strong, healthy and very valuable horses for their journey. In 1855 the Salish Indians were relocated from their original Homelands to what is now the Flathead Indian Reservation North of Missoula on Highway 93.

Come spend time in the land of the Confederated Salish & Kootenai Tribes of the Flathead Indian Reservation where you will find the National Bison Range, The People's Center, Salish Kootenai College and many other Tribal Enterprises including: **Best Western KWATAQNUK Resort.**

- 112 Guest Rooms
- 6,000 Sq. Foot Meeting Space
- Break Out Rooms
- Full Catering/Banquet
- 50 Passenger Cruise Ship
- Boat Rental
- White Water Rafting
- Close to 5 Golf Courses
- AAA & AARP Rates
- Indoor & Outdoor Pool
- Call for Special Packages
- 24 Hour Casino
- Full Serve Restaurant
- Complimentary Fry Bread Served with Lunch & Dinner

Take a stroll along our lakefront waterway or walk through time...with the original caretakers of this land at the People's Center and learn the story of our people from the perspective of our elders, our leaders today and from our youth, who hold in their hands the future of our tribes.

Proudly owned and operated by the Confederated Salish & Kootenai Tribes of the Flathead Indian Nation.
303 US Hwy 93 East • Polson, MT 59860
406-883-3636 or Toll Free 800-882-6363 • www.kwataqnuk.com

See the Trail from the Air

DISCOVERING LEWIS & CLARK FROM THE AIR

Photography by Jim Wark
Text by Joseph A. Mussulman

From Monticello in the east to Fort Clatsop on the Pacific Coast, the wild continent the expedition crossed is revealed anew in breathtaking full-color photographs. Well-researched text accompanies each photo, including quotes from the explorers' journals. The view from above provides new information about the Corps' experience and stirs fresh wonder at their achievement.

264 pages • 9½ x 9½ • 111 color photographs
6 color maps • bibliography • index
paper $24.00 • ISBN 0-87842-489-X • Item No. LCTP 676
cloth $40.00 • ISBN 0-87842-490-3 • Item No. LCTP 677

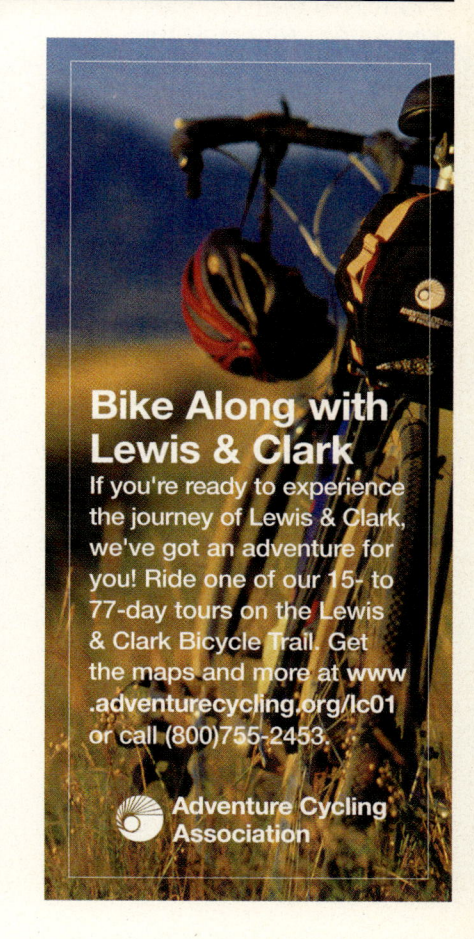

Please include $3.00 shipping and handling per order!

Mountain Press Publishing Company
P.O. Box 2399 • Missoula, MT 59806
406-728-1900 • fax: 406-728-1635
toll free: 1-800-234-5308
email: info@mtnpress.com
web: www.mountain-press.com

Bike Along with Lewis & Clark

If you're ready to experience the journey of Lewis & Clark, we've got an adventure for you! Ride one of our 15- to 77-day tours on the Lewis & Clark Bicycle Trail. Get the maps and more at www.adventurecycling.org/lc01 or call (800)755-2453.

ADVENTURE CYCLING ASSOCIATION

Montana

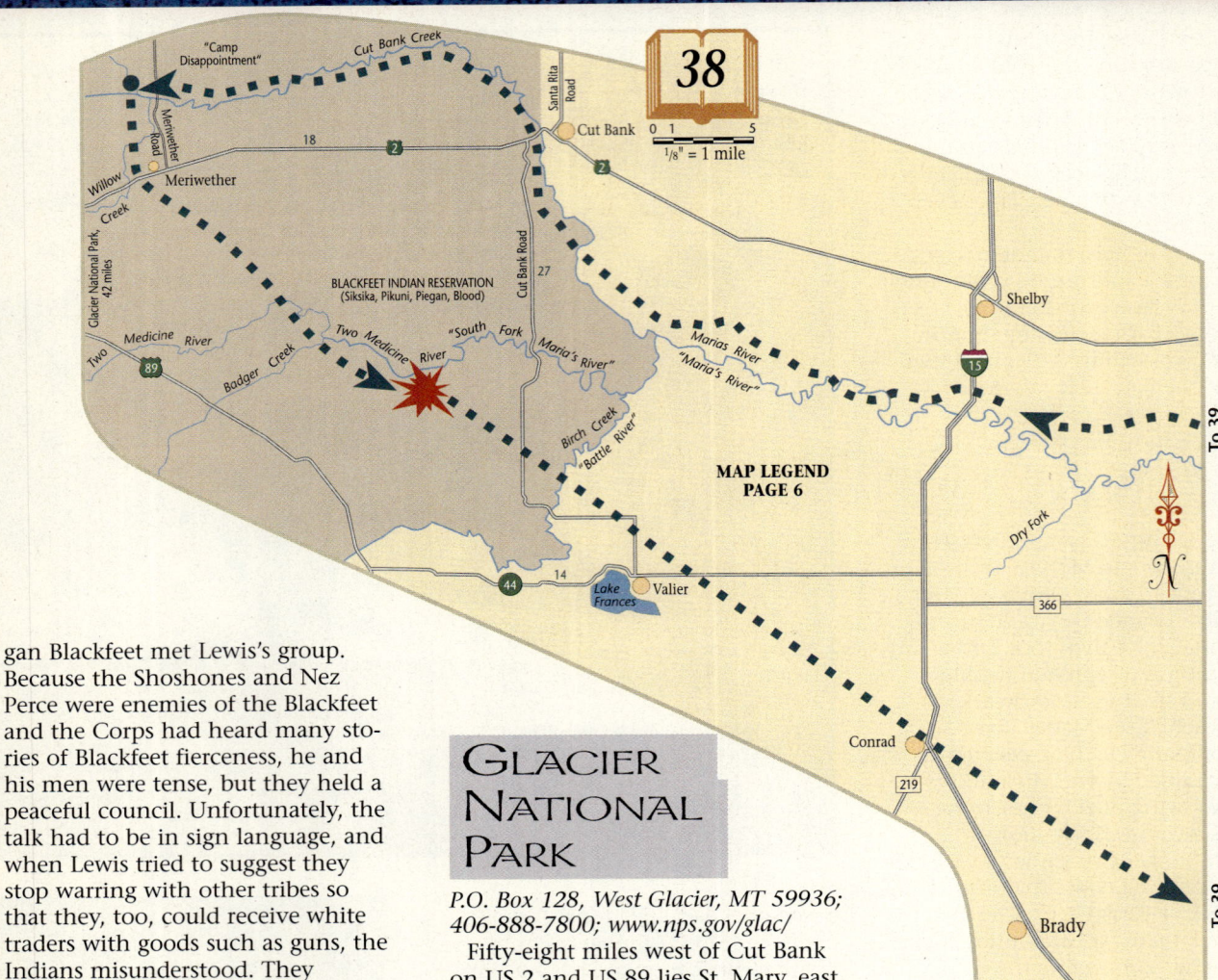

gan Blackfeet met Lewis's group. Because the Shoshones and Nez Perce were enemies of the Blackfeet and the Corps had heard many stories of Blackfeet fierceness, he and his men were tense, but they held a peaceful council. Unfortunately, the talk had to be in sign language, and when Lewis tried to suggest they stop warring with other tribes so that they, too, could receive white traders with goods such as guns, the Indians misunderstood. They thought he said he had allied the Blackfeet's enemies and supplied them with guns. But, when invited, the Blackfeet camped with Lewis's men. Lewis and his men took turns standing guard.

Upon rising, three Blackfeet reached for three of the Corps' guns, and a fight followed, leaving one Blackfeet man dead and another wounded. The others fled, and Lewis was sure they'd return with a war party. His group packed and rode off as quickly as possible.

Frequently hosting the nation's coldest winter days, modern Cut Bank at least has a sense of humor about it: witness the 27-foot-tall talking penguin.

Glacier County Historical Museum
1121 E. Railroad; 406-873-4904
See a restored oil derrick, general store, 1914 schoolhouse, antique farm machinery, arrowheads, dinosaur bones, and railroad displays.

Glacier National Park

P.O. Box 128, West Glacier, MT 59936; 406-888-7800; www.nps.gov/glac/
Fifty-eight miles west of Cut Bank on US 2 and US 89 lies St. Mary, east entrance to this million-acre preserve of glacier-sculpted mountains, 200 lakes, and 50 glaciers. Trail hiking and backpacking are permitted throughout, but the only automobile through-road is Going-to-the-Sun Road, from St. Mary to West Glacier, open in summer except to vehicles over 40 feet long. Campgrounds, historic hotels, guided boat tours on Lake MacDonald.

west of Glacier National Park
Libby
Gateway to man-made Lake Koocanusa, a name created from this Kootenai area of Montana, Canada, and U.S.A.

Lewis's return: July 27, 1806
Conrad 38

Lewis and his men galloped across the prairie just south of here. Having fled Cut Bank Creek in the early morning, they rode until 3:00, stopping then for an hour and a half of rest. They rode 17 more miles, rested two hours and killed a bison for food, then rode 20 more miles by moonlight, stopping at 2 in the morning. Even thought exhausted and sore, Lewis awakened the men at dawn on the 28th to get moving again.

www.lewisandclark.com

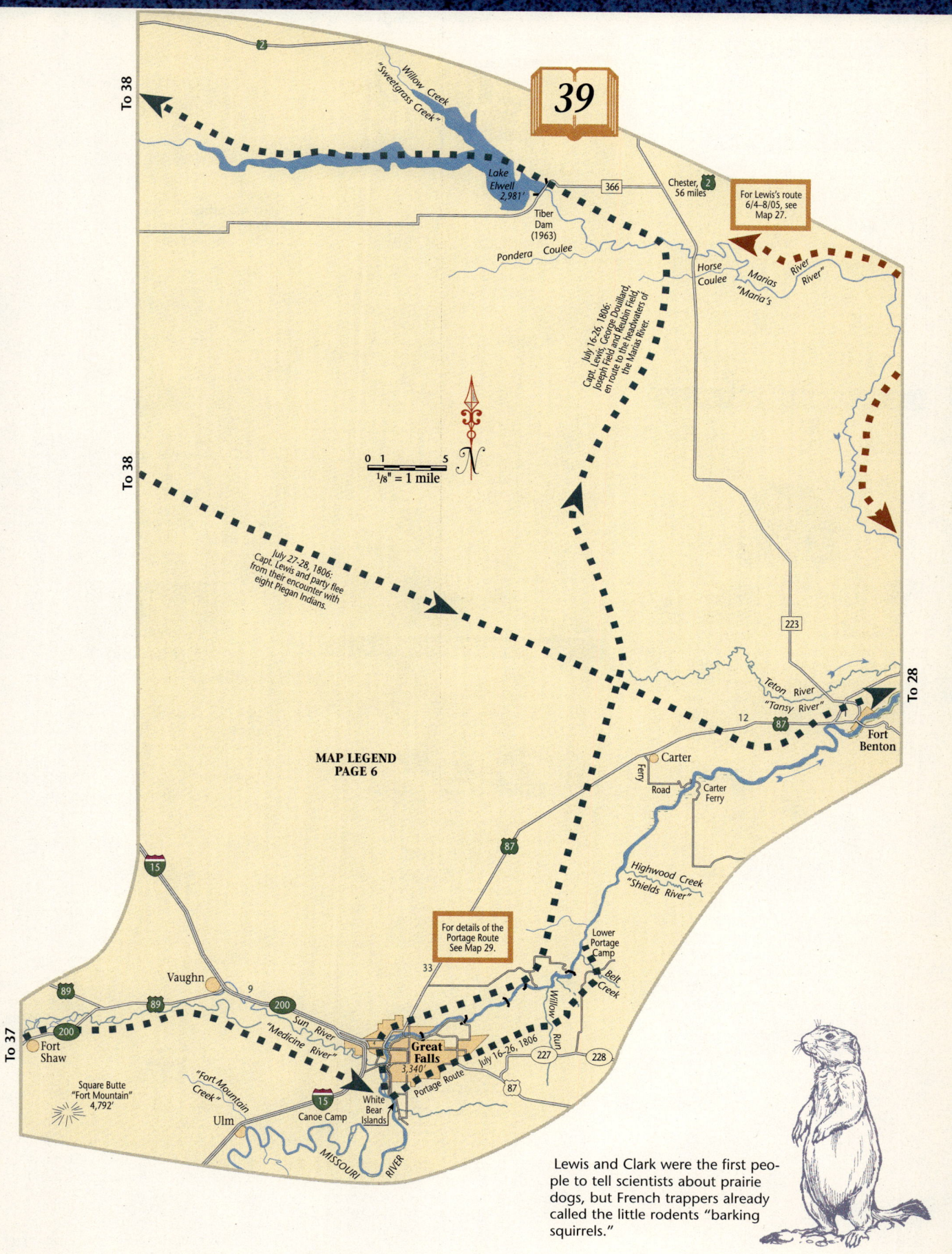

Lewis and Clark were the first people to tell scientists about prairie dogs, but French trappers already called the little rodents "barking squirrels."

91 MONTANA

MONTANA DINING ALONG THE LEWIS & CLARK TRAIL

A SPECIAL ADVERTISING SECTION

CUSTER COUNTRY

GUADALAJARA

GUADALAJARA FAMILY MEXICAN RESTAURANTS
17 N. 29th St. • (406) 259-8930
444 South 24th St. W. • (406) 652-5156
1341 Main (Heights) • (406) 245-2151
Billings, MT 59101

The best authentic Mexican food! Open seven days a week. Daily luncheon and dinner specials. Banquet facilities, orders to go.

GLACIER COUNTRY

The Bridge
A Neighborhood Bistro

515 South Higgins Ave • Missoula, MT 59801
(406) 542-0638 • www.bridgebistro.com

L&C specialties, seasonal offerings: elk, buffalo, venison, trout, salmon, wild mushrooms & berries, etc... Truly a Missoula "Find." Same owners, David & Shirley, 32 years. Just across the Higgins Bridge from historic downtwon in an old "Dime-A-Dance" hall. Beer & wine. Reservations & credit cards gladly accepted.
Open every day at 5 P.M.

JAKER'S
STEAK RIBS FISH PASTA

3515 Brooks St • Missoula, Mt 59801
(406) 721-1312 • www.jakers.com

Jaker's features absolutely the best choice and prime graded steaks and prime rib. We also feature seafood, BBQ ribs, pasta and Stone-fired pizza. We have menus for both kids and seniors. Reservations accepted but never required and the dress is casual.
Lunch M-F, dinner daily.

Lost Horse Creek Lodge

Gourmet Dining in a Mountain Forest Setting
"Carolyn's"
1000 Lost Horse Rd • Hamilton, MT 59840
(406) 363-1460
www.losthorsecreeklodge.com

The best Prime Rib in Ravalli County—also featuring charbroiled steak, pork tenderloin, buffalo, pork chops, fresh pasta, and seafood menu. Fresh baked rolls and buns, fresh fruit, vegetables and desserts. Full service bar and casino. Now open for Lunch and Dinner 7 days a week. Just 8 miles South of Hamilton on Hwy 93 and 3.8 miles West.

Two Sisters OF MONTANA

127 W. Alder • Missoula MT 59802
(406) 327-8438
Hwy 89 • Babb, MT 59411 • (406) 732-5535
napigirl2@hotmail.com

Come and dine with the Sisters! Experience the Best of Montana with fabulous handmade cuisine at either location: near Babb outside Glacier National Park, or downtown Missoula.

GOLD WEST COUNTRY

7 Gables Resort
at Georgetown Lake

Montana 1 • Georgetown Lake
Anaconda, MT 59711 • (406) 563-5052
www.sevengablesmontana.com

Enjoy all the fun, recreation, and relaxation that's offered high in the Pintler Mountains. Great accommodations and fantastic restaurant! Southwest Montana's favorite year-round playground at scenic Georgetown Lake.

Bert & Ernie's
SALOON and EATERY

361 N. Last Chance Gulch
Helena, MT 59601 • (406) 443-5680
www.bertanderniesofhelena.com

Fine dining—lunch and dinner. Steaks, seafood, burgers, subs, salads, pizzas, kids menu. Imported, microbrews, fine wines, best service and atmosphere in town! Catering, take-out. Large groups welcome.

Brewhouse Pub & Grille

939½ Getchell • Helena, MT 59601
(406) 457-9390

Great lunches & extensive dinner menu—featuring steaks, seafood, & pasta. Wide hand-crafted beer & wine selection. Enjoy our non-smoking atmosphere.
Open 11:00 A.M. daily.

The Grasshopper Inn

P.O. Box 460511 • Polaris, MT 59746
(406) 834-3456 • www.grasshopperinn.com

The Inn is located in southwestern Montana in the spectacular Grasshopper Valley. It is 40 miles west of Dillon & 35 miles south of Wise River on the Pioneer Mountain Scenic Byway. There is a Motel, Lounge, Restaurant, & RV Park. Hot Springs are nearby.

Holiday Inn EXPRESS

701 Washington St • Helena, MT 59601
(406) 449-4000

Offering convenient, spacious and affordable lodging in Helena's Capital City. 100% non-smoking guest rooms & suites with complimentary breakfast bar, business & fitness centers, meeting space, and high speed internet access.

Joe's Pasty Shop

1641 Grand Avenue • Butte, MT 59701
(406) 723-9071

Since 1947, the traditional Cornish pasty has been standard fare at Joe's. The miners, reaching for one in their lunchbox, fondly referred to them as "a letter from 'ome."

Montana City Grill & Saloon

Montana City Exit on I-15
Montana City, MT 59634
(406) 449-8890 • www.montanacitygrill.com

Voted Helena's Best Prime Rib, Seafood & Steaks! Huckleberry BBQ pork ribs, seafood, and nightly homemade specials. Dinner daily at 4:00 P.M., and breakfast lunch and dinner on Sunday. The "Saloon" features a full bar and comfortable casino, all smoke-free. Just four miles south of Helena.

Montana Dining Along the Lewis & Clark Trail

A SPECIAL ADVERTISING SECTION

The Stonehouse Restaurant

120 Reeder's Alley • Helena, MT 59601
(406) 449-2552 • www.stonehousehelena.com

Experience exquisite cusine set in historic 1890's Reeder's Alley. Enjoy elegant dining in our Garden & Vineyard rooms or relax in our lounge with your favorite beverages & sandwiches.

Uptown Cafe

47 East Broadway • Butte, MT 59701
(406) 723-4735 • www.uptowncafe.com

Unique dishes are the rule at this surprising spot in Butte. Convenient cafe lunches weekdays; fine dining and early dining specials every night with French, Italian, Cajun, and other specialties.
Full bar. AAA 3 Diamond rating.

Russell Country

3D International Restaurant & Lounge

1825 Smelter Avenue • Black Eagle, MT 59414
(406) 453-6561

Family-owned and operated since 1946, Italian, steaks, prime rib, seafood, Cantonese, Szechuan, Thai, and Mongolian grill in unique Art Deco surroundings. Lunch and dinner. Major credit cards accepted.

Union Grille Restaurant

1 Grand Union Square • Fort Benton, MT 59442 • 1-888-838-1882 • (406) 622-1882
www.grandunionhotel.com

Enjoy our historic ambiance, exquisite cuisine, and superb service at the Union Grille restaurant overlooking the Wild & Scenic Missouri river. Specializing in gourmet western cuisine. Our extensive wine list will delight the novice to the connoisseur. Reservations suggested.

Jaker's Steak Ribs Fish Pasta

1500 10th Ave. S. • Great Falls, MT 59405
(406) 727-1033 • www.jakers.com

Jaker's features absolutely the best choice and prime graded steaks and prime rib. We also feature seafood, BBQ ribs and pasta. We have menus for both kids and seniors. Reservations accepted but never required and the dress is casual. Lunch M-F, dinner daily.

Penny's Gourmet To Go

815 Central Ave • Great Falls, MT 59401
(406) 453-7070
Mon.-Fri. 10 a.m. - 4 p.m.
Closed Sat. & Sun.

Fresh, healthy gourmet food to take out or eat-in. Soups, salads, sandwiches, daily dinner specials, great desserts and many vegetarian delights. Espresso. Juice Bar. Catering. We invite you to come in & enjoy our delicious "made from scratch" food.

Willow Creek Steak House

1700 Fox Farm Rd • Great Falls, MT 59404
(housed inside the Best Western Heritage Inn)
(406) 761-1900
www.bestwestern.com/prop_227029

The Willow Creek Steak House serves breakfast, lunch and dinner, featuring Certified Black Angus Beef, poultry, and pasta. Our certified chef guarantees that your experience here will be delicious!

Yellowstone Country

Bennigan's Grill & Tavern

1320 North 19th Ave. • Exit 305 I-90
Bozeman, MT 59718 • (406) 586-2332

Casual Family dining featuring American fare in a friendly, smoke-free, Irish Tavern atmosphere. Full bar, burgers, steaks, seafood, sandwiches, salads, and fantastic BBQ ribs. Lunch and dinner, 7 days/week.

M-C mint bar & cafe

A ROADHOUSE IN THE MONTANA TRADITION SINCE 1904
27 East Main • Belgrade, MT 59714
(406) 388-1100

Fresh seafood, hand-cut steaks, hand-crafted cocktails, and daily specials. Lunch 11:30 a.m.—3:00 p.m. Monday-Friday. Dinner 5:00 p.m.—10:00 p.m. Reservations accepted.

Sir Scott's Oasis

204 West Main • Manhattan, MT 59741
(406) 284-6929

Your favorite dining choice in the Gallatin Valley...a full steak and seafood menu including prime rib Wednesday, Friday, Saturday, Sunday. Full-service bar and lounge. Now open for lunch Tuesday–Friday. Open every evening for dinner menu.

The Along the Trail with Lewis and Clark Travel Planner & Guide encourages you to check out these fine restaurants.

See you along the way.℠

Vacations are Wonderful... when you get comfortable with us!

SUPER 8 MOTEL

There's always a Super 8 nearby:

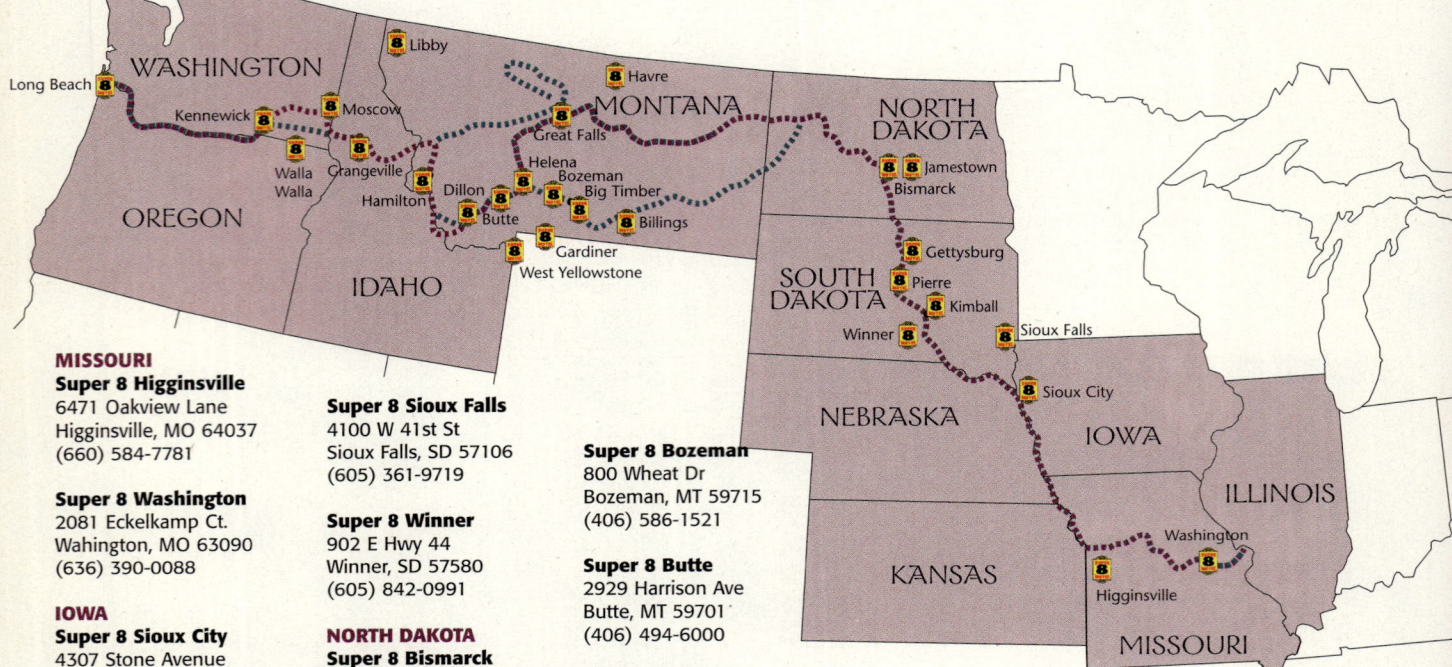

MISSOURI
Super 8 Higginsville
6471 Oakview Lane
Higginsville, MO 64037
(660) 584-7781

Super 8 Washington
2081 Eckelkamp Ct.
Wahington, MO 63090
(636) 390-0088

IOWA
Super 8 Sioux City
4307 Stone Avenue
Sioux City, IA 51106
(712) 274-1520

SOUTH DAKOTA
Super 8 Gettysburg
719 E Highway 212
Gettysburg, SD 57442
(605) 765-2373

Super 8 Kimball
PO Box 310
Intersection Hwy 45 & I-90
Kimball, SD 57355
(605) 778-6088

Super 8 Pierre
320 W Sioux Ave
Pierre, SD 57501
(605) 224-1617

Super 8 Sioux Falls
I-90 EXIT 399
4808 North Cliff Ave
Sioux Falls, SD 57104
(605) 339-9212

Super 8 Sioux Falls
4100 W 41st St
Sioux Falls, SD 57106
(605) 361-9719

Super 8 Winner
902 E Hwy 44
Winner, SD 57580
(605) 842-0991

NORTH DAKOTA
Super 8 Bismarck
1124 East Capitol Ave
Bismarck, ND 58501
(701) 255-1314

Super 8 Jamestown
I-94 & Hwy 281 South
Jamestown, ND 58401
(701) 252-4715

MONTANA
Super 8 Belgrade/Bozeman Airport
6450 Jackrabbit Lane
Belgrade, MT 59714
(406) 388-1493

Super 8 Big Timber
I-90, Exit 367
Big Timber, MT 59011
(406) 932-8888

Super 8 Billings
5400 Southgate Dr
Billings, MT 59102
(406) 248-8842

Super 8 Bozeman
800 Wheat Dr
Bozeman, MT 59715
(406) 586-1521

Super 8 Butte
2929 Harrison Ave
Butte, MT 59701
(406) 494-6000

Super 8 Dillon
550 N Montana
Dillon, MT 59725
(406) 683-4288

Super 8 Gardiner/Yellowstone
Hwy 89 South • Box 739
Gardiner, MT 59030
(406) 848-7401

Super 8 Great Falls
1214 13th St South
Great Falls, MT 59405
(406) 727-7600

Super 8 Hamilton
1325 N. 1st - Hwy 93 N.
Hamilton, MT 59840
(406) 363-2940

Super 8 Havre
1901 Hwy 2 West
Havre, MT 59501
(406) 265-1411

Super 8 Helena
2200 11th Ave
Helena, MT 59601
(406) 443-2450

Super 8 Libby
448 West Hwy 2
Libby, MT 59923
(406) 293-2771

Super 8 West Yellowstone
1545 Hwy 20 South
(Old Targhee Pass Hwy)
W. Yellowstone, MT 59758
(406) 646-9584

IDAHO
Super 8 Grangeville
801 West South 1st St
Grangeville, ID 83530
(208) 983-1002

Super 8 Moscow
175 Peterson Drive
Moscow, ID 83833
(208) 883-1503

WASHINGTON
Super 8 Kennewick
626 N. Columbia Center Blvd
Kennewick, WA 99336
(509) 736-6888

Super 8 Long Beach
500 Ocean Beach
Long Beach, WA 98631
(888) 478-3297

Super 8 Walla Walla
2315 Eastgate St. North
Walla Walla, WA 99362
(509) 525-8800

For Reservations, Call Superline® 1-800-800-8000 • www.Super8.com

www.lewisandclark.com

Lewis's return: July 28, 1806

With the luck or coincidence usually found in movie scripts, Lewis's party reached the Missouri River just as Ordway's canoe party came into view. Turning the horses loose, the stiff riders jumped into the canoes. Moving quickly downstream, they left Montana on August 7.

CHOTEAU

On the Rocky Mountain Front, where mountains abruptly meet prairie, Choteau offers dinosaur fossils, mountain hiking, wildlife viewing sites, and stream and lake fishing for trout, walleye, and pike.

Old Trail Museum
US 89 & US 2897;
406-466-5332

Exhibits focus on dinosaur fossils from nearby Egg Mountain, which proved that some dinosaurs were hatched in nests tended by their vegetarian parents. The area's gold rush & homesteading eras are covered also.

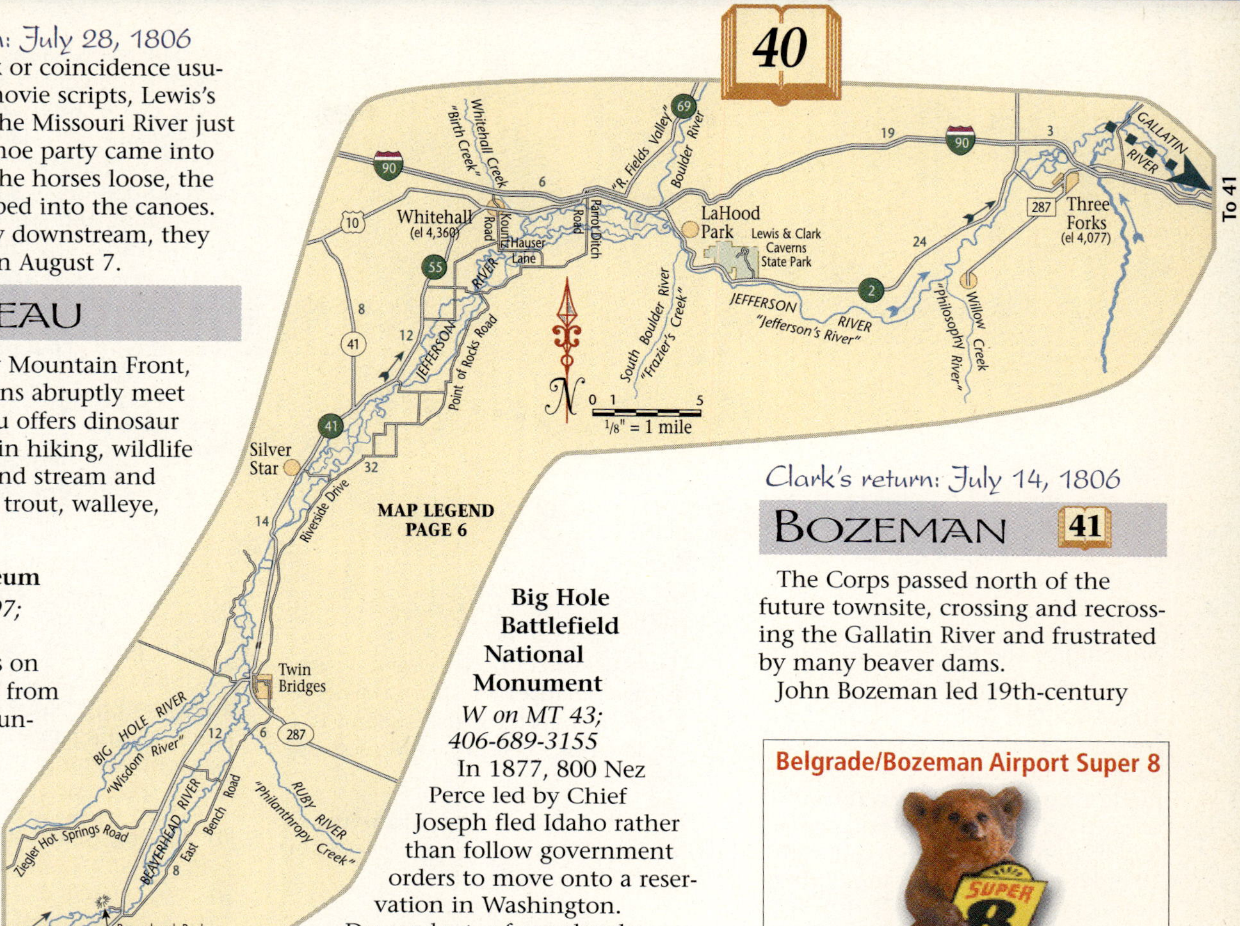

Clark's Return July 6, 1806

WISDOM 33

With a herd of 48 horses, Clark's group traveled south down the Bitterroot Valley then through the Big Hole south of Wisdom. Sacagawea pointed out Big Hole Pass as the way toward Camp Fortunate, where canoes and supplies were cached. In open country, the party suffered a violent wind- and rainstorm but rode five more miles before camping and building fires to dry out.

On the Bighole River, Wisdom is home base for summer and winter outdoor recreation. In 1805, Lewis and Clark had named the river Wisdom for one of President Jefferson's virtues.

Big Hole Battlefield National Monument
W on MT 43;
406-689-3155

In 1877, 800 Nez Perce led by Chief Joseph fled Idaho rather than follow government orders to move onto a reservation in Washington. Descendants of people who aided the Corps were camped here when the U.S. Army attacked; while warriors made a stand, the camp packed and moved out. Visitor center exhibits artifacts and has audiovisual story of the flight; self-guided walking tour of battlefield.

Clark's return: July 14, 1806

BOZEMAN 41

The Corps passed north of the future townsite, crossing and recrossing the Gallatin River and frustrated by many beaver dams.

John Bozeman led 19th-century

Belgrade/Bozeman Airport Super 8
2 MILES FROM AIRPORT
Belgrade, MT • 406-388-1493
www.belgradesuper8.com

STAGE STOP INN
CHOTEAU ■ MONTANA

Lewis & Clark roughed it!
You don't have to!

❖ 43 Classy Rooms
❖ Indoor Pool · Spa
❖ Continental Breakfast

Call Toll Free 1-888-466-5900
www.stagestopinn.com

At the Wild Edge of the Rockies!

Montana

wagon trains to this rich agricultural area and left his name on the town—and the pass that Sacagawea knew. Bozeman is home to Montana State University.

Museum of the Rockies
S. 7th Ave. & Kagy Blvd.
406-994-2251;
www.montana.edu/wwwmor
  Dinosaur remains and life-size models based on Montana fossil discoveries, planetarium, Montana history from Native Americans onward. Living history farm operates during summer.

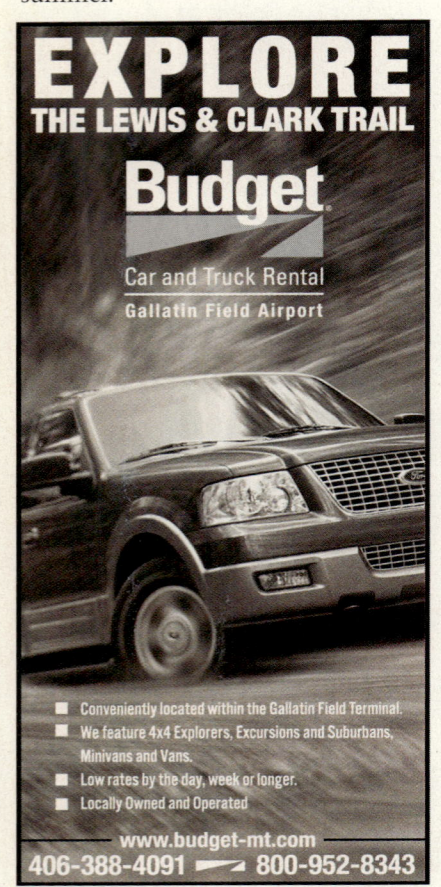

east of Bozeman
BELGRADE 41

Founded in 1882, this small town on the Gallatin River is a gateway to blue-ribbon trout fishing and to public lands for year-round recreation.

Belgrade Chamber of Commerce
P.O. Box 1126, 10 East Main, Belgrade, MT 59714; 406-388-1616

south of Bozeman
GALLATIN CANYON

The Gallatin River, which Lewis and Clark named for President Jefferson's secretary of the treasury, Albert Gallatin, flows at the bottom of this beautiful mountain-sided canyon. Blue-ribbon trout fishing, camping, winter skiing, and resorts both modest and deluxe are available today.

Clark's return: July 15, 1806
LIVINGSTON 41

Following Sacagawea's guidance, Clark's party crossed the pass later named for John Bozeman, which I-90 crosses today. They reached the Yellowstone River at 2 in the afternoon after seeing several 100- to 200-animal "gangs of elk" and "great numbers" of pronghorn. Passing the mouth of the Shields River on the Yellowstone, Clark named it for their valued gunsmith and carpenter John Shields; this is among the expedition names that stuck.
  During the golden age of rail travel, Livingston was the Northern Pacific Railway's "Gateway to Yellowstone National Park" (a change of trains and 90 miles south). Today it's a fly-fishing and arts mecca at the head of Paradise Valley.

Depot Center Museum
200 W. Park St.;
406-222-2300
  Permanent and changing art and history exhibits in the restored 1902 Northern Pacific depot.

Yellowstone Gateway Museum of Park County
118 W. Chinook St.;
406-222-3406
  Exhibits on Native Americans, homesteading, Northern Pacific Railway (including a caboose), and Yellowstone National Park (with a tourist stagecoach).

Fly Fishing Discovery Center
I-90, Exit 337; Corner of B & Lewis Sts.
406-222-9369
  The museum of the International Federation of Fly Fishers now includes a U.S. Park Service–certified exhibit on fishing and the Lewis and Clark Expedition: methods, fish species, Indian and expedition uses of fish.

south of Livingston
EMIGRANT

Twenty-two miles south of Livingston via US 89 and along the Yellowstone River, Emigrant wasn't on the direct path of Clark's group, so they missed its hot springs. Looking off in that direction, though, Clark noted "immense herds of elk."

south of Emigrant
GARDINER

On US 89 and the Yellowstone River also is the north entrance to Yellowstone National Park. Though the Corps of Discovery didn't visit here, Pvt. John Colter soon did. Begging an early discharge from the army in August 1806, Colter returned up the Missouri to trap and

---

EXPLORE THE LEWIS & CLARK TRAIL

Budget
Car and Truck Rental
Gallatin Field Airport

- Conveniently located within the Gallatin Field Terminal.
- We feature 4x4 Explorers, Excursions and Suburbans, Minivans and Vans.
- Low rates by the day, week or longer.
- Locally Owned and Operated

www.budget-mt.com
406-388-4091   800-952-8343

www.lewisandclark.com

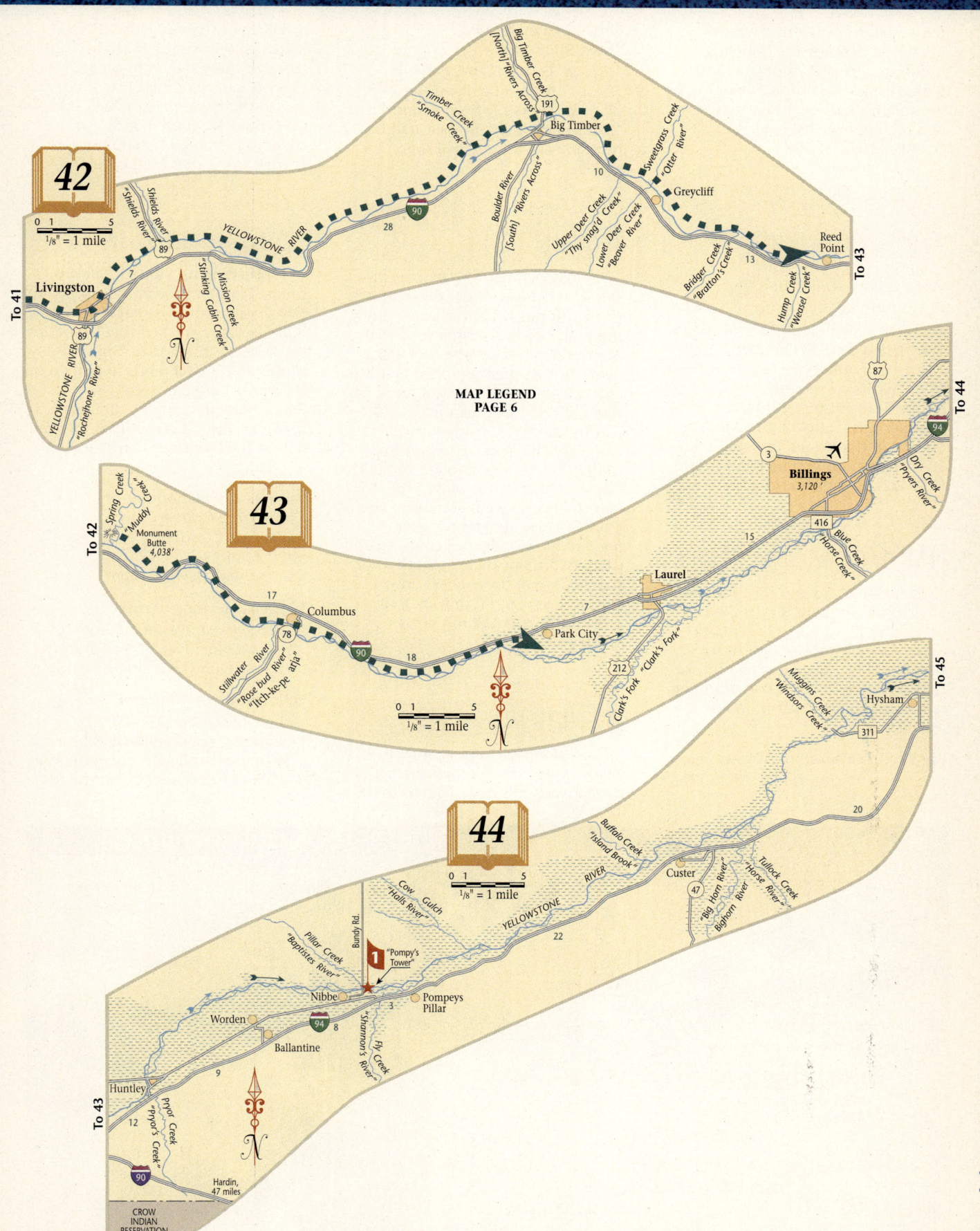

MAP LEGEND
PAGE 6

MONTANA

97

Montana

trade furs. He is the first white known to describe the bubbling mudpots and geysers of the future park. His listeners thought the mountain man was spinning lies and jokingly labeled the area "Colter's Hell."

West Yellowstone 42

West Yellowstone Chamber of Commerce
30 Yellowstone Avenue; P.O. Box 458 West Yellowstone, MT 59758
Lodging and service center just out of the park's west entrance; this center for trout fishing and hiking by summer turns into "Snowmobile Capital of the World" in winter. Pre-1840s mountain men/Indian Burnt Hole Rendezvous occurs in August.

Clark's return: July 17, 1806

Big Timber 43

Clark called the halt for their midday "dinner" where Big Timber Creek and the Boulder River both enter the Yellowstone, but from opposite sides. His party had hit the trail early this day, after an all-night rain made for an uncomfortable night's rest.

Big Timber Chamber of Commerce
P.O. Box 1012, Big Timber, MT 59011; 406-932-5131

Greycliff Prairie Dog Town State Park
I-90 exit 377; 406-247-2940
East of Big Timber is this great place to observe & learn about the "barking squirrels" in their natural habitat, with interpretive signs added.

Clark's return: July 19-24, 1806

Park City 43

The day before, Pvt. George Gibson suffered one of the expedition's worst injuries when his horse threw him and he landed on a snag that pierced two inches into his thigh. Even though the men piled blankets and skins on their gentlest horse so that Gibson could lean back, riding was torture. They camped south of Park City the next day when they found timber large enough to build canoes. On the morning of the 21st, half the horses were gone, and the tracks looked like they'd been herded off. Two canoes completed, Clark had them lashed together for stability when they set off downstream. Sergeant Pryor took four men and the remaining horses overland.

Clark's return: July 24, 1806

Laurel 43

Clark stopped the party on an island where the Yellowstone narrowed (east of today's Laurel) to await Pryor's group, ferry the men across, and drive the horse herd through the water. That accomplished, non-swimmer Pvt. Hugh Hall joined the horse party, which Pryor said could use more hands because these were trained buffalo hunters & tried to go after each herd met.

Clark's return: July 24, 1806

Billings 43

"Proceeding on" for a total of 69 miles, Clark's canoe party camped on Dry Creek at the east edge of today's Billings. They ate well that night, for the area was filled with "immense number[s] of deer, elk and buffalo on the banks. Some beaver."
Montana's largest city, Billings is a financial and oil center that was laid out by the Northern Pacific Railroad in 1882.

Billings Area Chamber of Commerce Convention & Visitors Council
800-735-2635; www.billingscvb.visitmt.com

Western Heritage Center
2822 Montana Ave.; 406-256-6809
Yellowstone River history and culture are themes of changing exhibits.

Yellowstone Art Musem
401 N. 27 St.; 406-256-6804
Changing regional artist exhibits & a permanent collection of contemporary Western art are here in the former county jail.

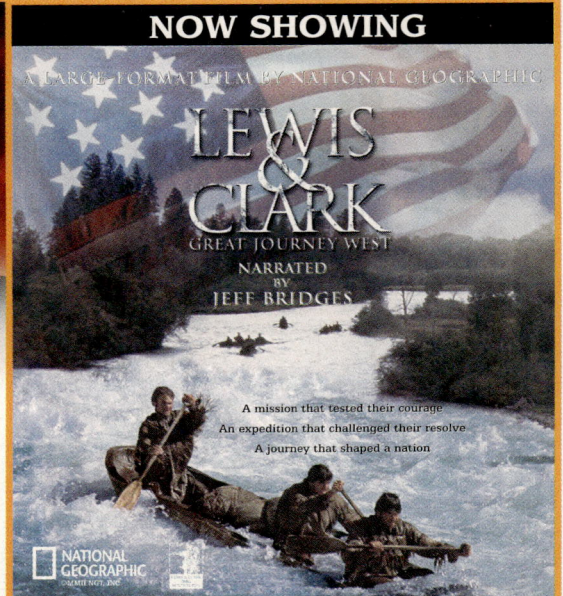

We can take you places you've only dreamed of!

YELLOWSTONE IMAX THEATRE

Experience IMAX®, the largest motion picture system in the world.

Everything Else is Just a Movie

Call for Shows and Showtimes
406-646-4100
Open Year Round
101 S. Canyon ▪ West Yellowstone, MT 59758
888-854-5862 toll free
Next to the West Entrance of Yellowstone National Park
Schedule subject to change without notice, please call for confirmation.

NOW SHOWING

A LARGE FORMAT FILM BY NATIONAL GEOGRAPHIC

LEWIS & CLARK
GREAT JOURNEY WEST
NARRATED BY JEFF BRIDGES

A mission that tested their courage
An expedition that challenged their resolve
A journey that shaped a nation

www.lewisandclark.com

Pryor's return: July 24, 1806

HARDIN

Sergeant Pryor, with Pvts. Hall, Shannon, and Windsor, camped on Fly Creek (which Clark had named Shannon's Creek). They were driving most of the horse herd toward the Mandan-Hidatsa villages, then into Canada, to trade for supplies. During the night, though, Crow Indians took the horses and left the men afoot. Horse taking was a Plains Indian war skill, and this was the Crow's home country. Pryor and his men walked north to the Yellowstone River, where they made two bullboats in the Mandan style: bowl-shaped bent-willow frames covered with bison hide. They caught up with Clark's return party on August 8 at Tobacco Creek in future North Dakota.

Big Horn County Historical Museum
RR 1, Box 1206A; 406-665-1671
www.museumonthebighorn.org

Demonstrations and living history enrich tours of 20 buildings moved here from around the area, including

---

Countryside Photography

Original Photos of Montana

Follow Lewis & Clark through Montana. See the Rivers, Mountains, Buffalo, Bear, Elk, and Wildflowers much as they saw them. You can enjoy all of this with our Notecards, Prints and Other Products

406-628-8613 • Fax: 406-628-2335
P.O. Box 235, Laurel, MT 59044
E-mail: countryside@twoalpha.net
www.countrysidephotogallery.com

Thomas Haukaas, *Lakota Special Boy Shirt*, 2002

Lewis & Clark Territory
Race, Place, and Memory
July 2, 2004 - November 7, 2004

Kevin Red Star
June 18, 2004 - January 16, 2005

A Western Icon
The Art & Stories of Will James

YELLOWSTONE ART MUSEUM

401 N. 27th Billings, MT 406-256-6804
http://yellowstone.artmuseum.org

EMBRACE THE LEGACY

Recapture the dramatic events of America's greatest quest with Lewis & Clark Designs' collector series of original illustrations. Entitled *"Legends of Discovery"*, each of six 15.5" x 30" unframed prints is reproduced on high quality watercolor paper recounting the expedition's voyage throughout Montana and its rivers.

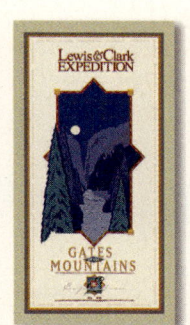

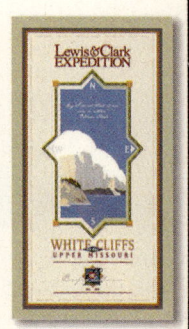

For those who share a passion for art and history, the Legends of Discovery Series provides striking artwork gracing your home and enriching the soul as a lasting keepsake. Created as a colorful tribute to the spirit that shaped our land, we invite you to relive the journey. *Visit www.lewisandclarkdesigns.com today.*

Legends of Discovery Series: $129.95
Individual Prints: $28.95

Order Now! 1-866-248-7117

2004•2006

Montana

a 1911 farmhouse, cabin of army scout Thomas LaForge, barn and blacksmith shop with early gas-powered farm machinery, Fly Inn café and gas station (1937-1958), completely stocked 1918 general store and post office, replica stage station from Fort Custer cavalry post (1877-1898), Christ Evangelical Lutheran Church (1917), Campbell Farming Corporation cookhouse, a bunk house, shower house and commissary from a massive 1923 wheat farm, school, doctors' office.

Clark's return: July 25, 1806

Pompeys Pillar National Historic Monument
I-94 exit 23; 406-875-2233

"At 4 P M arrived at a remarkable rock…which I shall call Pompy's Tower," Clark wrote. He had nicknamed Jean Baptiste Charbonneau (now a year and a half old) "Pompy." The first editor of the expedition journals changed "tower" to "pillar." On the 200-foot-tall sandstone tower, Clark carved his own name & the date—the only surviving physical sign of the expedition's path.

The park has a picnic area and visitor center and offers living history and other programs. Stairs lead to Clark's signature.

Clark's return: July 27, 1806

HYSHAM

Clark wrote (probably with relief), "I take my leave of the view of the tremendous chain of Rocky Mountains white with snow, in view of which I have been since the 1st of May last." The Yellowstone was wide and fast, and the party made an astonishing 80.5 miles this day.

Treasure County 89ers Museum
Highway 311; 406-342-5452

Tells of the hardships and rewards of early homesteading in the Yellowstone River valley.

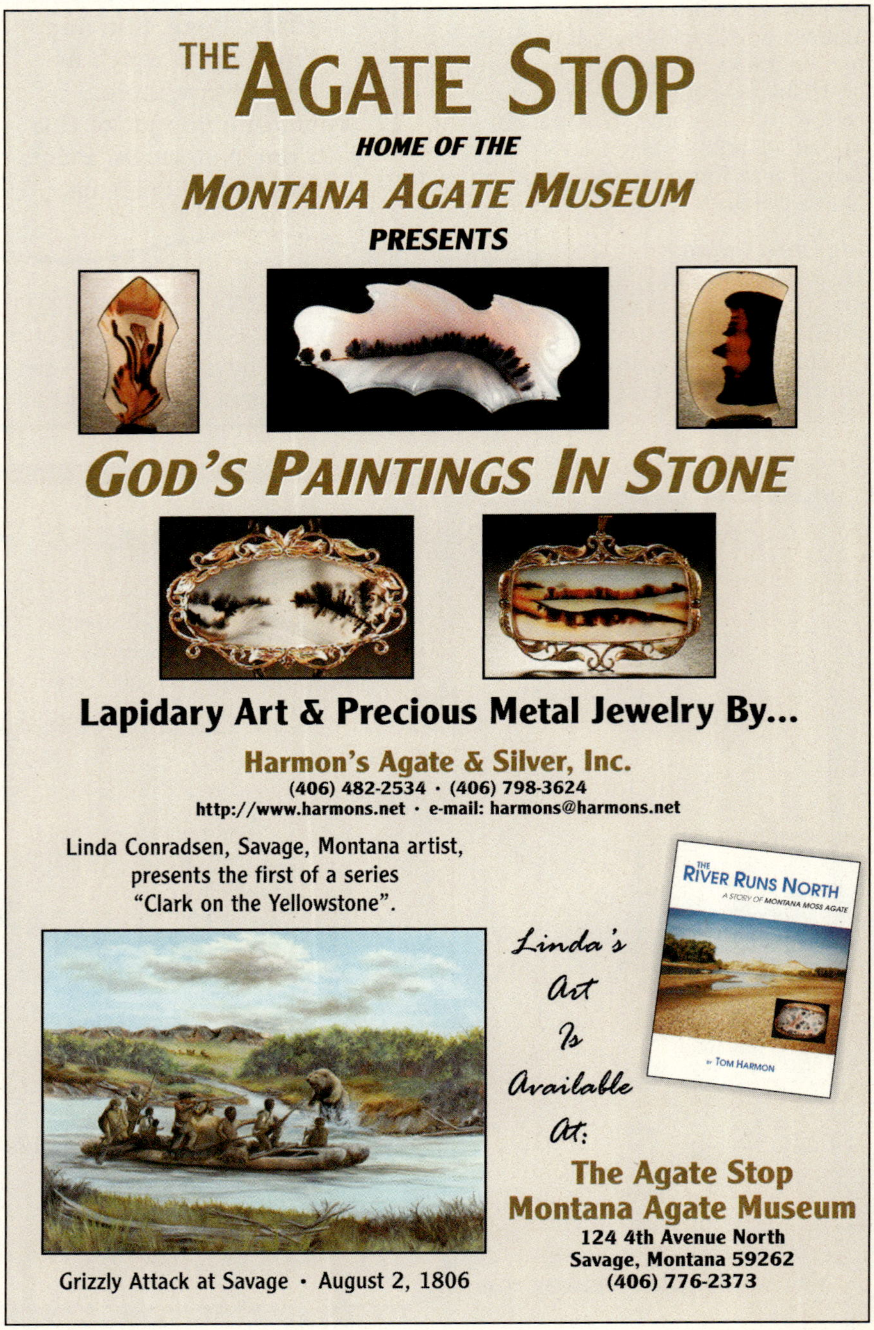

THE AGATE STOP
HOME OF THE MONTANA AGATE MUSEUM
PRESENTS

GOD'S PAINTINGS IN STONE

Lapidary Art & Precious Metal Jewelry By…

Harmon's Agate & Silver, Inc.
(406) 482-2534 • (406) 798-3624
http://www.harmons.net • e-mail: harmons@harmons.net

Linda Conradsen, Savage, Montana artist, presents the first of a series "Clark on the Yellowstone".

Grizzly Attack at Savage • August 2, 1806

Linda's Art Is Available At:

The Agate Stop Montana Agate Museum
124 4th Avenue North
Savage, Montana 59262
(406) 776-2373

www.lewisandclark.com

Clark's return: July 29, 1806

MILES CITY 46

Beaver were plentiful in the river, and seams of coal showed on the banks and in rugged hills to the east, Clark noted. Camp that night was just north of future Miles City.

The town grew up around Fort Keogh, built here in 1877 in response to Sioux and Cheyenne warfare. Saloons and brothels once lined one side of Main Street, and respectable businesses the other.

Miles City Area Chamber of Commerce
901 Main St., Miles City, MT 59301; 406-232-2890

Range Riders Museum
1 mile W on US10/I-94 Business Loop; 406-232-4483

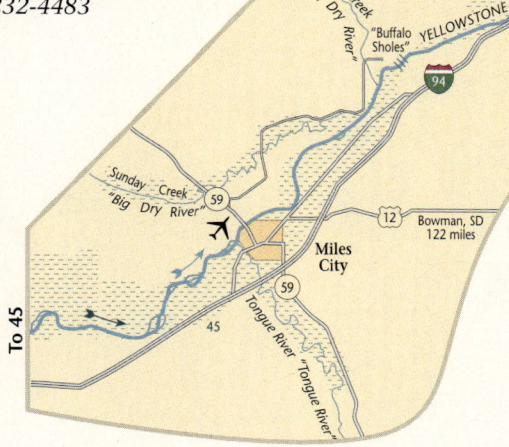

Eight buildings (including Fort Keogh officer quarters) hold a 500-item gun collection, fossils, archaeological finds, and antiques.

Custer County Art Center
Water Plant Rd.; 406-232-0635

Overlooking the Yellowstone River, Montana & Rocky Mountain artwork in changing exhibits.

Clark's return: August 1, 1806

GLENDIVE 47

After passing future Glendive, Captain Clark's party had to stop for half an hour while a herd of buffalo "as thick as they could swim" crossed the Yellowstone near today's Thirteenmile Creek.

Although Clark didn't see them, paddlefish must have lived in the river then as they do now. Seasonal fishing is permitted for these six-foot-long primitive fish with sharklike fins and long flattened noses that look like canoe paddles, and Glendive calls itself the world's Paddlefish Capital. Moss agates and fossils also are plentiful in the area.

Glendive Chamber of Commerce
200 N. Merrill, Glendive, MT 59330
800-859-0824; www.glendivechamber.com

Makoshika State Park
3 miles S; 406-365-6256

Amazing badland rock formations fill Makoshika (muh-coe-sh'cuh), where many dinosaur and other fossils have been found. Visitor center has exhibits and guides to hiking and driving the park. Picnic area, small primitive campground.

Clark's return: August 2, 1806

SAVAGE 47

In the morning, while the boats passed "emence numbers of Elk Buffalow and wolves," a grizzly bear swam at the canoes, possibly smelling meat in them; it was wounded but got away. But it was only the first grizzly of the day! (See below.)

Montana Agate Museum
124 4th Ave. N.; 406-776-2373

Museum, gallery, and shop with interpretation on Clark's Yellowstone River return and exhibits of native Montana agates, lapidary art, and Western art.

SIDNEY 47

In the afternoon, seeing a large grizzly enter the river ahead of them, Clark had the lashed canoes pulled ashore and shot what proved to be an old animal, the largest female grizzly Clark had ever seen. By day's end, Clark's party had left the boundaries of future Montana.

Mon-Dak Heritage Center
120 Third Ave. S.E.; 406-433-3500

Seventeen buildings make up a Montana frontier main street, and other exhibits include dinosaur fossils, an art gallery, and a gun collection. Open daily during summer; Wednesday-Sunday from Labor Day to Memorial Day, but closed in January.

Montana

They Liked It Out There

Several men of the expedition apparently liked the rough living in the Rockies, and at least seven we know of returned—most for the rest of their (short) lives.

John Colter didn't even get home before returning to the mountains. When the Corps met some fur traders heading upriver in August 1806, Colter asked for an early discharge to join them. The captains agreed, and off he went. Two years later, he and John Potts (see below) were trapping on Montana's Jefferson River when they were attacked by Blackfeet. For sport, Colter was stripped of his clothing and moccasins and given a head start to outrun warriors who fully expected to kill him. Running across prairie covered with prickly pear cactus, Colter managed to kill one of the warriors and reach the Madison. He hid in the water under driftwood until dark, then hiked to a fur post at the confluence of the Bighorn and Yellowstone rivers, 200 miles away. What took him 11 days became famous in mountain man lore as "Colter's Run." Colter also was the first white to tell of the amazing sights now in Yellowstone National Park, hot bubbling pots of mud, and springs in rainbow colors, and boiling water spouting into the sky were received merely as tall tales. Mountain men (for a while) referred to the seemingly imaginary locale as "Colter's Hell."

> 8/3/06, Clark: "at 8. A. M. I arived at the Junction of the Rochejhone with the Missouri, and formed my Camp imediately in the point between the two river at which place the party had all encamped the 26th of April —1805."

> 8/2/06, Clark: "about 8 A. M this morning a Bear of the large vicious Species being on a Sand bar raised himself up on his hind feet and looked at us as we passed down near the middle of the river. he plunged into the water and Swam towards us."

> 8/1/06, Clark: "at 2 P. M. I was obliged to land to let the Buffalow Cross over. not withstanding an island of half a mile in width over which this gangue of Buffalo had to pass and the Chanel of the river on each Side nearly 1/4 of a mile in width, this gangue...was entirely across and as thick as they could Swim."

> 8/1/06, Clark: "we had Showers of rain repeetedly all day at the intermition of only a fiew minits between them. My Situation a very disagreeable one. in an open Canoe wet and without a possibility of keeping my Self dry."

> 7/31/06, Clark: "I was much disturbed last night by the noise of the buffalow which were about me. one gang Swam the river near our Camp which alarmed me a little for fear of their Crossing our Canoes and Splitting them to pieces."

Journal excerpts courtesy of University of Nebraska Press.

MAP LEGEND PAGE 6

John Boley of the return party was back in St. Louis in 1805 after a winter at Fort Mandan. The next year, he volunteered for another army expedition west: Zebulon Pike's trip to Colorado.

John Collins trapped for William Ashley's fur company, and was killed by Arikaras in 1823.

George Drouillard, already an Upper Missouri traveler before the Corps hired him, partnered with Manuel Lisa in the Missouri Fur Company, and built a post at the Three Forks of the Missouri, where Blackfeet killed him in 1810.

John Newman trapped on the Missouri, and was killed in 1838 by the Yankton Sioux, who had been friendly to the Corps.

John Potts was back in Montana by 1808, when he was killed in the fight Colter barely survived.

Peter Weiser worked for fur traders Lisa and Drouillard (see above), and may have been killed in 1810 in the raid that got Drouillard.

MONTANA OUTFITTERS AND GUIDES
A SPECIAL ADVERTISING SECTION

Adventure Bound Canoe & Shuttle Co.
Fort Benton, MT
1-877-538-4890 toll-free
www.montanarivertrip.com

Experience the splendor of the Upper Missouri River Breaks National Monument with us, or on your own. Our guided trips offer the best in service, and cuisine. Our livery offers a large selection of quality rental equipment and canoes: Old Town, Wenonah, Mad River, rec. & touring kayaks. Best Quality, Service & Price!

Adventure Yellowstone, Inc.
P.O. Box 746 • Bozeman, MT 59771
(406) 585-9041 phone/fax
www.national-park-tours.com
seemontana@aol.com

- Private, naturalist-guided, grizzly bear and wolf safaris
- Hiking, animal tracking, photography, skiing and more
- Explore inside a bear den
- Custom-designed vacations for families, groups, or individuals
National Park Service/Forest Service License

BRIDGER OUTFITTERS
15100 E. Rocky Mtn. Rd
Belgrade, MT 59714 • (406) 388-4463
www.BridgerOutfitters.com

- On the Lewis & Clark Trail near the Headwaters of the Missouri
- Historic tours of Ghost Towns– gold panning
- Scenic wilderness horse camps
- Day trips or overnight in Wilderness tent camp, tipis or lodge
- Backcountry trail rides or cattle drives
- High Mountain Lake fishing
- River Floats
- 15 minutes from Bozeman

CANOE MONTANA
1312 Front St • PO Box 591
Fort Benton, MT 59442
1-800-500-4538 • (406) 622-5882
www.canoemontana.net

Come have some fun! Canoe or kayak the Lewis & Clark Trail on the Upper Missouri River Breaks Monument. Enjoy guided 1/2 day to 6 day guided tours and guided scenic floats. We also offer canoe and kayak rentals and shuttles.

FLY FISHING DISCOVERY CENTER
Corner of "B" & Lewis
Downtown Livingston, Montana
(406) 222-9369
www.fedflyfishers.org

Fishing with the Lewis & Clark Exhibit

Fishing for food, science and recreation was a significant part of the Lewis & Clark expedition. This is the only fish focused exhibit on the entire Trail and everyone interested in Lewis & Clark should experience this learning opportunity.

GREAT FALLS HISTORIC TROLLEY
315 5th St South
Great Falls, MT 59405
1-888-707-1100 • (406) 771-1100
www.GreatFallsHistoricTrolley.com

Enjoy daily two-hour "Historic" tour aboard climate-controlled fun trolley along L&C Trail. See Waterfalls, Historic Downtown, Railroad District, Museums, Churches, Giant Springs, Historic Home District, Saloons, River's Edge Trail. FUN!!

Hole-in-the-Wall Educational Adventures
117 Park St. • Lewistown, MT 59457
(406) 538-2418
www.hole-in-the-wall.org

Canoe Trips • Shuttle Service
Auto & Bus Tours

We offer services on Montana's Wild & Scenic Missouri River and the C.M.R. National Wildlife Refuge. Whether on the river or by vehicle, we can customize your trip to make it one you will remember for a lifetime.

JAKE'S HORSES & Outfitting
Big Sky, MT • www.jakeshorses.com
Mailing address: 5645 Ramshorn
Gallatin Gateway, MT 59730
1-800-352-5956 • (406) 995-4630

"Once you've been camping with Jake; everything else is less than," says one of our clients. Elk hunts, Yellowstone pack trips, trail rides year-round. Promises to be the highlight of your vacation. Call for a reservation.

Lewis Clark HERITAGE TOURS
Kent Watson, President
P.O. Box 4013 • Missoula, MT 59806
(406) 721-3500 • (406) 541-3541 fax
Kentwla@aol.com

Experience Lewis and Clark sites throughout western Montana with your personal historian/interpreter. Learn about the plants, animals and Native Americans the Expedition "discovered," as well as the local history, cultural features and landmarks. Call for information and reservations.

MISSOURI RIVER CANOE COMPANY
VIRGELLE MONTANA
1-800-426-2926
www.PaddleMontana.com

"Touch the Trail" with us...canoe and kayak trips along the Wild & Scenic Missouri River. Offering historic eco-tours and adventure in our backyard for over 20 years.
- Guided or Unguided River trips
- Historic Accommodations
- Full Outfitting Services

ROCKY MOUNTAIN SCHOOL
1001 Bon Accord Rd
Dillon, MT 59725
(406) 834-3499

Guides • Packers • Horsemen
Now offering "WOMEN WEST"
Education • Vacation • Employment

Learn Natural horsemanship & packing skills in the heart of Lewis & Clark country. Ride into the Ghost town of Bannack, first territorial capitol. Wildest west town ever. Experience the "Montana Frontier" horseback. Day, week, and monthly rates!

UDAP Pepper Power INDUSTRIES
P.O. Box 10808
Bozeman, MT 59719
1-800-232-7941
www.PepperPower.com

Be Prepared in Bear Country! FREE 36 page Bear Safety Tip Booklet with every purchase of PepperPower™ Bear Pepper Sprays. Developed by a grizzly attack survivor, PepperPower™ works on all bear species to deter bears from aggressive attacks.

UPPER MISSOURI RIVER KEELBOAT
1-888-721-7133
www.mrkeelboat.com

Step back in time on Montana's scenic and historic Marias and Missouri Rivers. Travel the watery trails of Lewis and Clark in comfort aboard a historic keelboat or oldtown canoe. 1 to 5 day trips available.

WTR OUTFITTERS
380 Outfitter LAne
Ovando, MT 59854
1-800-987-5666 • (406)793-5666 fax
www.wtroutfitters.com
info@wtroutfitters.com

Come - Explore like Lewis and Clark in the Bob Marshall Wilderness Complex. Make a magical memory with a Summer Pack Trip, Nature Observation Trip or Fall Hunting Trip. Call for more information and reservations.

YELLOWSTONE SAFARI CO
PO Box 42 • Bozeman, MT 59771
1-866-586-1155
(406) 586-1155
www.yellowstonesafari.com

Experience the wildlife and landscape of Lewis and Clark at the Missouri Headwaters and throughout Montana. Family suitable, professionally guided motor vehicle, hiking and river safaris.

Idaho

The Corps of Discovery struggled through very rugged country in Idaho, and much of it remains wilderness today. Following the trail by auto here means keeping close to it, rather than on it, much of the way. Two-laned US 12 runs closest to the route traveled by the Corps; Interstate 90 crosses the panhandle farther north. Choosing to follow the interstate won't prevent you from seeing how rugged the Bitterroot Mountains are as it weaves over passes and along mountainsides.

Colt Killed Creek, Clearwater National Forest. RANDY BEACHAM

Statewide resources on Idaho

Idaho Travel Council
Box 83720, Boise, ID 83720-0093
800-714-3246; www.visitid.org

Idaho Department of Parks and Recreation
P.O. Box 83720, Boise, ID 83720-0065
208-334-4199; www.idahoparks.org

Headquarters, Nez Perce National Historic Park
on US 95 at Spalding; 208-843-2261

southeast of expedition's trail
IDAHO FALLS

Museum of Idaho
200 N. Eastern Ave.; Idaho Falls, ID
208-522-1400; www.museumofidaho.org

"Discovering Idaho: The World of Lewis and Clark" exhibit features more than 300 artifacts from the era, a Shoshone village, the Corps' four boats, plants and animals including a preserved grizzly bear, items on loan from a Clark descendent, and "Discovering the Rivers of Lewis and Clark" film from American Rivers.

Relive the Lewis & Clark Adventure in Idaho...

Visit one of the largest Lewis & Clark exhibits in the nation. Over 10,000 square feet and over 400 items tell the story of
Discovering Idaho: The World of Lewis & Clark
through artifacts, portraits, documents, maps, animals and plants.

FOR INFORMATION REGARDING SHOPPING, DINING, AND LODGING IN IDAHO FALLS CALL
1·866·ENJOY I.F.
(365·6943)

IDAHO www.visitid.org

IDAHO FALLS CONVENTION AND VISITORS BUREAU

MUSEUM of IDAHO

Monday thru Saturday 9 am – 8 pm
Sunday 11 am – 5 pm
1 (208) 522-1400
200 North Eastern Ave., Idaho Falls
www.museumofidaho.org

Coming home... the birthplace of Sacajawea

The Natural Choice on the Lewis & Clark Trail

Salmon, Idaho

Sacajawea Heritage Days— 3rd weekend in August

For information & free brochure contact Salmon Valley Chamber of Commerce 1.800.727.2540 • www.salmonchamber.com

IDAHO www.visitid.org

WE INVITE YOU TO EXPERIENCE A QUALITY LEWIS & CLARK ADVENTURE WITH THESE SALMON BASED OUTFITTERS...

---

100 Acre Wood Bed & Breakfast Resort
Outdoor Adventure......Indoor Pampering

2356 Hwy 93 North
North Fork, ID 83466
(208) 865-2165
www.100acrewoodresort.com

Outdoor adventure, Indoor pampering. Build your own adventure from our list of 20 one-day tours. Includes lodging, dinner, breakfast, lunch and the guide and tour of your choice. Experience all the adventure the Salmon River country has to offer.

BIGHORN OUTFITTERS

11 Tom Boyle Road
Carmen, ID 83462
(208) 756-6963
www.huntidaho.com
dmelton@huntidaho.com

Bighorn Outfitters offers guided full day and half day horseback trail rides in the Lewis & Clark trail systems well as the Bighorn Crags in the Salmon Idaho Area. These trips can also be combined with whitewater float trips.

GEERTSON CREEK TRAILRIDERS

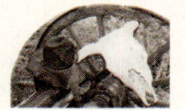

151 Geertson Creek Road
Salmon, ID 83467
(208) 756-2463 • (208) 940-0711
www.geertson.com • val@geertson.com

Geertson Creek Trail Rides is located in the beautiful Salmon, Idaho area, among the Lewis & Clark trails. Our guides and gentle mountain horses are ready to accommodate you and your family or friends. We offer all types of trail rides, ranging from 2 hours around the ranch and cattle, to all day trail rides into the majestic Geertson Lake. Stay at the rustic caBin at the lake, or the cozy homestead cabin on our ranch.

Happy Hollow Guest Ranch & Vacations

1035 Hwy 93 South
Salmon, ID
(208) 756-3954
happyhollowvacation@juno.com

We have been a permanent fixture here on the banks of the Salmon River for over 40 years. For Lewis & Clark enthusiasts we offer:

• Scenic Van Tours
• Trail Rides
• Working Ranch Vacations

IDAHO ADVENTURES
Live the Journey!

1-800-789-WAVE
www.idahoadventures.com

Along the Trail...

• 1/2 day wooden scow float on working historic replica.
• 1-6 day Salmon River Rafting Journeys.
• Mountain Biking Tours.
• Fishing Trips.
• Options for every budget or time constraint.
• Interpretive programs on all trips.
• Serving families since 1973.

KEATING OUTFITTERS

LEWIS AND CLARK ADVENTURES

On the Salmon
"RIVER OF NO RETURN"
at the base of Lost Trail Pass.

We have put together packages to give you several options for following this portion of the Lewis and Clark Trail.

White water rafting & Horseback

(208) 865-2252 or (208) 865-2534
www.LewisandClarkadventures.com

KOOKABURRA RAFTING TRIPS

Salmon, Idaho
1-888-654-4386
www.raft4fun.com
kookaburra@raft4fun.com

• 1-day Float along Clark's reconn. to the "impassible canyon"
• 1-day Whitewater Trip through the "impassible canyon"
• 2- & 3-day Rafting Adventure to, through and beyond...
• 1/2-day Sacajawea Discovery Trip along the Salmon cliffs
• 2-day, 3-night & 4-day, 5-night Raft and Ride packages

Lewis & Clark Interpretive TOURS

RAWHIDE OUTFITTERS
204 Larson St • Salmon, ID 83467
(208) 756-4276
www.rawhideoutfitters.com

Experience the rich historical sites of Lewis & Clark in the Lemhi & Salmon River Valleys. Tours for all ages and adventure levels. Interpretation conducted by knowledgeable L&C enthusiast.

Van Tours • Lemhi Pass
Trail Rides • Wagonhammer Springs
Saddle to Paddle Combination Tours

Idaho

August 12, 1805

Lemhi Pass

33 2 Lemhi Pass National Historic Landmark
from Grant, MT, drive 10 miles W on MT 324, then 2 miles N to a fork. Follow the left fork for 10 miles. Road is closed to vehicles over 40 feet long. Call 208-768-2500 or 406-683-3900 for road conditions.

When Lewis and his advance party stood atop the Continental Divide for the first time, he saw many ranges of mountains ahead—not at all what they hoped for.

August 13, 1805

Tendoy 48 and 33

Here at last the Corps met the Shoshones, the people they hoped would supply horses and help crossing the Continental Divide. Captain Lewis, with Pvts. Shields and McNeal and interpreter Drouillard, traveled ahead of the main group, who were towing canoes upstream on the Montana side. Lewis's group crossed the Divide at 7,372-foot Lemhi Pass. The captain was determined to take as long as a month to find the Shoshones, because without horses the Corps could not reach the Pacific by winter.

On the 11th, Lewis spotted a man he thought Shoshone, riding "an elegant horse." Lewis tried Plains sign language, but the rider galloped away. Two days later, more Indians were seen, but ran off. Then Lewis's group met an elderly woman and two girls. One girl fled, but the others sat down awaiting capture. When Lewis instead gave them gifts, they agreed to take him to their village.

Warned by the first three people Lewis had met, 60 warriors galloped toward them, ready for battle. Lewis put down his gun and walked forward to greet them. Finally, Chief Cameahwait agreed to go back with Lewis to "my brother chief" and "a woman of [your] nation." The Shoshones, ready to leave for their annual bison hunt on the plains, shared what little food they had.

33 3 Lewis and Clark Back Country Byway
Information kiosk near Tendoy Store, 20 miles S of Salmon on ID 28; 208-756-5400

This winding, 39-mile, one-lane, gravel loop road is a summer-only trip, and then not in rainy weather. Allow three to four hours driving time. Interpretive signs, hiking trails, picnic areas, and primitive camping are available.

33 4 Sacajawea Monument
just N; 208-756-4562
Information on her Shoshone homeland.

August 20, 1805

Salmon 48

Salmon Valley Chamber of Commerce
200 Main St., Ste. 1; 800-727-2450

Stop here for free brochures about expedition sites in the area, including one from the Bureau of Land Management and a color map of Lemhi County.

Withington Creek Campsite
10 miles S on ID 28

Near here, Lewis first met with the Shoshones. Clark and 11 men camped here their second night west of the Continental Divide. Today there's an informative turnout near the actual site.

Sacajawea Interpretive, Cultural & Education Center
200 Main St.; 208-756-1188; www.sacajaweacenter.org

Exhibits, amphitheater, and interpretive pathways on 72 acres present the stories of the young interpreter and her Lemhi Shoshone nation.

Lemhi County Historical Society Museum
210 Main St.; 208 756 3342; open June–September

Exhibits include a large collection of Lemhi Shoshone artifacts, the Ray Edwards Asian collection of early Chinese miners and others, and artifacts from early white settlers.

Clark: August 21, 1805

Carmen

Clark took 11 Corpsmen and a few Shoshones downriver to see if it was unnavigable. At the future site of Carmen he named "Sammon Creek," today's Carmen Creek.

Four-season outdoor recreation is the hallmark of Carmen for modern travelers.

Clark: August 22, 1805

North Fork 48

While most of Cameahwait's village crossed the mountains with the Charbonneaus to help the Corps, Clark hired a guide he nicknamed Toby, an abbreviation of one of his names that meant "furnished white man brains."

At future North Fork, Clark's party turned downriver. Within three days they saw that the Indians were right. Clark sent Pvt. Colter back to Camp Fortunate with a note for Lewis that the Salmon was out.

August 23, 1805

Gibbonsville

Clark's reconnaissance party passed west of here looking for a good canoe stream to the Columbia River. They traveled "with great dificuelty" because steep hillsides and plentiful rocks put their horses in the "greatest risque."

Driving the Salmon Scenic Byway now, travelers can view Clark's actual path from US 93. They can also enjoy many kinds of outdoor recreation in Salmon National Forest.

September 13, 1805; return: June 29, 1806

Outward bound, the Corps crossed the Continental Divide via Lolo Pass (see Montana section on this date).

De Voto Memorial Grove of Cedars
US 12, 5 miles W of Powell Ranger Station

The grove and picnic area honor Western historian Bernard De Voto, who stayed here in the 1950s while preparing his one-volume abridgment of the captains' journals.

www.lewisandclark.com

September 14, 1805
return: June 28, 1806

Toby lost the Nez Perce Trail and accidentally led the Corps south to the Lochsa River. Absolutely no game was found, so a colt was killed to provide dinner. The captains named this site Colt Killed Camp.

Powell Ranger Station
11 miles W of Lolo Pass on US 12; 208-942-3113
Exhibit tells of Colt Killed Camp.

DRIVING LOLO PASS 49

US 12 east over Lolo Pass into Montana runs slightly south of the Lewis and Clark Trail. USFS Rd. 500 is closer to the Trail, but you need a 4-wheel-drive vehicle, good weather, water, provisions, and a good map. This route is nearly as wild today as it was for the Corps. Information at 208-476-4541.

September 15, 1805

The expedition climbed a steep mountainside to return to the Nez Perce Trail. Horses fell down the slope, including Clark's. His portable writing desk was smashed.

49 2 Whitehouse Pond
US 12, 16 miles W of Lolo Pass; 208-942-3113
Interpretation of the Corps at a summer-only primitive campground; ATV trails, hiking, fishing.

Triple "O" Outfitters
Experience Idaho the Triple "O" Way

Triple "O" Outfitters were the guides for Ken Burn's television mini-series on Lewis and Clark.

**HUNTING • FISHING • BIKING
SNOWMOBILING • LEWIS & CLARK**

Visit the historic campsites of Lewis & Clark by horseback and van and enjoy the primitive outdoors, all within the care and comfort of experienced outfitters. This trip is an ideal way to experience the outdoors like Lewis & Clark did on their historic journey through America.

Idaho Outfitters and Guide Licensed and Bonded

PH: 208-464-2349 PH: 208.464.2761 FX: 208.464.2238
Harlan & Barb Opdahl, Box 217, Pierce, Idaho 83546

September 20, 1805: return: May 1-24 & June 10-15, 1806

WEIPPE 49

After climbing up and down the Bitterroots in snow (their only source of water) and being "as wet and as cold in every part as I ever was in my life," Clark led a party of hunters down to Weippe (WEE-ipe) Prairie. Nez Perce people were there collecting camas roots and shared those plus fish, berries, and bison with the men. Pvt. Reubin Field and a Nez Perce man took roots and three large salmon back to Lewis and the main party at once. The others reached Weippe Prairie on the 22nd. Returning in 1806, the Corps camped here to prepare for their Rockies crossing. Against advice of the Nez Perce, they tried to cross too early, met deep snows, and returned to wait at Weippe before the second, successful, try.

49 1 Weippe Prairie/Nez Perce National Historical Park
E of Greer on ID 11 (Park headquarters at Spalding, ID, on US 12 at US 95; 208-843-2261); www.nps.gov/nepe
Interpretive signs on the economic and cultural importance of the Nez Perce annual gatherings here, and on their meeting with Clark's party.

north of Weippe

PIERCE

In the heart of Idaho's gold rush and logging country, Pierce is a center for fishing, hunting, and photography. The Bradbury Logging Museum exhibits the gear of that bygone era.

September 26-October 5, 1805

OROFINO

After following the Clearwater downstream to good timber, the Corps set up "Canoe Camp" to make canoes for the trip west. Many were ill from near-fasting and the abrupt change from red meat to fish and roots. The Nez Perce agreed to care for the Corps horses until they returned.

Canoe Camp/Nez Perce National Historic Park
4 miles W of Orofino on US 12 (Park headquarters is at Spalding, ID, on US 12 at US 95; 208-843-2261)
Exhibits on the Corps and Nez Perce include canoe building. More Clearwater River frontage recently added to the site.

IDAHO

return: May 14–June 10, 1806

KAMIAH 49 and 50

South of Orofino is where the Corps stayed longest in one place other than winter forts. They didn't name it, but today it's called Camp Chopunnish, from what the captains thought the Nez Perce called themselves, or Long Camp. While waiting for the snow to clear off so they could start the Bitterroot crossing, the Corps hunted and preserved meat, offered medical care, and traded with the Nez Perce.

Long Camp and Asa Smith Mission/Nez Perce National Historic Park
Pullout on US 12, 1 mile E (Park headquarters is at Spalding, ID, on US 12 at US 95; 208-843-2261)

Interpretive signs cover the Corps' stay 2 miles from here (now private land.) Also told is the story of the Rev. Mr. and Mrs. Asa Smith's mission to the Nez Perce (1839-1841), during which Mr. Smith worked on a Nez Perce/English dictionary with the esteemed leader named Lawyer.

return: June 1, 1806

KOOSKIA 49 and 50

From Camp Chopunnish on May 27, Sgt. Ordway led Pvts. Frazer and Weiser overland west to the Snake River to purchase salmon. This area was new to the men, because in 1805 they had traveled via the Clearwater River north of here. The Indians they traded with at Wild Goose Rapids suggested a better route to Camp Chopunnish, which took them through the future site of Kooskia (*koos-kee*) on this date.

return: June 1, 1806

GRANGEVILLE 50

Ordway's party passed north of here on the edge of the Gospel Hump Wilderness Area. Grangeville is the starting point for the Elk City Wagon Road scenic drive to the east, Fish Creek Loop Mountain Bike Trail seven miles south, and snowmobile trails and Fish Creek Meadows Nordic Ski Trails for winter visitors.

White Bird Battlefield/Nez Perce National Historical Park
US95, 15 miles S; 208-843-2261

Only 71 years after the Nez Perce last showed great friendship and generosity to the first U.S. army men they met, the same army fought them here. Fleeing from deportation to a reservation, Nez Perce were pursued by the army in the 1877 "Nez Perce War," whose first battle occurred here. Interpretive trail and shelter on the highway tell tale.

Bicentennial Historical Museum
305 N. College; 208-983-2104

Covers local history, including the Nez Perce people and mining.

October 8-10, 1805

SPALDING

For the first time since leaving St. Louis the Corps was going downstream rather than against a river's flow. But the Clearwater had many rapids, so it wasn't easy. Passing through one set of 15 rapids, a canoe split and dumped men and goods. That night the Corps put in here to dry out goods and repair the canoe. Nez Perce chiefs Tetoharsky and Twisted Hair traveled with the Corps to introduce them to Upper Columbia nations.

Following the Corps three decades later were Catholic and Protestant missionaries. Lapwai Mission boasted future Idaho's first flour mill, sawmill, and printing press.

50 **Headquarters/Nez Perce National Historic Park**
On US 95; 208-843-2261

Visitor Center has exhibits on Nez Perce history and culture; Spalding Site offers a self-guided tour of Lapwai Mission, founded 1838.

October 10, 1805
return: May 5, 1806

LEWISTON 50

The expedition progressed 12 miles and reached the Snake River. All along the Clearwater, as on the Snake and Columbia, Indians camped to fish. This night the Corps purchased dogs (for food) and dried fish from some Nez Perce. Clark wrote that he couldn't eat dog, but that the others "relish[ed]" it—including Lewis, who traveled with his pet dog! (and see Clarkston, WA)

BARKER RIVER TRIPS

The Lewis and Clark Experience
Experience everything.
Join our Historians as we fly, float, tour, and learn about the Lewis and Clark Expedition in North Central Idaho. See the route from the air, the water and visit the important sites.

Follow the Corps of Discovery
down the Clearwater River. Day float trips from Canoe Camp in our safe guided rafts. Float a part of the actual river route of the Corps.

For additional information visit our website or call:

www.barker-river-trips.com
800-353-7459

Barker River Trips providing quality outdoor programs for 27 years
2124 Grelle Ave. Lewiston, ID 83501

Follow the Rivers to the LEWIS & CLARK DISCOVERY FAIRE

June 25th-27th
PIONEER PARK
LEWISTON, IDAHO

- Arts & Crafts
- Interactive Family Fun
- Music
- Vendors
- Food
- Historical Exhibits

IDAHO www.visitid.org
Lewiston CHAMBER

108

Lewiston Chamber of Commerce
111 N. Main, Lewiston, ID 83501; 800-473-3543
www.lewistonchamber.org

Pioneer Park
5th Street at 2nd Avenue; 208-746-6857

Fountain portrays Sacagawea, and park interprets the Corps; picnic area, playground.

Lewis and Clark Visitor Center
US 12 Bypass & D Street

Replica canoe and other Corps exhibits, across from Snake and Clearwater confluence where they camped. The U.S. Army Corps of Engineers center features Nez Perce history.

Hells Canyon National Recreation Area

Raft or jet-boat trips available from Lewiston to tour this rugged, 100-mile-long, 8,000-foot deep canyon of the Snake; get information from Lewiston Chamber of Commerce. Hiking trails, fishing, camping, and hunting.

north of Lewiston

Moscow

Home to the University of Idaho, Moscow offers art, theater, and music—right in a center of four-season outdoor recreation.

Moscow Chamber of Commerce
411 S. Main; 800-380-1801
www.moscowchamber.com

Appaloosa Horse Club & Museum
2720 W. Pullman Rd.
www.appaloosamuseum.org

Excellent horsemen and breeders, the Nez Perce developed the Appaloosa strain, which they called "raindrop horses" because of the distinctive spotted markings. Here are Appaloosa art and artifacts, as well as historical Nez Perce gear.

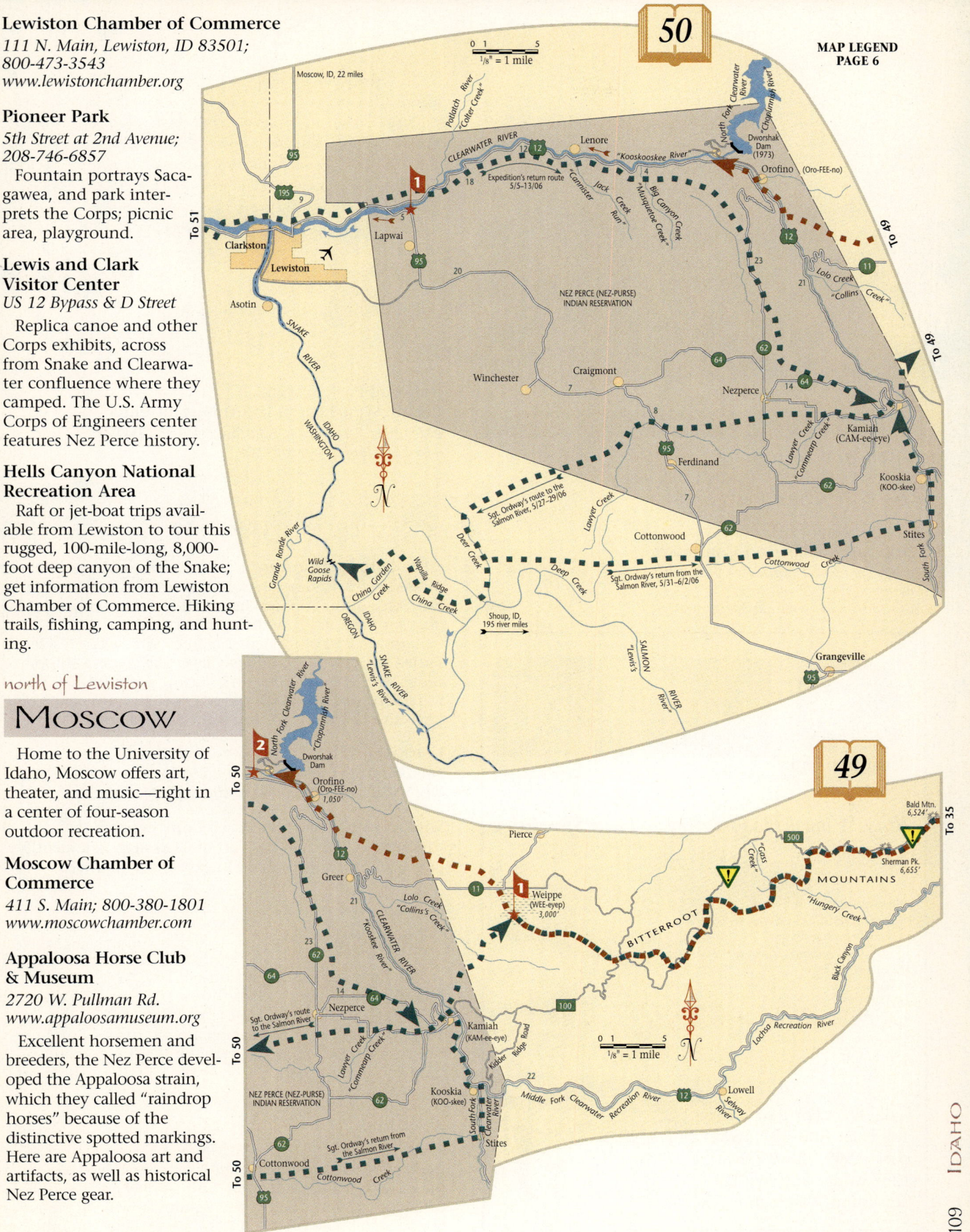

www.lewisandclark.com

MAP LEGEND PAGE 6

WASHINGTON

Not long after entering today's Washington via the Snake River, the Corps of Discovery were delighted to reach the Columbia River at last. Soon, they believed, they'd arrive at the Pacific and halt for the winter. But it took thirty-nine days to reach Long Beach on the coast. The north shore of the Columbia Estuary didn't pass muster for a winter camp, though, and the Corps crossed to future Oregon. On the way home the following spring, the friendly chief of the Wallula Indians revealed a welcome shortcut in southeastern Washington.

Lower Granite Lake, Snake River. FRED PLUGHOFT

Statewide resources on Washington

Washington Tourism
Box 42500, Dept. 323, Olympia, WA 98504
800-638-8474; www.tourism.wa.gov

**Washington State
Parks and Recreation Commission**
7150 Cleanwater Lane, P.O. Box 42650
Olympia, WA 98504-2650
800-233-0321; www.parks.wa.gov

Best Western RiverTree Inn

Stay Where Hospitality Is Our Specialty

- Refrigerators in All Rooms
- Some Rooms w/Recliners/Microwaves
- Non-Smoking Rooms
- Two Non-Smoking Suites
- Fitness Room
- Sauna
- Hot Tub
- All TV's with Remote & Showtime
- Ironing Boards & Irons
- In Room Coffee
- Pool
- BBQ Area
- Continental Breakfast
- Free Local Calls
- Fax Service
- Copy Service
- Data Ports on all Phones
- Hairdryers

Call Direct For Reservations
Toll Free: **800-597-3621**
Local: **509-758-9551**
1257 Bridge St. (Hwy 12)
Clarkston, Washington

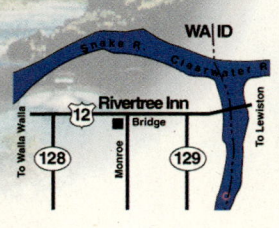

**National Park Service
Pacific West Region Information Center**
Bldg. 201, Fort Mason, San Francisco, CA 94123
415-556-0560; www.nps.gov

October 11, 1805; return: May 4, 1806

CLARKSTON 📖 50

The Corps of Discovery passed this site and went six miles downstream before stopping for breakfast among Nez Perce of the Alpowai band. They purchased more dogs for food, along with dried fish.

Clarkston had other names before 1902, when residents settled on honoring William Clark. The city is a shipping center of the Snake River and starting point for waterborne excursions of the river's Hells Canyon.

See also Lewiston, ID, across the Snake River.

Clarkston Chamber of Commerce
502 Bridge St., Clarkston, WA 99403
800-933-2128; www.clarkstonchamber.org

Snake and Clearwater River Confluence
Interpretive signs at the Port of Clarkston park identify plants and trees mentioned in expedition journals.

Today's northern route, via I-90

SPOKANE

Only four years after the Corps of Discovery headed home south of here, the Northwest Fur Company opened a trading post, Spokane House, near today's Spokane. In 1872, the city began to develop around nearby Spokane Falls, a center for processing eastern Washington agricultural and forest products. Today, the falls are at the heart of Riverfront Park.

Riverfront Park
Follow signs from I-90 into Spokane
Fifty acres along the Spokane River downtown were the site of Expo '74, a world's fair. Visitors now enjoy a 1909 carousel, monorail, outdoor sculptures & walking paths, surrounded by restored buildings, stores, & restaurants.

Northwest Museum of Arts and Culture
2316 W. First Ave., Spokane; 509-456-3931
www.cheneycowles.org

Exhibits include art, regional and Native American artifact exhibits. Campbell House on the grounds is a restored 1898 Tudor mansion of a mining baron, with carriage house and five acres of grounds.

October 16–18, 1805
PASCO-KENNEWICK-RICHLAND 53

At last, on October 16, the Corps reached the "great Columbia River," the long-sought goal. Where the Snake River poured into the Columbia, they paused for rest and local exploration. Captain Clark and two men, on the 17th, went far enough up the Columbia to see the Yakima River's mouth (at today's Richland). The Nez Perce chiefs had gone ahead to notify Yakama and Wanapam Indians of the visitors, and these local residents welcomed the Corps with singing and drumming, and gifts of horse jerky and fish. The captains in turn held a council and presented gifts.

Today's "Tri-Cities" are in the center of Washington's best wine-grape–producing area, and also river shipping.

Tri-Cities Visitor and Convention Bureau
6951 Grandridge Blvd.
Kennewick, WA 99336-7768
800-254-5824; www.visittri-cities.com

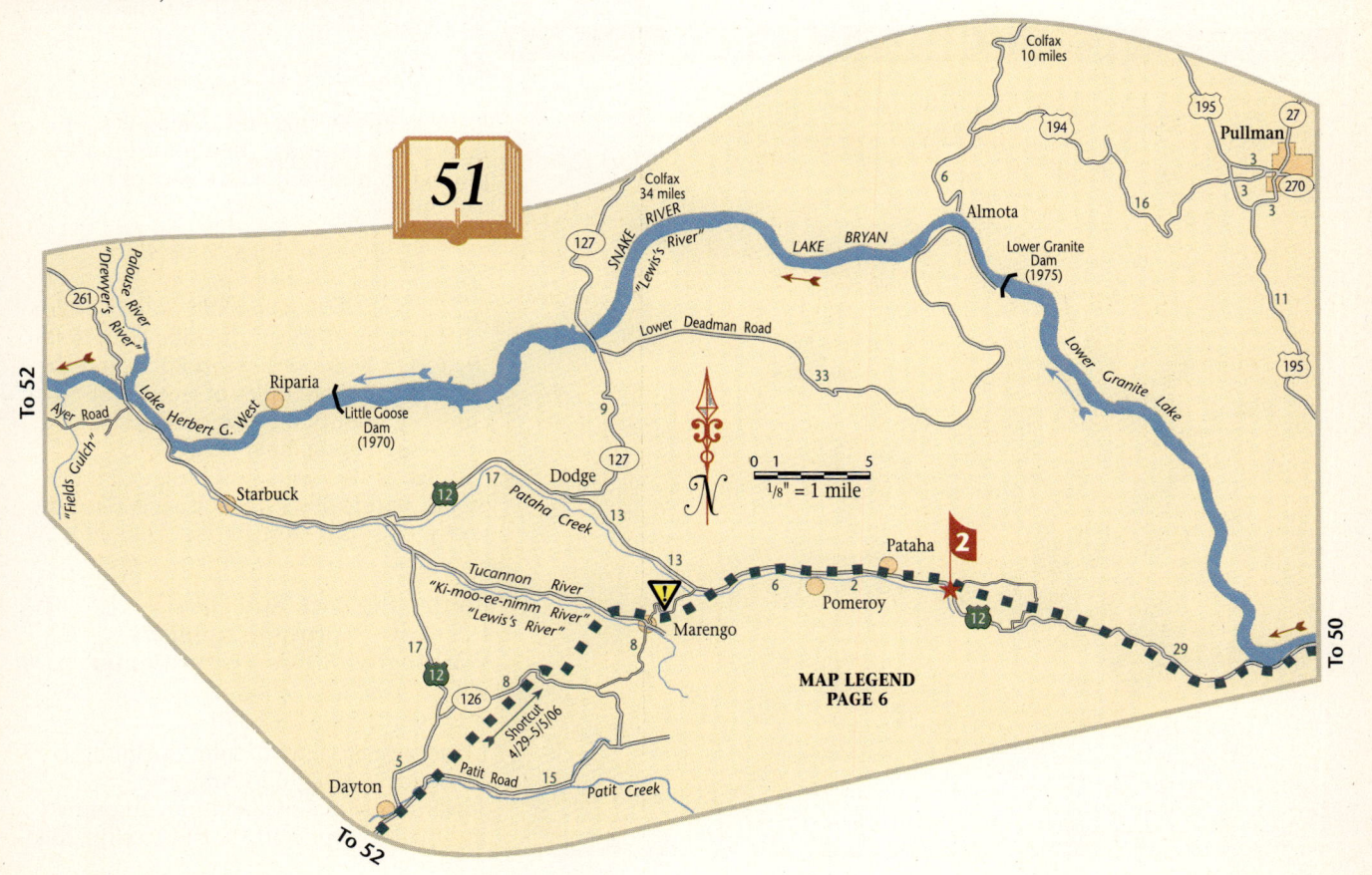

Hampton Inn Richland
Located on the Columbia River!

- 24-Hour Indoor Pool & Spa
- FREE Continental Breakfast Buffet
- FREE 24-Hour Airport Shuttle
- In-Room Coffee & Mini-Refrigerators
- FREE Wireless DSL
- Explore Nearby Parks & Wineries!

Hampton Inn (509) 943-4400 • 1-800-HAMPTON
486 Bradley Blvd. • Richland, WA 99352

For a Grand Tour visit www.northwestinns.com

WASHINGTON

54 Sacajawea State Park
2 miles east of Pasco, US 12
509-545-2361

The expedition's campsite was in this area, and today a visitor center has exhibits about the expedition, Sacagawea, and tools made by local Native Americans. Picnic area, playground, fishing, boating.

October 22, 1805; return: April 21, 1806

WISHRAM 54

54 Celilo Falls Overlook
US 14 above Wishram

Inundated in 1957 under the waters of Lake Celilo, the falls in 1805 demanded a full day to pass, even with the help of Indians who brought horses to assist the Corps. People and horses passed along the Washington side, empty canoes were carried on the Oregon side and dropped back into the water to be caught downstream.

October 24, 1805; return: April 19-21, 1806

MURDOCK

Columbia Hills State Park
WA Highway 14

Living history interpretive programs tell of the expedition's portages of the Columbia River's Celilo Falls and the Long Narrows, and friendly trading with area Indians. The park, formerly Horsethief Lake State Park, also includes Native American pictographs and petroglyphs.

October 29-November 1, 1805

Columbia River Gorge National Scenic Area
WA 14 parallels the Columbia through the area from Maryhill to Washougal. Highway crossings of the gorge are: US 97 at Maryhill, US 197 west of Wishram, WA 141 at Bingen, and east of North Bonneville.

October 30-31, 1805

STEVENSON 56

Faced with the Cascades of the Columbia, expedition members camped to plan their portage (made on November 1). Lewis visited a small village of Yehuh Indians, and saw manufactured items white traders had brought to the Pacific Coast.

56 Columbia River Gorge Interpretive Center
900 Rock Creek Dr., Stevenson, WA 98648;
509-427-8211

The story of Columbia River Gorge from its geological formation through the Lewis and Clark Expedition and Oregon Trail emigrants.

November 1, 1805

NORTH BONNEVILLE 56

The Corps viewed and named Beacon Rock on October 31, then passed it after portaging around the Cascades of the Columbia.

56 Beacon Rock State Park
WA 14, three miles west of North Bonneville; 509-427-8265

It's a steep climb up the mile-long trail to the top of 848-foot Beacon Rock, and the park has 13 more miles of steep trails, rock climbing, mountain bike trails, primitive camping, fishing, boat access.

Bridge of the Gods (toll bridge) 3 miles east of Bonneville Dam connects Cascade Locks, OR, with North Bonneville, WA. See also Cascade Locks in Oregon section.

**Bonneville Lock and Dam
U.S. Army Corps of Engineers
Washington Shore Visitor Center**
WA 14 2 mi. west of Bridge of the Gods; 541-374-8820

Underwater views of salmon climbing fish ladders, self-guided tour of powerhouse, exhibits and film about fish and hydropower. Fort Cascades self-guided

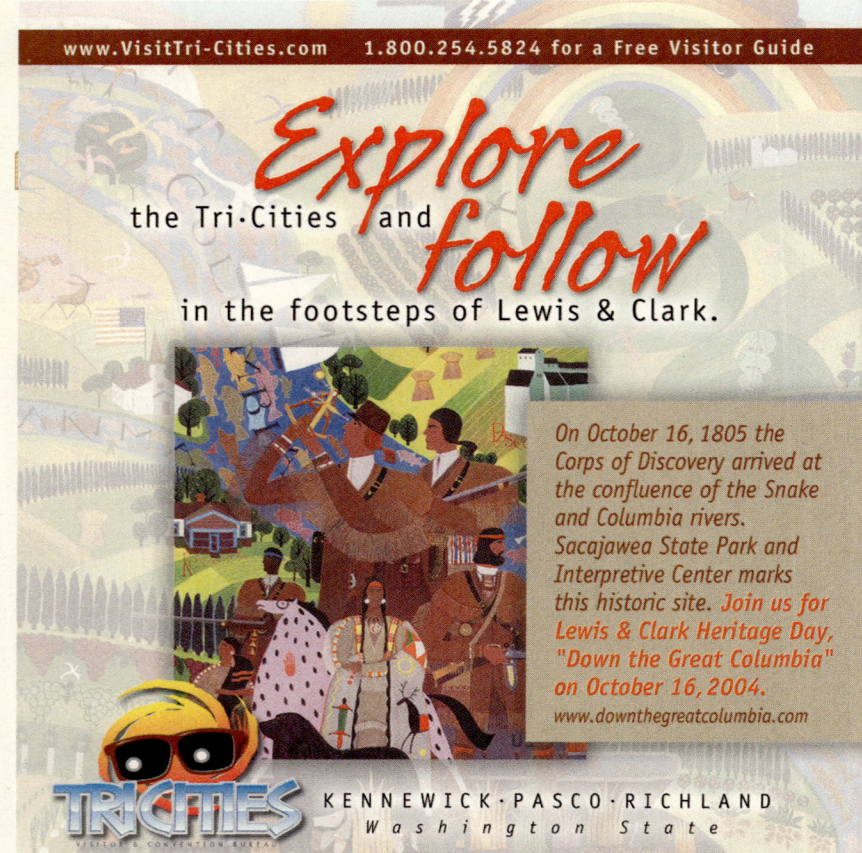

---

www.VisitTri-Cities.com   1.800.254.5824 for a Free Visitor Guide

Explore the Tri-Cities and follow in the footsteps of Lewis & Clark.

On October 16, 1805 the Corps of Discovery arrived at the confluence of the Snake and Columbia rivers. Sacajawea State Park and Interpretive Center marks this historic site. *Join us for Lewis & Clark Heritage Day, "Down the Great Columbia" on October 16, 2004.*
www.downthegreatcolumbia.com

TRI-CITIES
KENNEWICK · PASCO · RICHLAND
Washington State

historical trail and picnic areas are nearby. Summer ranger programs.

November 4, 1805

Vancouver 57

It was a "cloudy cool morning" as the Corps passed the site of future Vancouver. They also had the first taste of wapato, an underwater plant whose starchy roots were a staple for lower Columbia Indian peoples.

Only 19 years later, the Hudson's Bay Company built Fort Vancouver, starting Washington's oldest city. At the head of deep water on the Columbia River, Vancouver's port serves oceangoing and river vessels. Its shipyard built about 100 vessels that served the U.S. forces during World War II.

Southwest Washington CVB
101 E. 8th St., Suite 110, Vancouver, WA 98660
360-750-1553

Fort Vancouver National Historic Site
I-5 exit 1C, then 0.5 mile east; 800-832-3599

Experience the fur-trade era in the partially reconstructed post that the Hudson's Bay Company operated 1825-1849. In 1849, the U.S. military built its first Pacific Northwest fort nearby, which was used until 1860. Visitor center has audiovisual program and exhibits of trade goods.

Officers Row
East Evergreen Blvd., Vancouver, WA 98661; 360-693-3103

Now shops and offices, these 21 homes date from 1849 to 1906. Marshall House at 1031 Officers Row offers a slide show about the homes and a tour.

November 7, 1805

Pillar Rock
view from WA 401, east of Dahlia

The Corps spent a miserable night opposite Pillar Rock: it was hard to find a big enough spot to camp above the "tide." They had to lie on rocks, and it rained continuously. When the fog lifted the next morning, though, Clark wrote there was "great joy in camp" because they though they were "in view of the ocean…this great Pacific ocean which we have been so long anxious to see." But this was the Columbia Estuary, and they still had another month of cold, wet travel before settling in for winter.

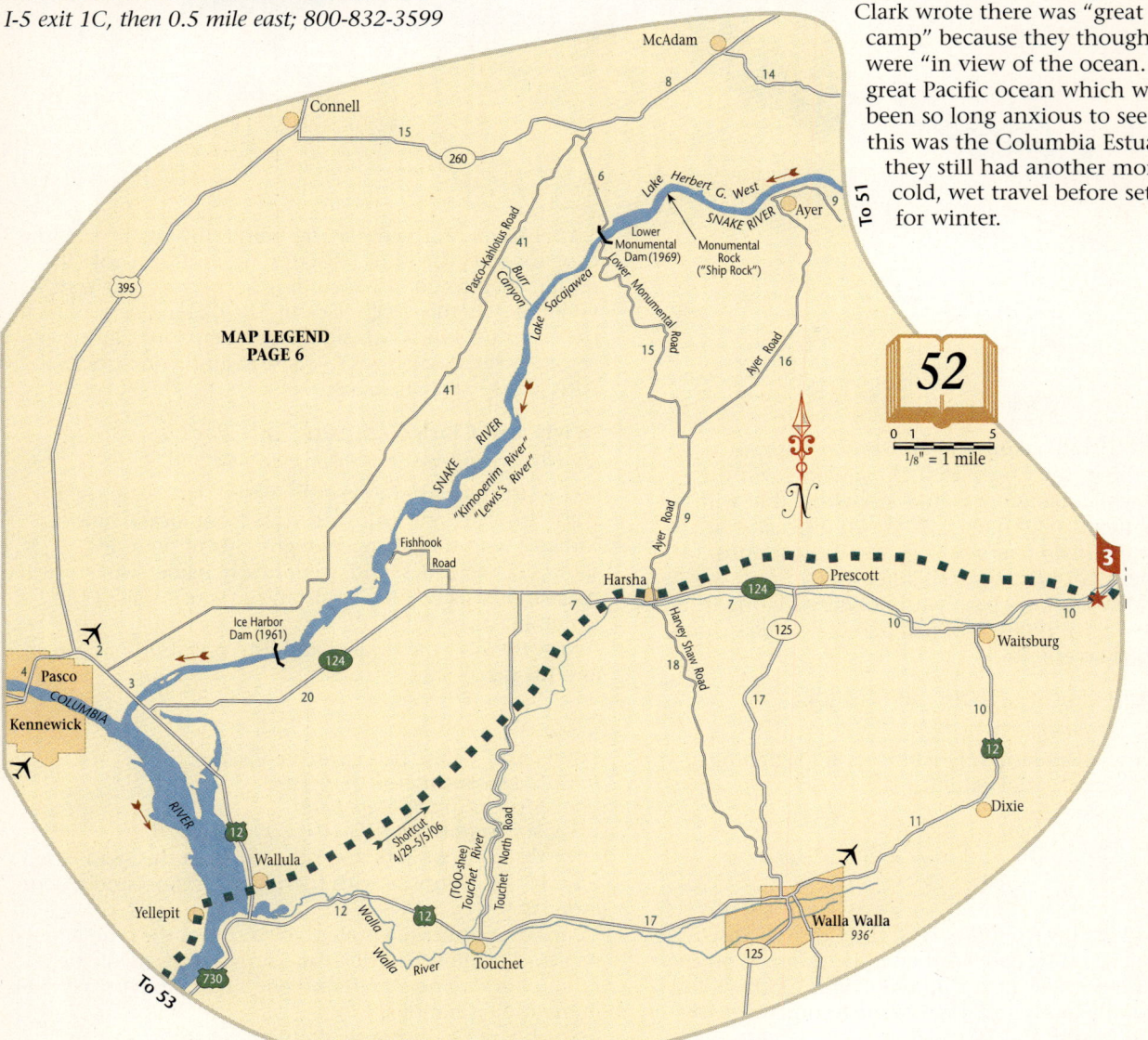

Washington

November 10–15, 1805
Point Ellice 58

So close, yet so far from the ocean coast! The Corps sheltered from rain in what Clark called a dismal niche on the eastern side of Point Ellice, which they named "Point Distress." Today's WA 401 follows the shoreline to the point, where it joins US 101 to cross the bridge to Astoria, OR.

On the 13th, pvts. Colter, Willard, and Shannon were sent downstream to look for a good harbor, thus becoming the first members of the Corps of Discovery to see the Pacific Ocean. They returned by land the next day, reporting a sandy beach, but no trading posts as had been hoped. Wind and high waves kept the expedition at Point Distress until mid-afternoon on the 15th. They made only three miles and were forced to camp again at today's Chinook Point.

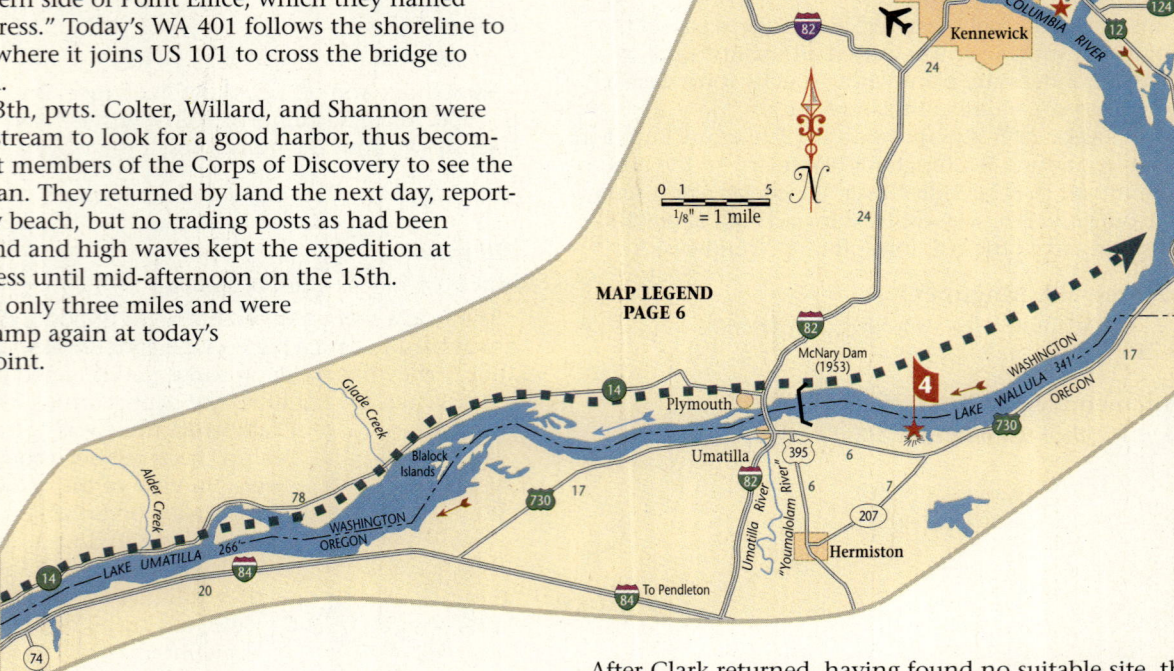

November 6, 1805
Cathlamet 55

Piloted by a Wahkiakum Indian wearing European sailor's clothing, the Corps' canoes paddled down the Columbia while the tide was in. Clark wrote that without this guide, they would have had "much dificuelty" in moving to the main channel from the shore islands.

Today the small town of Cathlamet (cath-LA-met) is a view into Washington's past, with buildings dating from the 1860s to early 1900s, antiques and collectibles shops, and dockside tavern.

Wahkiakum County Historical Museum
65 River St., Cathlamet, WA

Portrays the area's farming, fishing, and logging history, including extensive tool exhibits.

November 15–25, 1805
Ilwaco 58

East of today's Ilwaco (ill-WAH-co), the Corps of Discovery was stopped again by bad weather and encamped on the east side of Baker Bay, near Chinook Point. Clark wrote that he "could plainly see" they could go no farther by water. He took York and 10 other men overland to the coast on the 18th to 20th, scouting for a winter site.

After Clark returned, having found no suitable site, the captains took the unusual action of holding a vote to decide what to do. All, including Sacagawea and York, voted on whether to go back up the Columbia or cross it to "examine" the south side. The latter won. Clark recorded that Sacagawea's vote was simply for a place with plenty of roots to eat.

Lewis and Clark Campsite State Park
US 101 five miles east of Ilwaco; 360-642-3078

The larger group waited here while Clark explored the coast, hunting and enjoying visits from local Chinook Indians, who traded and brought gifts of pounded salmon, cranberries, and "very neatly made" woven-rush mats and baskets. Clatsops from the south side of the Columbia also visited.

Now there's a picnic area and interpretation of Clark's and his men's stay.

November 18–20, 1805 (Clark)
Lewis and Clark Interpretive Center
In Cape Disappointment State Park
(formerly Fort Canby State Park)
2.5 miles southwest off US 101; 360-642-3078

For three days, Clark and his men from this field base for a winter campsite with friendly neighbors and a good food supply.

Today's multimedia presentation covers the whole journey, and exhibits describe the Corps' foods, medicine, military discipline, entertainment, and help received from many Indian nations.

North Head Lighthouse, dating from 1898, is open for tours during summer.

"in full view of the Ocian"

—Captain William Clark, November 15, 1805

Lewis & Clark Interpretive Center at Cape Disappointment

In November of 1805, after 18 months of courageous travel through unknown landscapes, members of the Lewis & Clark Expedition fulfilled their quest for the continent's edge on the shores of the Pacific.

Overlooking the mouth of the Columbia River and the Pacific Ocean, the newly remodeled Lewis & Clark Interpretive Center and Gift Ship provides a unique experience for all members of the family. Here you will find a full spectrum of exhibits, related book and gift selections, and hiking opportunities to explore and learn about the Expedition's pioneering experiences along the Columbia River.

The center is located 3 miles west of Ilwaco, Washington in Cape Disappointment State Park (formally Fort Canby State Park). Open daily 10 a.m. to 5 p.m. P.O. Box 488, Ilwaco, WA 98624; 360-642-3029; lcic@parks.wa.gov

Gift Shop, Friends of the Columbia River Gateway, P.O. Box K, Ilwaco, WA 98624, toll free 888-874-4882, e-mail: fcrstore@pacifier.com and on-line store: www.lewis-clark-expedition.com

For additional information on the Lewis and Clark Expedition's 18 days in what is now Pacific County, Washington, visit www.capedisappointment.org, www.lewisandclarkwa.org, and www.funbeach.com

Lewis and Clark Interpretive Center

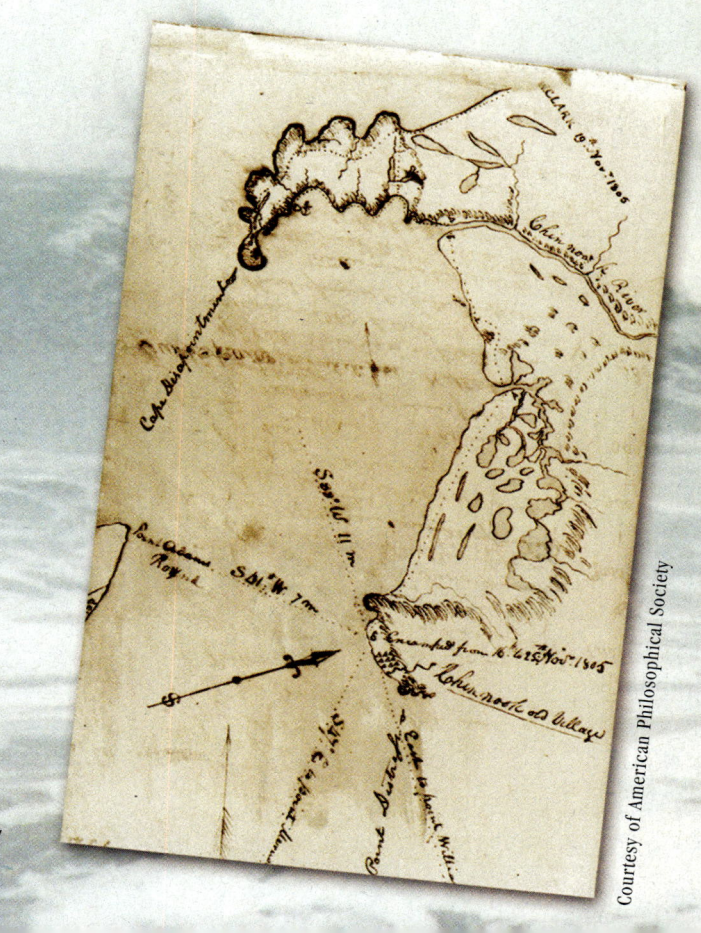

Captain William Clark's map of Station Camp and overland route to Cape Disappointment.

Courtesy of American Philosophical Society

WASHINGTON

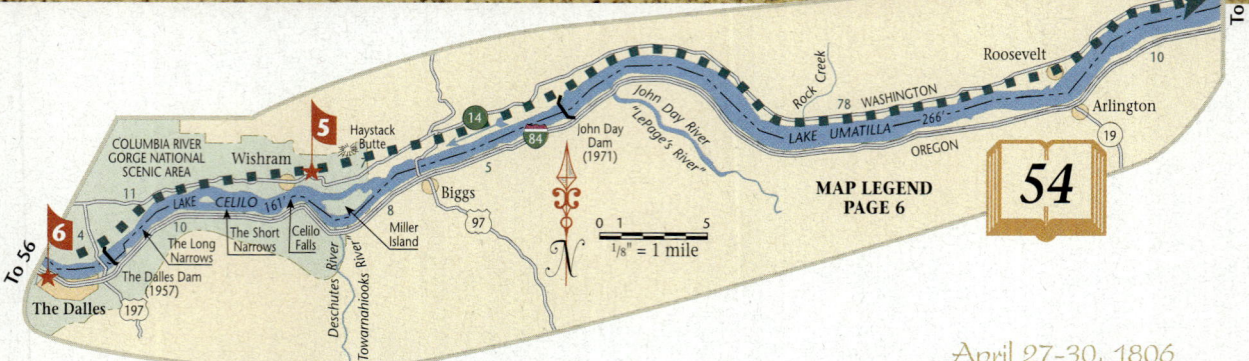

Ilwaco Heritage Museum
115 S.E. Lake St.; 360-642-3446;
www.ilwacoheritagemuseum.org

Located right on Clark's path through the area, the museum's exhibits include Chinook Indian culture, Lewis and Clark Expedition, seaside village life of 1900, Columbia Estuary, Ilwaco Railway & Navigation Co. narrow-gauge railroad (with Pullman Palace car).

STAY AT THE END OF THE TRAIL

If Wm Clark could visit the spot on Long Beach where he ended his famous journey, he would find our beautiful resort situated on 24 beachfront acres of lawn and dunes. He would also be pleased to see 'Clark's Tree' monument marking the spot in the dunes where he carved his name on a pine then turned back.

We offer affordable ocean view rooms and suites with balconies, fireplaces, kitchens and living rooms. (One low price - no charge for extra persons.) Pets OK. Indoor pool & spa. Playground, game courts & more.

THE BREAKERS
Long Beach Washington
1-800-219-9833

Visit our webcam of the ocean & Clark's End of The Trail Monument
www.breakerslongbeach.com

November 19, 1805 (Clark)
LONG BEACH 58

Clark said that he carved his name and the date on a pine tree in this area, the farthest reach of his Washington coast exploration, before returning to base camp.

Even if uninviting for an all-winter campout then, Long Beach Peninsula's 28-mile sand beach and oyster farming industry now make it a popular vacation site. A wide, half-mile-long, elevated boardwalk (reached from Bolstad Street off WA 103) has three interpretive natural-history displays with telescopes for scenic views of Cape Disappointment and lighthouses. A British captain named Cape Disappointment in 1788 when he couldn't find the Columbia's mouth beyond it.

Long Beach Peninsula Visitors Bureau
US 101 at WA 103, P.O. Box 562,
Long Beach, WA 98631
800-451-2542

Cranberry Museum
2907 Pioneer Rd.; 360-642-5553

Museum of cranberry farming and processing equipment, product labels, photographs; self-guided tour of working cranberry farm. Open daily April–mid-December, free admission.

Return shortcut, 1806

Upon reaching the Columbia River the previous October, the Corps of Discovery had met Chief Yelleppit of the Wallula (Walla Walla) Indians, who urged them to stop and visit. Anxious to keep moving, the captains gave him a small peace medal and promised a longer visit on their return. In spring 1806, they found Yelleppit's village opposite the mouth of today's Walla Walla River, and enjoyed keeping their promise.

April 27-30, 1806
WALLULA 52

The Wallula campsite is now under the waters on the west side of Lake Wallula. Chief Yelleppit was a warm host, and his village generously shared scarce firewood shrubs and fish. Yelleppit described an overland trail on the Columbia's east side that would save the Corps 80 miles in getting to the Clearwater River (compared to returning upstream on the Snake). This was a great gift, too.

On the 28th, the captains treated medical problems among their hosts, including setting a broken arm. Yelleppit invited neighboring Yakamas to come to dance that evening, and it was quite a party. First the fiddle was played and men of the Corps danced, then the Indians, and then some of Lewis and Clark's men joined in again. Until 10:00 P.M., about 550 Indians and the 30-some of the Corps relaxed.

Trading and getting horses and baggage—plus dogs purchased from the Wallulas for food—across the Columbia occupied the 29th. The night was cold and windy, so the Corps turned down suggestions for more dancing. They left "these friendly honest people" the next morning, guided by a Wallula and accompanied by a Nez Perce family.

WALLA WALLA 52

South of Yelleppit's shortcut is where Walla Walla grew at the base of the Blue Mountains. Today it's a center for more than 30 wineries, & honored with a Great American Main Street Awards by a division of the Bational Trust for Historic Preservation, boasts the oldest continuous symphony west of the Mississippi River, & has many art, theater, blues, jazz, & acoustic-music venues.

www.lewisandclark.com

Walla Walla Chamber of Commerce
29 E. Sumach; 509-525-0850

Fort Walla Walla Museum
755 Myra Rd.; 509-525-7703
www.fortwallawallamuseum.org

View a life-size Lewis and Clark diorama, and walk through a village of original and reconstructed buildings that take you back to the early days of white settlers in southeastern Washington. Open daily April-October.

May 2, 1806

DAYTON 51

Following the Touchet River then Patit Creek upstream, the meat-eating Corps was happy to find game more abundant in this area. Lewis noted camas in bloom, and tasted stems of young cow parsnip that the Wallulas ate after removing toxic outer layers. He liked it and ate "heartily" with no ill effects.

Today, Dayton's historic train depot (built in 1881, it's Washington's oldest) is a museum of railroad memorabilia and antique furniture. Self-guiding tours cover the town's three historic districts, which also include the state's oldest courthouse.

Dayton Chamber of Commerce
166 E. Main, Dayton, WA 99328
800-882-6299; www.historicdayton.com

51 **Lewis and Clark Trail State Park**
5 miles west of Dayton on US 12
509-337-6457

Kiosks and a mile-long interpretive trail tell of the Corps in this area, and re-enactments are featured. Birding trail, picnic sites and small tent/RV campground.

52 **3 Forks Indian Trail Turnout**
On US12, 15 miles east of Dayton; 509-758-9580

Sign gives information about nearby trails, including the one the Wallulas told the Corps about and they used for their 1806 return shortcut.

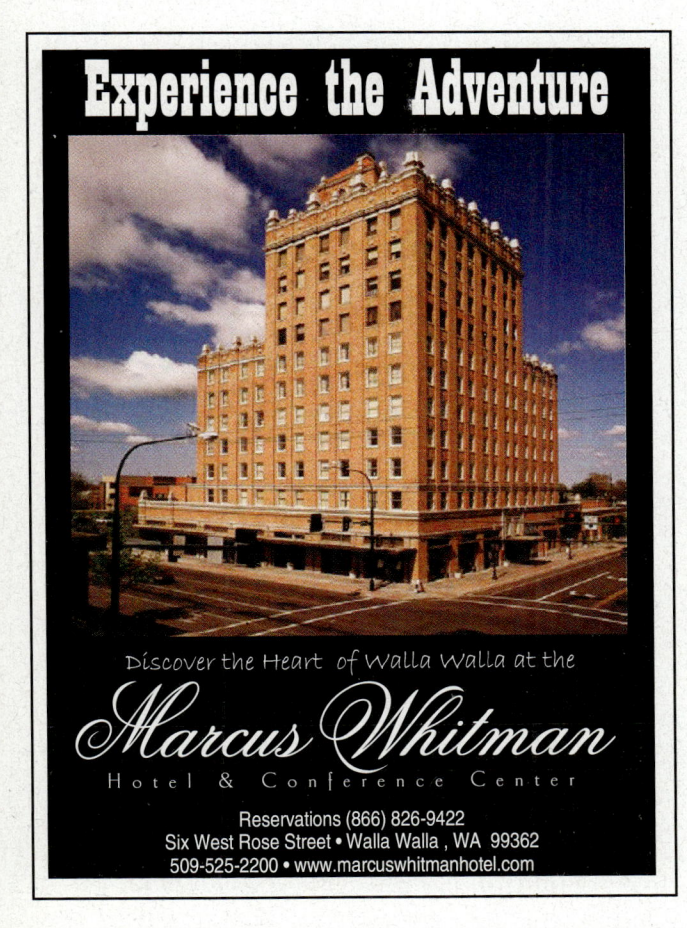

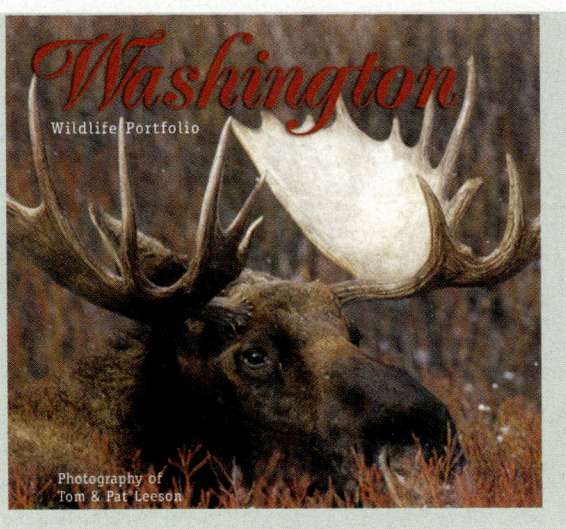

Experience the Adventure

Discover the Heart of Walla Walla at the
Marcus Whitman
Hotel & Conference Center

Reservations (866) 826-9422
Six West Rose Street • Walla Walla, WA 99362
509-525-2200 • www.marcuswhitmanhotel.com

Washington Wildlife Portfolio
Photography by Tom and Pat Leeson.
Experience the natural rhythms of animal lives as these wild Washingtonians interact with their distinct environments and each other in the state's 10 million acres of undeveloped lands.
131 color photos. 120 pages, 10½" x 12". HB. $24.95

1-800-821-3874

OREGON

Traveling west, downstream on the Columbia River, the Corps of Discovery entered future Oregon on October 18, 1805. All along the river, Indians of several nations were camped to harvest the fall salmon run. The expedition camped on both sides of the Columbia during the next month, and first explored the Pacific Coast from Washington, scouting for a winter campsite. On November 27, they crossed to the Columbia's south side, and ten days later began building the cramped huts they named Fort Clatsop.

Historic Columbia River Scenic Highway. CHUCK HANEY

Statewide resources on Oregon

Oregon Tourism Commission
775 Summer St. N.E., Salem, OR 97310
800-547-7842; www.traveloregon.com

Eastern Oregon Visitors Association
P.O. Box 1087, Baker City, 97814; 800-332-1843
www.eova.com

Northwest Oregon Tourism Alliance
26 S.W. Salmon, Box S5, Portland, OR 97204; 800-962-3700

Oregon Parks and Recreation Department
1115 Commercial St. N.E., Salem, OR 97310
800-452-5687; www.prd.state.or.us

National Park Service
Pacific West Region Information Center
Bldg. 201, Fort Mason, San Francisco, CA 94123
415-556-0560; www.nps.gov

October 19, 1805
return: April 27, 1806

HERMISTON, IRRIGON, BOARDMAN 53

The Corps passed "a rock...resembling a hat" on a day that included running rapids where today's McNary Dam sits. Camp was on an island, perhaps Blalock Island between Irrigon and Boardman. About 100 Umatilla Indians crossed the river to visit, so Pvts. Pierre Cruzatte and George Gibson took turns playing the fiddle for singing and dancing—much to the Umatillas' delight.

53 **Hat Rock State Park**
US 730, nine miles east of Umatilla; 541-567-5032
Open from spring to fall, the park around Hat Rock includes interpretive signs, picnic area, sand volleyball court, stocked trout-fishing pond, waterfowl habitat, and boat access to Lake Wallula on the Columbia for waterskiing, jetskiing, and fishing.

PENDLETON

Southeast of Hermiston, Pendleton is near the Umatilla Indian Reservation, home to descendants of nations that the Corp met. Held in the second full week of September, the Pendleton Round-up is one of the West's most famous rodeos. Local history is served up in intriguing ways.

Pendleton Chamber of Commerce
5015 Main St., Pendleton, OR 97801; 800-547-8911;
www.visitpendleton.us

Tamastslikt Cultural Institute
72789 Hwy. 331 (4 miles east of Pendleton via I-84)
Pendleton, OR 97801; 541-966-9748; www.wildhorseresort.com
Exhibits on the history of the three distinct peoples who now form the Confederated Tribes of the Umatilla Indian Reservation: Cayuse, Umatilla, and Walla Walla. The Institute is part of a larger resort complex.

Umatilla County Historical Society
108 S.W. Frazer, Pendleton, OR 97801; 503-276-0012
In a restored 1909 railroad depot are exhibits on the area's sheep industry, Pendleton Woolen Mills, Umatilla County history, Indian artifacts.

Pendleton Underground Tours
37 SW Immigrant, Pendleton, OR 97801; 503-276-0630
Guided tours of tunnels built by Chinese immigrants in the late 19th century show cardroom, laundry, butcher shop, bordello, and residences.

October 21, 1805

RUFUS 54

Passing today's John Day River, the captains named it for Jean Baptiste Lepage, a French boatman hired in St. Louis who had enlisted at Fort Mandan.

The Corps had used the last of their whiskey on July 4, 1805, but tonight at camp near here they had a pleasant surprise: Pvt. John Collins "presented us with some very good beer" made by accident—it was bread from the Nez Perce of Idaho that had gotten wet and then fermented.

www.lewisandclark.com

LePage Park
I-84 exit 114; 541-296-1181

Water sports park at the mouth of John Day River, with picnic sites, small campground, fishing, boating.

October 25-28, 1805
return: April 15-18, 1806

THE DALLES 54

Getting through the Columbia's Short Narrows (a quarter mile long) and then its Long Narrows (five miles) took planning and caution. Men who couldn't swim walked around, carrying freight to lighten the canoes. Others stood ready to throw lifelines to the canoeists who ran the rapids that Clark called "shocking." The Dalles Dam has raised the Columbia's waters above these rapids.

The Corps reached here during the fall salmon run, and so native people were camped on the shores in the greatest numbers yet seen. To French fur traders, the narrows were "the trough," or *les dalles*, where they met Indian people to trade, and a settlement grew. Three museums in the area tell the stories of some of the nations who greeted white visitors. Now The Dalles is a center for whitewater river floating, sailboarding, fishing, and museum-going.

The Dalles Chamber of Commerce
404 W. 2nd St., The Dalles, OR 97058
800-255-3385; www.thedalleschamber.com

Columbia Gorge Discovery Center & Wasco County Historical Museum
5000 Discovery Dr.; The Dalles, OR 97058
541-296-8600; www.gorgediscovery.org

50,000 square feet of exhibits, art, Native American and immigrant craftwork, and the area's story from earliest residents to Lewis and Clark Expedition, Oregon Trail wagon trains and on to white settlement.

54 Lewis and Clark Rock Fort Site
I-84 exit 83, Webber St.
North to First St., and east
to Overlook; 541-296-9533

The two Nez Perce chiefs traveling with the Corps warned the captains that Wishram-Wasco Indians of this area planned to attack them, so the captains claimed a high point of rocks for their campsite and posted a guard each night while pausing here to dry out the soaked cargo. Their own name for the camp was Fort Rock. The site has interpretation about the expedition.

Fort Dalles Museum
15th and Garrison; 541-296-4547

Area history exhibits in Oregon's oldest museum include the surgeon's quarters that survive from the 1850 fort, the Anderson Home complex, and more.

The Dalles Art Center
220 E. 4th St.; 541-296-4759

Surrounded by gardens, the 1910 Carnegie Library building now houses changing exhibits by local artists.

LEWIS AND CLARK FOUGHT BEARS, SLEPT ON ROCKS AND BRAVED THE ELEMENTS IN SEARCH OF KNOWLEDGE.

PERHAPS YOU SHOULD DRIVE.

Almost 200 years ago, Lewis and Clark set off to explore the West. Meet the people who welcomed them. The Tribes of the Umatilla, Cayuse and Walla Walla invite you to visit the very homeland these great explorers crossed. You'll discover a thriving community with traditions that have stood the test of time. You'll also find the Tamástslikt Cultural Institute. And within its walls lie our stories of the past and our vision of the future. So come enjoy the hospitality that continues to make history.

· TAMÁSTSLIKT ·
CULTURAL INSTITUTE
OPEN DAILY 9AM-5PM

1.800.654.9453   WWW.TAMASTSLIKT.COM   PENDLETON, OREGON   I-84, EXIT 216
OWNED AND OPERATED BY THE CONFEDERATED TRIBES OF THE UMATILLA INDIAN RESERVATION

Cargo...

When Lewis and Clark packed for the journey west they carried 30 tons of supplies... you may want to pack a little lighter.

Photo Courtesy of Washington State Historical Society, Tacoma

In October 1805 a group of threadbare explores arrived in what would become The Dalles and the eastern gateway of the Columbia River Gorge National Scenic Area. They left Missouri with several tons of equipment and trade goods...enough supplies to get to the West Coast. Here, surrounded by bands of indigenous peoples, they camped on high ground at a place they named Rock Fort. Visit their encampment site, hear the sounds of powwows in spring and fall at nearby Celilo and experience the re-creation of the 30 tons of cargo at the Columbia Gorge Discovery Center and Museum. Come and stay for several days...just pack a little lighter. For a free vacation planner, call 800-255-3355.

Columbia Gorge Discovery Center & Museum
5000 Discovery Dr.
The Dalles, OR 97058
www.gorgediscovery.org

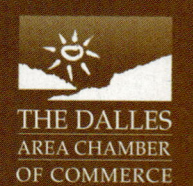

THE DALLES AREA CHAMBER OF COMMERCE

The Dalles Area Chamber of Commerce and Visitor Center
404 W. Second Street
The Dalles, OR 97058
www.thedalleschamber.com
www.tdedc.com

www.lewisandclark.com

October 29–November 1, 1805
Columbia River Gorge National Scenic Area

I-84 parallels the Columbia from the Deschutes River west of Biggs to the Sandy River at Portland. Higher up, the Historic Columbia River Highway (US 30 built in 1915) is open from Mosier to The Dalles for leisurely travel and great views.

Columbia Gorge crossings: US97 at Biggs, US 197 east of The Dalles, OR 35 east of Hood River, and Bridge of the Gods east of Bonneville Dam.

The Dalles Dam
I-84 east of US 197; 541-296-9778
Visitor center has exhibits on power generation, and guided tours are offered of the powerhouse, fish ladder, lock, and dam.

October 29, 1805
HOOD RIVER

Passing the Hood's mouth, the captains named it Labiche's River for Private Francois Labiche, but he lost the honor later to Samuel Hood, a British admiral who fought under Lord Nelson in the Napoleonic Wars.

Today, Hood River calls itself the Sailboarding Capital of the World.

Columbia River Gorge Visitors Association
2199 W. Cascade #106, Hood River, OR 97031, 800-98-GORGE

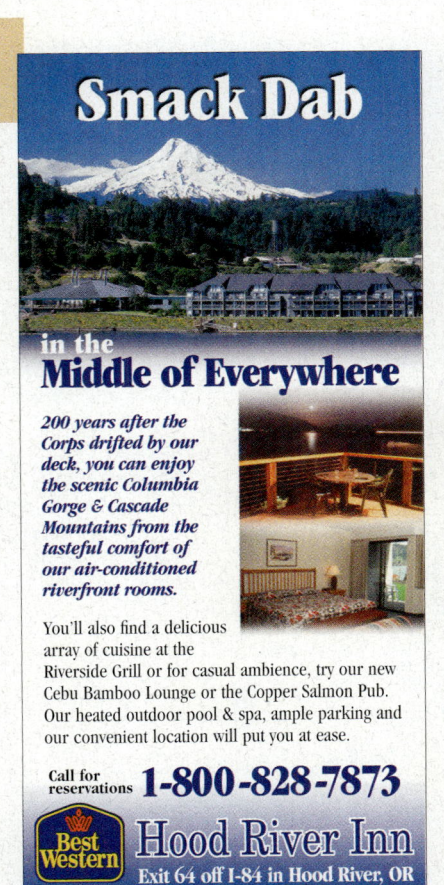

Hood River County Historical Museum
Port Marina Park, Hood River, OR 97031, 541-386-6772; www.crgva.org
Exhibits and artifacts on area history and homesteading.

November 2, 1805
CASCADE LOCKS

This day's portage around the Cascades of the Columbia was a mile and a half on land, and the lightened canoes ran the rapids "without much damage." Bonneville Dam raised the Columbia above these rapids.

Bridge of the Gods 3 miles east of Bonneville Dam connects Cascade Locks, OR, with North Bonneville, WA. See also North Bonneville, Washington.

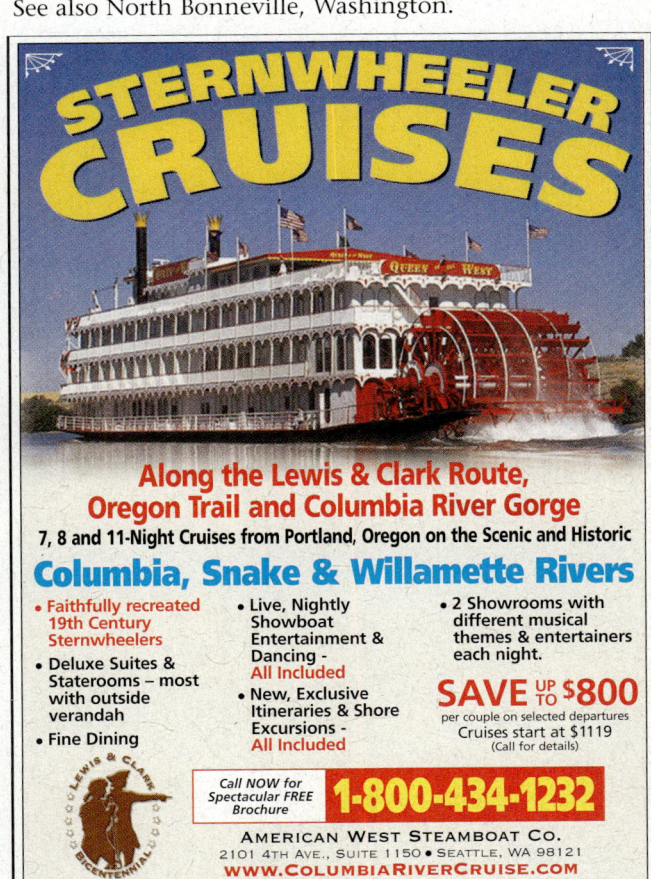

Smack Dab in the Middle of Everywhere

200 years after the Corps drifted by our deck, you can enjoy the scenic Columbia Gorge & Cascade Mountains from the tasteful comfort of our air-conditioned riverfront rooms.

You'll also find a delicious array of cuisine at the Riverside Grill or for casual ambience, try our new Cebu Bamboo Lounge or the Copper Salmon Pub. Our heated outdoor pool & spa, ample parking and our convenient location will put you at ease.

Call for reservations **1-800-828-7873**
Best Western Hood River Inn
Exit 64 off I-84 in Hood River, OR
www.hoodriverinn.com (online reservations available)

STERNWHEELER CRUISES

Along the Lewis & Clark Route, Oregon Trail and Columbia River Gorge

7, 8 and 11-Night Cruises from Portland, Oregon on the Scenic and Historic **Columbia, Snake & Willamette Rivers**

- Faithfully recreated 19th Century Sternwheelers
- Deluxe Suites & Staterooms – most with outside verandah
- Fine Dining
- Live, Nightly Showboat Entertainment & Dancing - All Included
- New, Exclusive Itineraries & Shore Excursions - All Included
- 2 Showrooms with different musical themes & entertainers each night

SAVE UP TO $800 per couple on selected departures
Cruises start at $1119 (Call for details)

Call NOW for Spectacular FREE Brochure
1-800-434-1232
AMERICAN WEST STEAMBOAT CO.
2101 4TH AVE., SUITE 1150 • SEATTLE, WA 98121
WWW.COLUMBIARIVERCRUISE.COM

OREGON

Visit BONNEVILLE LOCK and DAM

- Watch salmon climb fishladders through special underwater viewing windows.
- Explore a huge powerhouse.
- See a lock raise ships sixty feet.

BONNEVILLE LOCK and DAM is located in Oregon at Interstate 84, Exit 40 and in Washington at Highway 14, Mile 40. For visitor information call (541) 374-8820.

Multnomah Falls Lodge

One of Oregon's greatest treasures

Photo by Steve Terrill

Visitor and Interpretive Center
- Unique Northwest gifts & handcrafts
- Northwest cuisine, seafood & steaks
- For reservations: 503-695-2376

Cascade Locks Historical Museum

Marine Park, 355 Wanapa St., Cascade Locks, OR 97014, 541-374-8535

Artifacts tell of Native Americans and white settlers in the area; the museum is housed in what was a lockkeeper's house.

Bonneville Lock and Dam U.S. Army Corps of Engineers Bradford Island Visitor Center

I-84, exit 40; 541-374-8820

The island was named Brant Island by Corps of Discovery. Underwater views of fish ladder, films, displays, access to powerhouse. Navigation lock visitor center, picnic areas, fish hatchery. Summer ranger programs.

November 2, 1805
Rooster Rock State Park
I-84, exit 28; 503-695-2261

In camp at this site, the Corps watched the Columbia rise and fall from tidal effects while they ate well, "supping" on geese that four hunters brought in.

Today's park has picnic area, large swimming beach during low water (with separate clothing-optional beach at far eastern end of park), jet ski rentals, boat ramp, fishing.

TROUTDALE 57

Crown Point State Park
US-30, 11 miles east of Troutdale; 503-695-2261

Camp was "behind a large rock," today's Crown Point.

The octagonal, domed Vista House was built atop Crown Point in 1916 to provide views of the Columbia River Gorge; today it's open March through October, with exhibits on area history and geology, interpretive tours and signs, and frequent programs including music, living history, and celebrations.

November 3, 1805
Lewis and Clark State Park
US-30, 16 miles east of Portland; 503-695-2261

To the captains, the river meeting the Columbia here was "Quick Sand River," because it deposited "coarse sands" into the Columbia. That sand is from lava flows on Mount Hood. When the expedition voted on where to winter (see Washington section, Nov. 15-25, 1805), 10 men wanted to return here to the Sandy.

Today's park borders a popular swimming beach and offers fishing and boating. Climb the trail to the top of Broughton's Bluff, the boundary between Cascade foothills & the Willamette Valley.

www.lewisandclark.com

November 3, 1805
return: March 31–April 6, 1806

PORTLAND 57

The expedition camped on "Diamond Island" at Portland; since then, the river has split it into today's Government and McGuire islands. Now, the captains knew, they again were in territory previously explored by Europeans. Captain George Vancouver's British party had reached Diamond Island just 12 years earlier.

At Fort Clatsop, the captains learned of a big river flowing into the Columbia from the south, which they'd missed seeing because of a sandbar at its mouth. On April 2-3, 1806, Clark took an Indian guide, York, and six privates up the Willamette, pleased with its gentle current and great depth, which would allow "the largest ship."

The Chinook Indians were the first of many people to meet for trade at the confluence of the Willamette and Columbia rivers, and in 1844 two Americans laid out a townsite. By a flip of the coin, it was named for one man's hometown in Maine. From the beginning, residents preserved green areas and historical buildings as the city grew and modernized.

Portland Oregon Visitors Association
1000 SW Broadway, Ste. 2300, Portland, OR 97205
800-962-3700

Oregon History Center
1200 S.W. Park Ave., Portland, OR 97205; 503-222-1741; www.ohs.org
Environmental exhibits bring to life Portland and Oregon history.

Children's Museum
3037 S.W. Second Ave., Portland, OR 97201; 503-823-2227
Children can learn while exploring child-sized exhibits such as a grocery store, bistro, and medical center.

Portland Art Museum
1219 S.W. Park Ave., Portland, OR 97205
503-226-2811; www.pam.org
Galleries exhibiting the entire collection are devoted to Native American, Northwest, American, Contemporary, and European works of art.

November 27, 1805
Lewis and Clark National Wildlife Refuge
access from Knappa on US 30;
360-795-3915

After looking around on the Washington side of the Columbia Estuary (see Washington section, Nov. 15-25, 1805) and voting on how to proceed, the Corps went back upstream to Pillar Rock and made a rough canoe crossing to Tongue Point, Oregon, through today's refuge.

Modern visitors can reach the refuge by boat only, and a self-guiding canoe trail is offered.

south of Portland
CLACKAMAS

Clackamas County Tourism Development Council
619 High Street; 800-647-3843
www.clackamas-oregon.com

End of the Oregon Trail Interpretive Center
1726 Washington Street;
800-424-3002, 503-657-9336

At the end of the Oregon Trail, the center hosts living history interpretations and multimedia dramatizations to depict pioneers' struggles and successes.

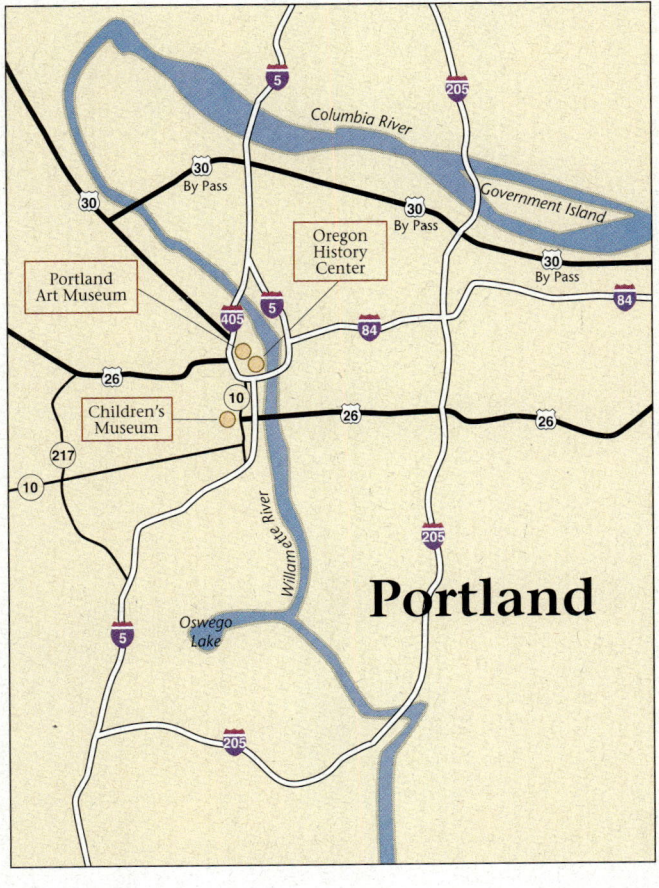

CLACKAMAS INN
Overlooking Mount Hood, Oregon

Amenities
- Complimentary Continental Breakfast
- Complimentary local phone calls
- Non smoking rooms (on request)
- Remote Cable TV and HBO
- Outdoor pool (seasonal)
- Fax and copy service
- Jacuzzi suites
- Microwave, refrigerator & hair dryer in room
- Handicap assist rooms
- Children 12 and under stay free
- 24 hour front desk
- Meeting space accommodates up to 25 people
- Guest laundry facilities
- Clackamas Town Center Mall minutes away
- Group & Tour rates available
- AAA, AARP, Corporate, & Gov't rates available

Reservations
800.874.6560
www.clackamasinn.com
16010 SE 82nd Drive • Clackamas, OR 97015
P:503.650.5340 • F: 503.657.7221

Portland

OREGON

123

OREGON

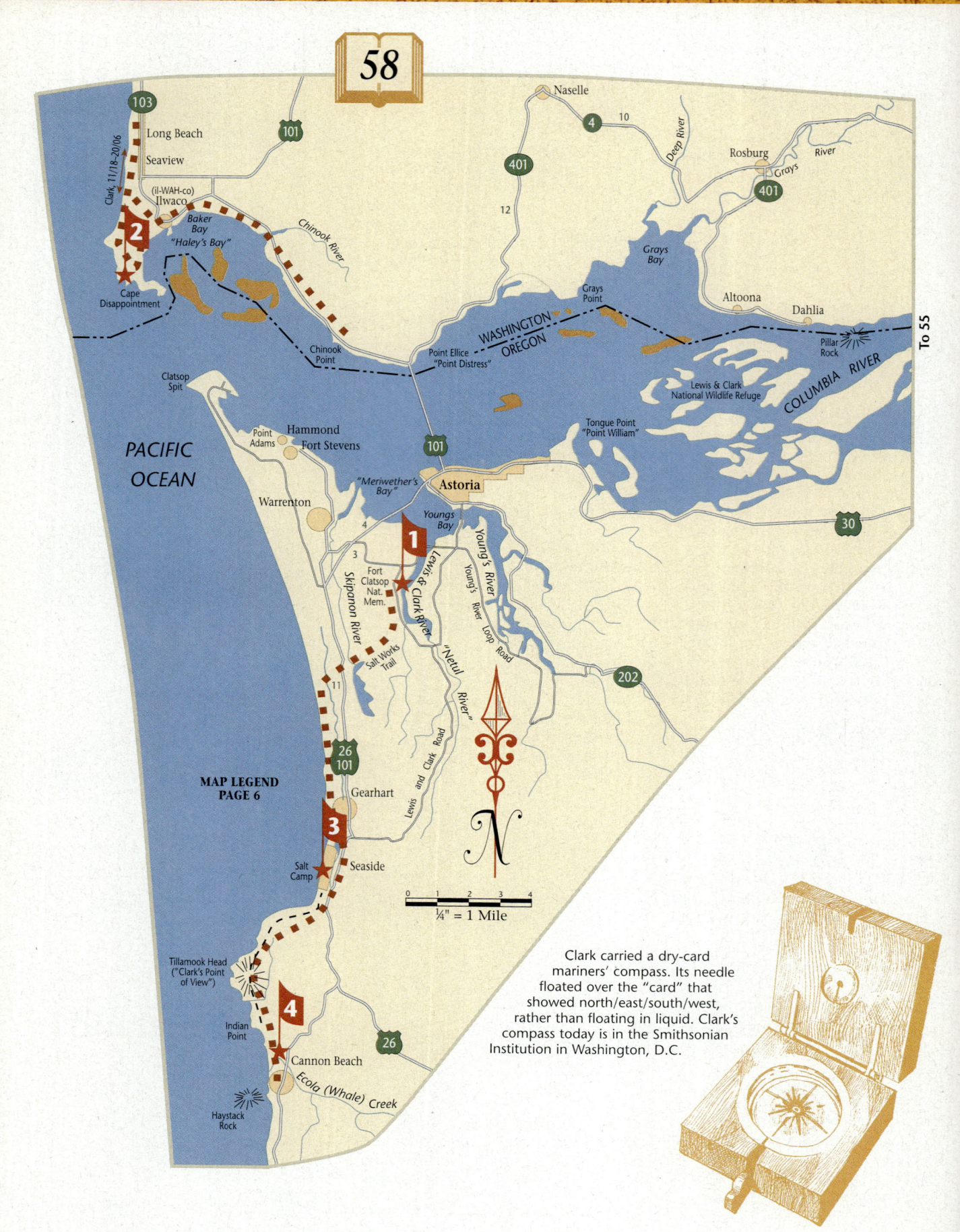

Clark carried a dry-card mariners' compass. Its needle floated over the "card" that showed north/east/south/west, rather than floating in liquid. Clark's compass today is in the Smithsonian Institution in Washington, D.C.

www.lewisandclark.com

south of Clackamas
Oregon City

Oregon City Chamber of Commerce
500 Washington; 503-656-1619

Museum of the Oregon Territory
211 Tumwater Drive; 503-655-5574
www.orcity.com/museum

The story of Oregon City's days as capital of vast Oregon Territory when it extended east to the Rockies.

Stevens Crawford Heritage House
603 Sixth Street; 503-655-2866
www.orcity.com/museum

An example of Foursquare Architecture, completed in 1908, filled with period furniture, toys, "modern" combination electric/gas lighting, operable kitchen and pantry, seasonal exhibits.

November 29-December 5, 1805
Astoria 58

Lewis and five men followed the shore of Youngs Bay and set up a base camp for seeking their winter home. Only six years in the future, John Jacob Astor's Pacific Fur Company built its Fort Astoria here.

Fort Astoria
Exchange and 15th Sts., Astoria, OR 97103; 503-325-2203

Part of the Pacific Fur Company post has been restored and is open for tours.

Columbia River Maritime Museum
1792 Marine Dr., Astoria, OR 97103; 503-325-2323

Touring a lightship is one highlight of exhibits on Columbia and Pacific coast maritime history.

December 7, 1805–March 23, 1806
Fort Clatsop National Memorial
5 miles southwest of Astoria
on US 101; 503-861-2471; www.nps.gov/focl

Lewis's advance party found elk, an important part of their winter needs, two miles up the Netul River (today's Lewis and Clark River). Leaving two men behind to hunt, Lewis and the others returned to lead the main party here. On the 8th, men began felling trees to build what they'd call Fort Clatsop in honor of neighboring Indians. They moved into the palisaded "huts" (Clark's term) on Christmas Eve.

Nearly constant cold rain made this winter unpleasant in many ways. On only 12 of their 141 days here was there no rain, and only six days showed clear sky. Meat rotted before they could eat it all or dry it, even though they built the smokehouse before their own shelter and kept fires burning constantly in it. Their leather clothing rotted while they continuously tanned hides to make clothing and moccasins for the return trip.

The Nez Perce had warned the captains they couldn't cross the Rockies until June, but the expedition left Fort Clatsop in March for a May arrival at the mountains, eager both to head home and to get out of the wet.

Today, tour the tiny "fort" reconstruction built from Clark's floor plan sketch, with rooms furnished as they might have been. The visitor center has exhibits and audio-visual presentations; living history programs occur daily during summer.

December 9-10, 1805 (Clark)
Seaside 58

On the 8th, Capt. Clark and five men had begun a two-day trip of 15 miles by creeks and trail to the coast. At the site of today's Seaside, he found a Clatsop village of four lodges beside the mouth of the Necanicum River. The people welcomed his party into their partially underground homes and seated them on new woven mats, serving dinner on rush "platters" and "neat" wooden trenchers and soup in horn bowls with cockleshell spoons.

Seaside developed as Oregon's first ocean resort town and today is its largest.

Seaside Visitors Bureau
415 1st, Seaside, OR 97138
888-306-2326; www.el.com/to/seaside

December 28, 1805–February 21, 1806

58 3 **Salt Works Memorial**
south end of Promenade in Seaside

This memorial imagines what the salt works looked like as small groups of enlisted men took turns staying here and boiling ocean water to produce four salt.

Seaside Museum and Historical Society
570 Necanicum Dr., Seaside, OR 97138
503-738-7065

Exhibits cover the area's Clatsop residents, logging and other local history and include a restored 1912 "beach cottage" rooming house.

MOTEL 6 ACCOR hotels

Motel 6 Seaside, Oregon - "At The End Of The Trail"
2369 S. Holiday Drive, Toll free: 866-738-6269 or 503-738-6269
Great Amenities And The Best Price Of Any National Chain
Toll Free 800 4 MOTEL 6 Or Book Online At motel6.com

OREGON

January 7, 1806

CANNON BEACH 58

Having heard from the Clatsops that a whale was beached down the coast, Clark decided to take some men and trade for blubber and oil. The night before he left, Janey (as he'd nicknamed Sacagawea) made her case for joining him: she'd come all this way to see the "great waters" and still hadn't been allowed to go there, and now a giant fish was also to be seen! Clark agreed that she and Charbonneau would go along.

The Tillamook Indians had nearly finished butchering the whale when Clark's party reached them at the mouth of **Ecola Creek**, which the captains named using the Chinookan word for whale. Clark persuaded the Tillamooks to part with 300 pounds of blubber, which the Corps ate for three weeks.

Today's "trading" in Cannon Beach includes handcrafts and clothing in specialty shops on Hemlock Street.

Cannon Beach Information Center
2nd and Spruce, Cannon Beach, OR 97110
503-436-2623; www.cannon-beach.net

Tillamook Head
in Ecola State Park

En route to the whale, their Indian guide led Clark's party up and over Tillamook Head, where Clark wrote, they "hauled our selves up by the assistance of the bushes." After Clark returned to Fort Clatsop and told Lewis of the view from the 1,136-foot "mountain," Lewis named it "Point of Clark's View." Hardy hikers today can follow Clark's path to the top; the view is one of Oregon's most photographed.

Ecola State Park
2 miles north off US 101; 541-436-2844

Park includes interpretive signs, picnic shelters, beach access from Indian Beach parking lot. A sea lion colony inhabits offshore rocks.

Cannon Beach Historical Society
1387 South Spruce; 503-436-9301; www.cannon-beach.net/cbhs

History of the Cannon Beach and Arch Cape area, introduced by a mural showing William Clark's perspective from Tillamook Head, a view he described as "the grandest and most pleasing prospects which my eyes ever surveyed."

Plains Indians, like those the Corps met, got horses from 1650 to 1750, but by 1800 they still had few guns and hunted bison with traditional weapons.

Subscribe for 3 years for $58 and receive our $9.⁹⁵ Lewis & Clark map FREE

Lewis & Clark stories running through 2006:

- Floating the rivers today that Lewis & Clark traveled
- Overland trips—by car, foot, and bicycle in the areas they explored
- Historic narrative & contemporary contributions to the legend and facts of the Corps of Discovery

Along the Trail with Lewis and Clark

Full-color poster outlines the trip from St. Louis to the Pacific and back, showing land and water routes, 53 sites to visit, 44 landmark or intriguing events. 36"x24" individually shrink-wrapped.

A $9.95 value FREE

MONTANA MAGAZINE

P.O. Box 5630, Helena, MT 59604

1-888-666-8624

www.montanamagazine.com

Don't miss a single issue!
Subscribe today! Simply call our toll-free phone number.

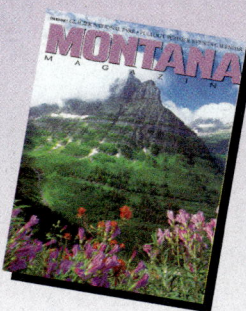

SAVE $21

MONTANA MAGAZINE PHOTO OF MEDICINE LAKE NATIONAL WILDLIFE REFUGE

Along The Trail
IMPRESSIONS

Rich full-color landscape photographs make these an excellent souvenir or remembrance at a cost not much more than a greeting card.
80 pages. 9⅛" x 8⅛". Softbound.

ONLY $9.95 + shipping

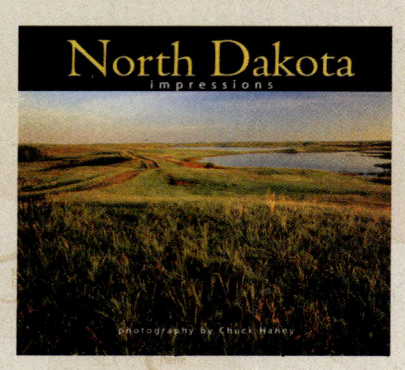

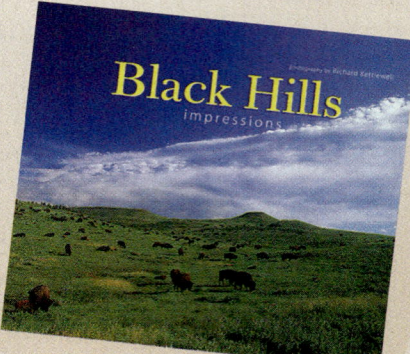

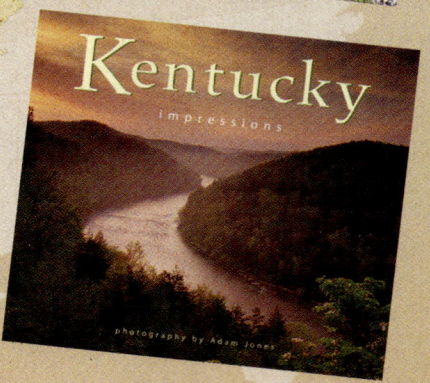

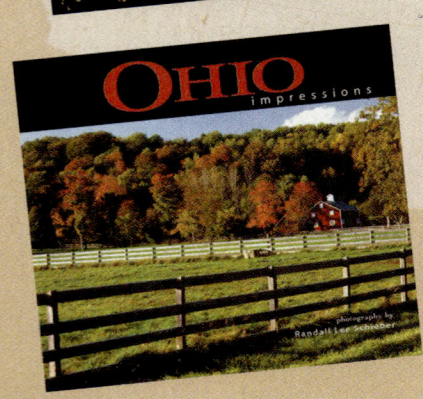

800-821-3874 • www.farcountrypress.com

Visit Us Online!

ALONG THE TRAIL WITH
LEWIS AND CLARK
Travel Planner and Guide

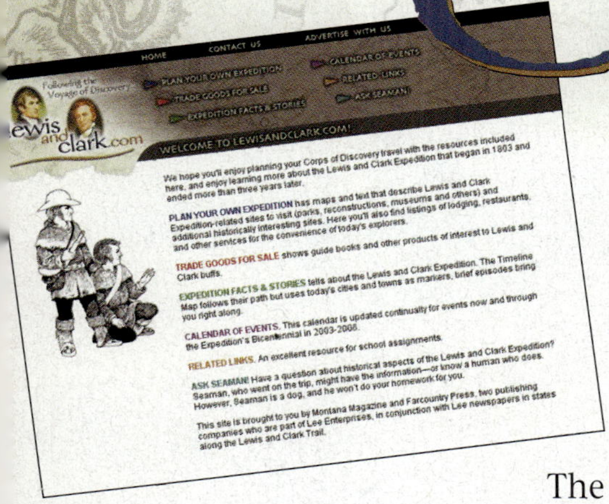

See more information to help you enjoy your travels on the Lewis and Clark Trail: what to see, where to stay, and what was happening to the Corps of Discovery there.

Covers the entire trail from Monticello to the Pacific!

The website offers these sections:

HISTORY, MAPS & TRAVEL INFO—maps and text that describe Lewis and Clark Expedition-related sites to visit (parks, reconstructions, museums and others) and additional historically interesting sites. Here you'll also find listings of lodging, restaurants, and other services for the convenience of today's explorers.

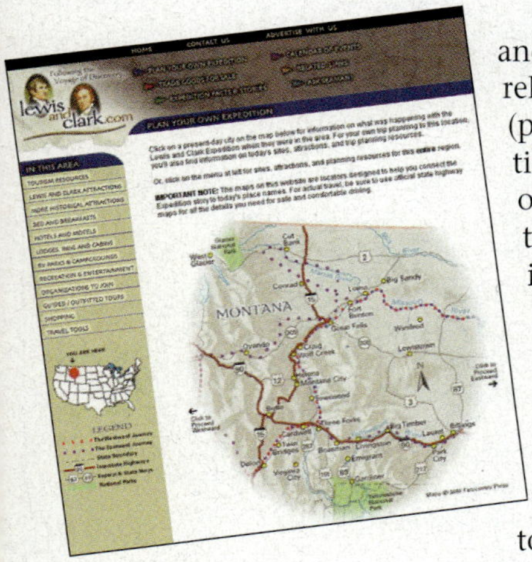

TRADE GOODS FOR SALE—guide books and other products of interest to Lewis and Clark buffs.

ASK SEAMAN! Have a question about historical aspects of the Lewis and Clark Expedition? Seaman, who went on the trip, might have the information—or know a human who does.

EXPEDITION FACTS & STORIES—includes a Timeline Map that follows their path but uses today's cities and towns as markers, and relates brief episodes of the expedition to bring you right along.

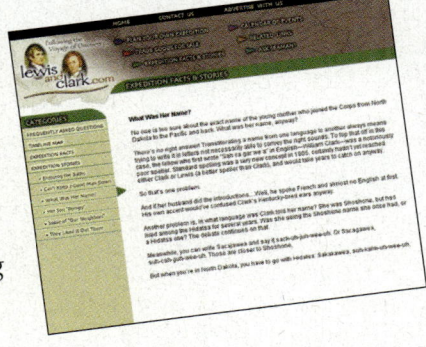

CALENDAR OF EVENTS—updated continually—for events through the Expedition's Bicentennial in 2004-2006.

RELATED LINKS—excellent resource for school assignments.

This site is brought to you by Montana Magazine and Farcountry Press, two publishing companies who are part of Lee Enterprises, in conjunction with Lee newspapers in states along the Lewis and Clark Trail.

www.lewisandclark.com

Red Lion Hotels...
Commemorates the 200-Year Anniversary of Lewis & Clark.

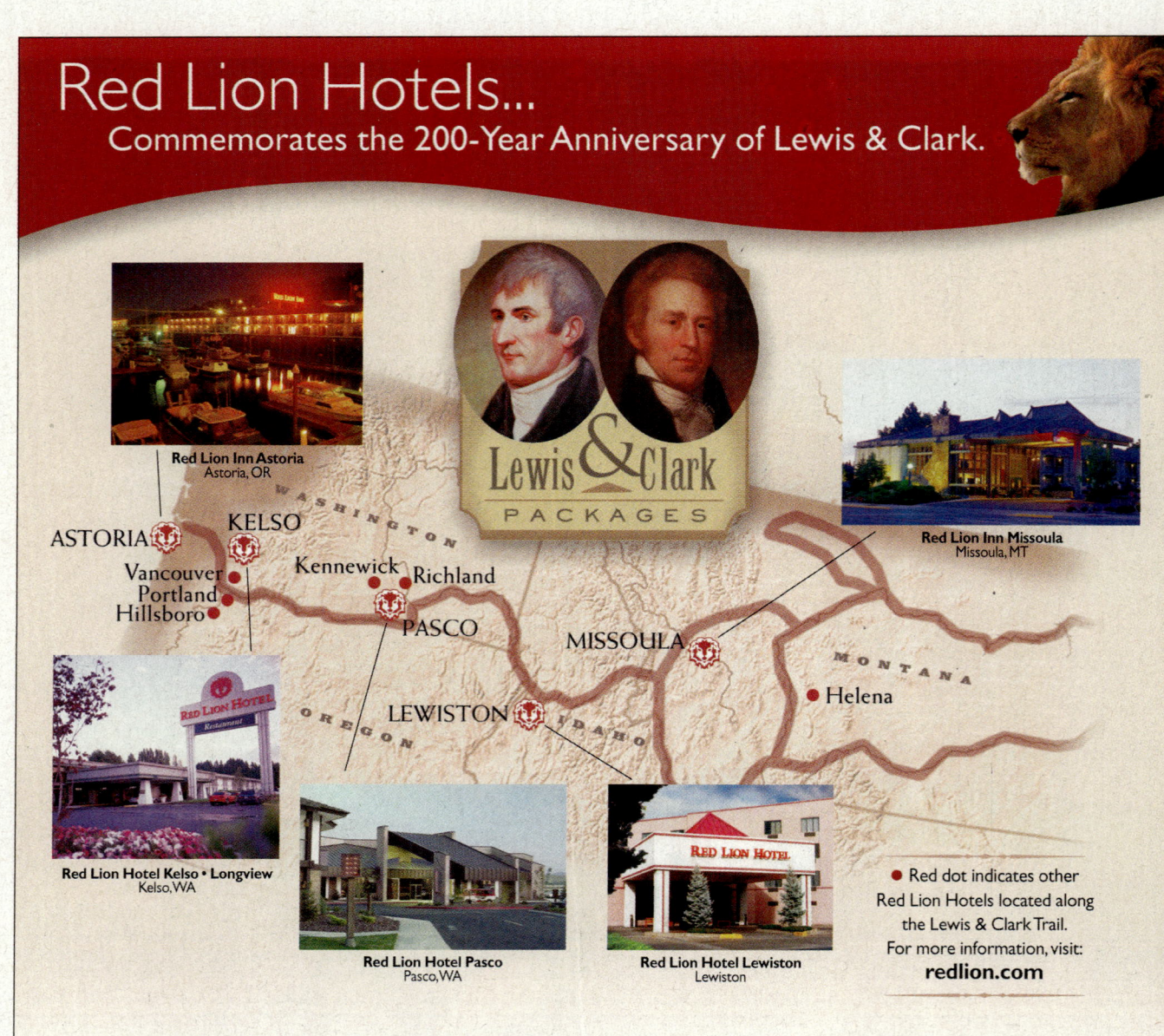

Lewis & Clark PACKAGES

Red Lion Inn Astoria — Astoria, OR
Red Lion Inn Missoula — Missoula, MT
Red Lion Hotel Kelso • Longview — Kelso, WA
Red Lion Hotel Pasco — Pasco, WA
Red Lion Hotel Lewiston — Lewiston

ASTORIA • KELSO • Vancouver • Portland • Hillsboro • Kennewick • Richland • PASCO • LEWISTON • MISSOULA • Helena

WASHINGTON • OREGON • IDAHO • MONTANA

● Red dot indicates other Red Lion Hotels located along the Lewis & Clark Trail. For more information, visit: **redlion.com**

Follow the route of the Lewis & Clark expedition through Montana, Idaho, Washington and Oregon. You'll find distinctive Red Lion Hotels conveniently located along this historic trail. Your family will enjoy learning the history of their journey at one or several of the numerous parks, historic sites and events along the way.

Our Hotels Feature:
- Deluxe Accommodations
- Entertainment Lounges
- Full Service Restaurants
- Meeting & Banquet Space
- Indoor & Outdoor Swimming Pools
- Corporate & Leisure Packages
- Golf and Ski Getaways

RED LION HOTELS®
redlion.com 800-Red Lion

GUESTAWARDS™

* Amenities vary at each property. GuestAwards is a trademark of WestCoast Hospitality Corp. © 2004 WHC 825-0012-1/0204

WESTCOAST FAMILY OF HOTELS